P9-EDG-533

MEDIA VIOLENCE AND ITS EFFECT ON AGGRESSION: ASSESSING THE SCIENTIFIC EVIDENCE

In this controversial work, Jonathan Freedman argues that the scientific evidence does not support the notion that exposure to TV and film violence causes aggression in children or adults. Based on his findings, far fewer than half of the scientific studies have found a causal connection between exposure to media violence and aggression or crime. In fact, Freedman believes that, taken to an extreme, the research could be interpreted as showing that there is no causal effect of media violence at all.

Media Violence and Its Effect on Aggression offers a provocative challenge to popular wisdom and various public statements by professional and scientific organizations. Freedman begins with a comprehensive review of all the research on the effect of violent movies and television on aggression and crime. Having shown the lack of scientific support for the prevailing belief that media violence is connected to violent behaviour, he then explains why something that seems so intuitive and even obvious might be incorrect, and provides plausible reasons why media violence might *not* have bad effects on children. He contrasts the supposed effects of TV violence on crime with the known effects of poverty and other social factors.

Freedman concludes by noting that although in recent years television and films have been as violent as ever and violent video games have become more and more popular, there has been a dramatic *decrease* in violent crime. He argues that it is thus unlikely that media violence causes an increase in aggression or crime and that both increases and decreases in violent crime are the result of major social forces.

JONATHAN L. FREEDMAN is Professor of Psychology at the University of Toronto.

JONATHAN L. FREEDMAN

Media Violence and Its Effect on Aggression: Assessing the Scientific Evidence

UNIVERSITY OF TORONTO PRESS
Toronto Buffalo London

© University of Toronto Press Incorporated 2002
Toronto Buffalo London
Printed in Canada

ISBN 0-8020-3553-1 (cloth)
ISBN 0-8020-8425-7 (paper)

Printed on acid-free paper

National Library of Canada Cataloguing in Publication Data

Freedman, Jonathan L.
  Media violence and its effect on aggression : assessing the scientific
  evidence

  Includes bibliographical references and index.
  ISBN 0-8020-3553-1 (bound). ISBN 0-8020-8425-7 (pbk.)

  1. Violence in mass media – Psychological aspects.
  2. Aggressiveness in children. I. Title.

  P96.V5F73 2002   155.4'018232   C2001-903806-2

This book has been published with the help of a grant from the
Humanities and Social Sciences Federation of Canada, using funds
provided by the Social Sciences and Humanities Research Council of
Canada.

The University of Toronto Press acknowledges the financial assistance
to its publishing program of the Canada Council for the Arts and the
Ontario Arts Council.

University of Toronto Press acknowledges the financial support for
its publishing activities of the Government of Canada through the
Book Publishing Industry Development Program (BPIDP).

P96
V5
F-73
2002

To Rona and Jacob

Contents

Preface

Many people are convinced that media violence is harmful. They believe that exposure to this kind of violence causes children and perhaps also adults to become more aggressive and even to commit violent crimes. This belief has been fostered and supported by some psychologists and representatives of health organizations, who have claimed that the scientific research has proven that media violence has this effect. As I shall attempt to show in this book, this is not correct. There is a considerable amount of research on the topic, and contrary to these claims, the results of the research generally do not demonstrate that exposure to media violence causes aggression.

For many years I followed the debate about media violence at a distance, without conducting any research or writing any articles on the topic. I got involved largely by accident. When I first came to the University of Toronto, some graduate students wanted me to teach a seminar. I wanted a topic that would involve many different kinds of research and that would also be inherently interesting. I chose television violence because it met these criteria, and also because I knew relatively little about the research and could thus start at about the same point as the students. I had read some of the research and was somewhat sceptical of the claims that had been made about it, but I had no fixed ideas about the subject.

The class was attended by five graduate students, and between three and five faculty members sat in on each session. We read quite a lot of the research during the term. Each week, we read several papers, analysed them, and discussed the results. As the term progressed, we were all surprised to find that the research often did not show what it had been described as showing. Many studies that were typically cited as showing that exposure to television violence increased aggression – what I call the causal hypothesis – did not show this effect, and sometimes they even showed the opposite effect. By the time the course ended I had decided that it was important to set the record straight. I spent a year or so reading the research, and wrote a review of the non-laboratory studies that concluded that the research did not support the causal hypothesis. The paper was published in the *Psychological Bulletin*, which is the main journal of the American Psychological Association for this kind of review.

Since that paper was published, I have been asked to give talks, appear at conferences, and contribute papers on the topic. I have continued to read the research and to be involved in the debate. Throughout these years I have argued that contrary to what is often claimed, the bulk of the research does not show that television or movie violence has any negative effects.

In 1999 I was approached by the Motion Picture Association of America and asked whether I would consider conducting a comprehensive review of all the research on media violence. Until then I had never received any support from any organization for this work. On the one hand, I was a little nervous because I knew there was a danger that my work would be tainted by a connection with the MPAA. On the other hand, I thought it was time for a complete review of the research, and I knew I could not do it without support. After some soul searching and consultation with a lawyer, I agreed as long as it was made absolutely clear that I was free to do and say what I wanted in the review. The MPAA would have no input into the review, would see it only after it was complete, and except for editorial suggestions, would be forbidden to alter what I wrote. Of course they asked me to do the review, rather than someone else, because they knew my position and assumed or at least hoped that I would come to the same conclusion after a more comprehensive review. But there was no quid pro quo. Although I was nervous about being tainted, I am confident that I was not. In any case, the conclusions of this review are not different from those of my earlier review or those I expressed in papers and talks between 1984 and 1999.

In 1999 I began systematically reading and reviewing every single scientific study I could find that dealt with the question whether exposure to film and television violence causes aggression. Having looked at all this research, I concluded that the results do not support the view that exposure to media violence causes children or anyone else to become aggressive or to commit crimes; nor does it support the idea that it causes people to be less sensitive to real violence. In this book I report on this comprehensive review. My purpose is to describe the evidence, indicate what it shows, and provide plausible reasons why media violence does not have bad effects on children.

In this book, I describe each study, analyse its results, present any relevant criticisms, discuss the study, and draw conclusions. All of this is transparent, so that readers will be able to decide whether they agree with my assessments instead of taking them on faith. In doing the review I considered each study in detail. For most types of research the book contains descriptions and discussion of every relevant study. Unfortunately, I could not provide this level of detail for the laboratory experiments, because there have been too many of them. Instead, I have summarized the findings, described some representative examples, and indicated how I classified each of the studies.

Some of the details in the book are technical, but as much as possible I have tried to make the research and this review of it accessible to those without specialized training. The book is directed at a general audience. However, since this is (I believe) the only thorough and detailed review of this literature, I think that psychologists and other social scientists will also find it valuable.

Acknowledgements

I would like to thank So-Jin Kang, who was an enormous help in locating, getting copies of, and organizing the papers that I reviewed. I am also grateful to all of those at the University of Toronto Press who helped bring this book into print, especially my editor, Virgil Duff, who shepherded the book through the long process from submission to publication and to Matthew Kudelka, who did an excellent but gentle and respectful job of copyediting. I also thank the Motion Picture Association of America for providing financial support for the review of the research. The Association and Vans Stevenson, who was the person there with whom I had most contact, honoured their agreement to maintain an arm's-length relationship, never attempting to interfere with or to influence my work. I am grateful to the Humanities and Social Sciences Federation of Canada and to the Canada Council for the Arts and the Ontario Arts Council for the financial assistance they provided to the press. Finally, I am continually grateful to my wife and son for their love and support and for the privilege of knowing them.

MEDIA VIOLENCE AND ITS EFFECT ON AGGRESSION: ASSESSING THE SCIENTIFIC EVIDENCE

1

Villain or Scapegoat? Media Violence and Aggression

On 20 April 1999, at around 11:20 a.m. local time, two students wearing black trenchcoats walked into Columbine High School in Littleton, Colorado. Eric Harris, eighteen, and Dylan Klebold, seventeen, were armed with semiautomatic handguns, shotguns and explosives. They killed twelve students, one teacher, and then themselves.

On 1 December 1997, Michael Carneal killed three students at Heath High School in West Paducah, Kentucky.

On 30 April 1999 a fourteen-year-old Canadian boy walked into the W.R. Myers High School in Taber, a quiet farming community of 7,200 people two hours southeast of Calgary, Alberta. He shot and killed one seventeen-year-old student and seriously injured another eleventh-grade student.

It is difficult to imagine events more terrible than our young people deliberately killing each other. These horrifying incidents have caused almost everyone to wonder what has gone wrong with North American society. How can it be that in quiet, affluent communities in two of the richest countries on earth, children are taking guns to school and killing their classmates?

Many answers have been suggested. It was the parents' fault; it was Satanism and witchcraft; it was lack of religion in the schools and at home; it was moral breakdown; it was the availability of guns; it was the culture.

One answer proposed whenever events like this occur is that they are a result of exposure to media violence. Children who watch television and go to the movies see thousands of murders and countless other acts of violence. They see fistfights, martial arts battles, knifings, shootings, exploding cars, and bombs. These acts of violence are committed by heroes and villains, by good guys and bad guys. They are committed by live actors and animated figures; they appear in the best movies and TV programs as well as in the worst. It is almost impossible for children to avoid witnessing these violent acts time and time again. All of this has caused many people to ask whether watching violent television programs and movies causes people, especially children, to be more aggressive and to commit crimes.

Another reason some people worry about the effects of media violence is that television became available in the United States and Canada in the 1950s and violent crime increased dramatically in both countries between 1960 and 1990. Many people see a connection. They think that watching violence on television makes children more aggressive and causes them to grow into adults who are more likely to commit violent crimes. Brandon Centerwall, a psychiatrist and epidemiologist, has even suggested that the increase in violent crime during this period was due entirely to television. As he put it, 'if, hypothetically, television technology had never been developed, there would today be 10,000 fewer homicides each year in the United States, 70,000 fewer rapes, and 700,000 fewer injurious assaults.'

The belief that media violence is harmful is widespread. In a recent poll in the United States, 10 per cent of people said that TV violence is the major cause of the increase in crime. This tendency to blame media violence has been fostered by some social scientists and whipped up by politicians and lobby groups. It has led politicians to propose bills restricting access to violent movies, banning violent television programs during certain hours, forcing television companies to rate every single program in terms of violence, and requiring that all television sets be fitted with V-chips to enable parents to block out programs they find offensive. We are told that all of this will reduce crime and make children better behaved, and that if we do not deal with media violence our society will continue to experience increased violence and crime.

Some people say they don't need science to know that watching violence makes children violent. To these people it is so clear, so self-evident, that we don't need to bother with research. They point to some horrible incidents to support this view.

On 14 October 1992 the headlines in many American papers read BOY LIGHTS FIRE THAT KILLS SISTER. Two days earlier a television program had shown young boys setting fires. The very next day, Tommy Jones (not his real name) an eight-year-old boy, set a fire that burned down the trailer in which he and his family lived. His baby sister was trapped inside and burned to death. All over the United States, newspapers, television stations, and politicians concluded that Tommy must have seen the television program and gotten the idea of playing with matches and setting a fire. Surely this was a perfect example of why children should not be allowed to watch violent programs.

In February 1993 the whole world shuddered at an awful crime committed by two young boys in England. That month a small boy who was about to turn three was taken from a shopping mall in Liverpool by two ten-year-old boys. Jamie Bulger had walked away from his mother for only a second – long enough for Jon Venables to take his hand and lead him out of the mall with his friend Robert Thompson. They took Jamie on a walk of over two-and-a-half miles, along the way stopping every now and again to torture the poor little boy, who was crying constantly for his mommy. Finally they left his beaten small body on the tracks so that a train could run him over.

Jamie's frantic mother noticed almost at once that he was missing, and a massive search began. Jon and Robert were identified from surveillance tapes in the mall. At first they denied any knowledge of Jamie, but eventually they admitted everything and led police to the dead body. Although they confessed to taking Jamie, each accused the other of doing the torturing and killing. During the trial, Jon cried a lot and looked miserable, while Robert seemed unaffected. They were convicted and sentenced to long prison terms.

The trial judge had observed the boys for many days and heard all the testimony. At the sentencing he denounced them as inhuman monsters. He also said he was convinced that one of the causes of their crime was television violence. According to the judge, shortly before the crime the boys had watched a television program, involving kidnapping and murder. They had imitated this program and the result was Jamie's kidnapping, torture, and murder. It was, he said, one more case of the harmful effects of television violence.

People think they see the effects of media violence in their daily lives. Every day, parents and teachers watch children practising martial arts at home and in schoolyards. Pass by a playground and you will see martial arts in action – slashing arms, jumps, kicks, the works. A generation ago young boys almost never used karate kicks; now they all do. And this goes along with increased violence in our schools. Again, surely television violence has caused it.

The terrible crimes related to television programs, the increase in violent crime since the introduction of television, and the ordinary occurrences of fighting in imitation of television heroes have convinced many people that television violence causes aggression, violence and crime. It seems so obvious that there is no need to worry about the scientific evidence. Why should anyone care what the research shows?

Don't be so sure. Not so terribly long ago it was obvious that the world was flat, that the sun revolved around the earth, and that the longer women stayed in bed after childbirth the healthier they would be. Scientific research has proven all of these wrong. An awful lot of people also knew that men were smarter than women, that picking babies up when they cried would only encourage them to cry more in the future, and that rewarding kids for playing games would make them like the games more. Research has proven all of these wrong too. Perhaps it will do the same for beliefs about the effects of media violence – that is why so many people have done so much research to establish whether watching violent programs really does make children more aggressive.

Anecdotes are not always very reliable. Let's look at the examples I offered above. Consider the case of the fire that killed the little girl. At first glance there seems no question what happened. The newspapers all reported that the boy was a well-behaved child who had never been in trouble before. He happened to watch the TV program about setting fires, and he imitated what he saw. What more could one ask? Clearly, this was a simple case of TV causing a tragedy.

But it wasn't. As those reporters who looked into the incident more carefully found out, the truth was quite different from the early reports. First of all, little Tommy was not a very well-behaved boy. He had been playing with matches and setting fires for some time – long before the program was aired. No one had been killed or hurt in any of the fires before this, so they did not make the news, but they were set nonetheless. Second, and more important, the TV program in question was shown only on cable, not on the regular networks. *And Tommy's family did not have cable television*. In fact, no one in the trailer park had it, and no one he knew had it. *So there was no way he could have seen the show*. The tragic incident had nothing whatsoever to do with the television program that had been shown the day before. Rather than it being a case of television causing the tragedy, it was simply one more instance of children playing with fire and someone getting hurt.

Also consider the case of the two boys who killed Jamie Bulger. The judge announced in court that he was convinced that TV played a crucial role in the crime – that the boys had watched a program about kidnapping and had imitated it. Again, an obvious case of TV violence producing violence?

Yet the judge's belief had no basis in fact. The police made it absolutely clear that the boys had not watched the program in question, that they did not watch television much, and that there was no reason to believe that TV had anything to do with the crime. The last time children of this age had been found guilty of murder in England had been several hundred years earlier. It hadn't been due to television then, so why in the world would the judge think so this time? This was a horrific crime beyond human comprehension. We have no idea how they could have committed it, but there is not the slightest bit of evidence that it was caused by television.

Yes, the rate of violent crime increased after television was introduced. But there is no reason to think the two are in any way related. As I shall discuss at length later, television was also introduced to France, Germany, Italy, and Japan at around the same time as it came to the United States and Canada. Yet crime rates did not increase in these other countries. If television violence were causing the increase, surely it should have had the same effect elsewhere. We have to remember that the availability of television in the United States and Canada coincided with vast changes in our societies. Between 1960 and 1985 – the period of the increase in crime – the divorce rate more than doubled, many more single parents and women began working outside the home, the use of illegal drugs increased, the gap between rich and poor grew, and because of the postwar baby boom, there was a sharp increase in the number of young males. Almost all of the experts, including police, criminologists, and sociologists, agree that these factors played a crucial role in the increase in crime, and no one seriously blames television for these changes in society. It is an accident, a coincidence, that television ownership increased during this same period. These important social changes are certainly some of the causes of the increase in crime; television ownership may be irrelevant.

Although it may seem as if youth violence is increasing, it is actually declining. In 1999 the rate of murder by white youths in California was at a record low, 65 per cent less than in 1970, and the rates for Black, Latino, and Asian youths were also low. According to FBI records, elementary-school students are much less likely to murder today than they were in the 1960s and 1970s. And, both Black and white children feel less menaced now by violence in their schools than twenty-five years ago. True, over the past seven years there has been an increase in incidents in schools in which more than one person was killed. However, the number of children killed in schools in the United States and Canada has dropped during the same period, from a high of fifty-five in the 1992–93 school year to sixteen in 1998–99. This last year included one killing in Canada, which shocked a country not used to this kind of violence in its schools, but it is the only case of its kind in this decade.

Moreover, the rates for all violent crimes have been dropping steadily and dramatically since the early 1990s. The number of homicides in the big American cities has plunged to levels not seen since the early 70s, and the numbers for other violent crimes have been falling as well. This, at a time when movies and television shows are as violent as ever. Add to this the rising popularity of rap music, with its violent language and themes; and of video games, which are just as violent and just as popular. If violence in the media causes aggression, how can real-life violence and crime be dropping?

None of this proves that television violence plays no role in aggression and violence. The point is that stories about its effects are often false and that obvious effects may be explainable in other ways. People's intuitions and observations are sometimes wrong, and may be this time. That is why we have to rely on scientific research to answer the question whether exposure to media violence really makes children more aggressive; and that is why I have conducted the extensive review of the research that is presented in this book.

What about Pronouncements by Scientific Organizations?

The public has been told by panel after panel, organization after organization, that media violence causes aggression. A long list of prestigious scientific and medical organizations have said that the evidence is in and the question has been settled. The American Psychiatric Association and the Canadian Psychological Association have all weighed in on this matter. Recently, under some prodding by a congressional committee, the American Medical Association, the American Academy of Pediatrics, the American Psychological Association, and the American Academy of Child and Adolescent Psychiatry issued a joint statement. According to these groups, it is now proven that media violence causes aggression and probably causes crime. The pediatric group went so far as to urge that children under two should watch no television because it interferes with their normal development. The National Institute of Mental Health has published an extensive report on television in which it concludes that media violence causes aggression.

If all these respectable scientific organizations agree that media violence is harmful, surely it must be. Well, it isn't. Although they have all made unequivocal statements about the effects of media violence, it is almost certain that not one of these organizations conducted a thorough review of the research. They have surely not published or made available any such review. If they made these pronouncements without a scientific review, they are guilty of the worst kind of irresponsible behaviour. If they were in court as expert witnesses, they could be convicted of perjury. It is incredible that these organizations, which purport to be scientific, should act in this manner. Yet that seems to be the case.

Consider the policy statement from the American Academy of Pediatricians published in August 1999. It states: 'More than 1000 scientific studies and reviews conclude that significant exposure to media violence increases the risk of aggressive behavior in certain children and adolescents, desensitizes them to violence, and makes them believe that the world is a "meaner and scarier" place than it is.' Apparently not satisfied, in its November 2001 Policy Statement on Media Violence the AAP stated: 'More than 3500 research studies have examined the association between media violence and violent behavior [and] all but 18 have shown a positive relationship.' That sounds pretty impressive. After all, if over 3500 scientific studies reached this conclusion, who could doubt it? The only problem is that this is not true. There have not been over 3500 or even 1000 scientific studies on this topic. This vastly exaggerates the amount of work that has been done. That the pediatricians give such an inflated figure is only one indication that they do not know the research. Imagine the response if an organization of economists asserted that there were serious economic problems in over 150 American states. No one would bother asking for their statistics, since if they were so sloppy as to think there were that many states, who could possibly trust the rest of their statement? In the same way, since the pediatricians say that they are basing their statement on over 3500 scientific studies, it must be clear that they have not read the research because there are not anywhere near that many studies.

To make matters worse, the studies that do exist do not all reach the conclusion that media violence has any of the effects listed by the AAP.

Indeed, as we shall see later, most of the studies show no ill effects of exposure to media violence. And there is virtually no research showing that media violence desensitizes people to violence. Why do these presumably well-meaning pediatricians make these unsupported and inaccurate statements? Who knows.

To cap it off, the policy goes on to 'urge parents to avoid television viewing for children under the age of 2 years.' It supports this extreme recommendation by saying that 'research on early brain development shows that babies and toddlers have a critical need for direct interactions with parents ... for healthy brain growth and the development of appropriate social, emotional and cognitive skills.' I am not a neuroscientist and I have not reviewed the relevant research. However, an article in the *New York Times* quotes neuroscientists at Rockefeller University, the University of Minnesota, and the Washington University Medical School, as saying that there is no evidence to support the pediatricians' advice. 'There is no data like that at all,' according to Charles Nelson. The author of the *Times* article goes on to say that the person who wrote the pediatric academy's report agreed that there was no evidence but that they had 'extrapolated' from other data.

This is incredible. This organization is giving advice to medical doctors who deal directly with millions of American parents and children. And it is telling these doctors to urge their patients (i.e., the parents of their patients) to keep children under two away from television – not just limit their exposure but to keep them away from television entirely. Given the role that television plays in the lives of most families, following this advice would be a major undertaking. In the first place, it would be very difficult for the parents to manage it. Television keeps children occupied, stimulates them, entertains them, and educates them. Even if it did none of these things, imagine how difficult it would be for parents who like to watch television themselves or have older children who like to watch. Would they have to turn off the television whenever the under-two children are in the room? Or are they supposed to keep the young children out of the room with the television? Be serious.

Yet the pediatricians are supposed to tell parents that watching television will harm their children by preventing them from developing normally. This is quite a threat. Many parents will presumably take it to heart, worry about doing damage to their children, and try to follow the advice. This is not a matter of reducing fat intake a little or giving them enough milk – this is telling them to alter the social environment in their home, supposedly on the basis of hard, scary, scientific facts. Do *this* or your child will not grow up normally.

But there is no scientific evidence that television harms children under two – nothing at all to support this recommendation. It is junk science; pop psychology of the worst sort based on nothing but some vague extrapolations from research that is not cited and may not exist. This is truly irresponsible. Fortunately, I think we can trust most pediatricians to ignore this nonsensical policy and not give the advice; and if they do give it, we can probably trust most sensible parents to ignore it.

Well, after all, pediatricians are not usually experts in this kind of research. Perhaps they can be forgiven for not bothering to read the research and for not understanding it fully. Besides, pediatricians are concerned mainly with the physical health of their young patients, and whatever effect television has is presumably mainly psychological rather than physical.

Psychiatrists, on the other hand, are concerned with mental health, so they should know better. Sure enough, the American Psychiatric Association also has a position on this issue – though not on the question of television and brain development, just on the social effects. On its website the APA describes the 'psychiatric effects of media violence' and offers a series of steps that parents should take regarding the media. This statement begins with strong words: 'The debate is over. Over the last three decades, the one overriding finding in research on the mass media is that exposure to media portrayals of violence increases aggressive behaviour in children.' It adds that 'countless studies have demonstrated that exposure to depictions of violence causes desensitization and creates a climate of fear.' Both these statements are false. The debate is obviously not over, and the one overriding finding of the research is *not* that media violence causes children to be aggressive. Moreover, it is not true that 'countless studies' have shown that media violence causes desensitization and/or a climate of fear. In fact, only a few studies – easily counted on the fingers of two hands – have dealt with desensitization, and they have not supported the hypothesis that media violence causes desensitization. I have not concerned myself in this review with the work on 'climate of fear,' but I do know that the research has not provided much support for it.

The psychiatrists are a little less extreme than the pediatricians, and a little less inaccurate since at least they do not refer to 'more than 1000 studies' or to problems of neurological development. Nevertheless, it is clear that no one involved in this policy statement has actually read the research. Like the pediatricians, the psychiatrists are probably basing their statement on their own personal beliefs and on what others have said about the research, rather than bothering with it themselves.

Even so, the psychiatrists do not hold back when it comes to their recommendations to parents. They tell them not to use television as a babysitter. It's not clear exactly what that means – although one hears the phrase all the time – but presumably it means that parents should not let their children watch television just to keep them occupied. If that were the children's only activity, this would make some sense; but if the children have other activities and interests, why in the world can't they watch television?

Parents are also told to limit their children's television use to one or two (get this) 'quality' hours per day. 'OK, kids, it's time for your quality hour of television – we've turned on the presidential debate.' Is *Sesame Street* quality enough? At least one believer in the harmful effects of television claims that *Sesame Street* makes kids aggressive, so maybe not. This is silly.

Parents are told to turn the television off during mealtimes. Now I have to admit, generally I can't stand television during meals. But what is the justification for this? If the family all want to watch a baseball game or a movie or a favourite show, and it happens to be showing during their normal mealtime, what possible harm could it do? If there were any solid (or for that matter not so solid) research showing that watching television at mealtimes was harmful, the APA would be justified in passing this on. But I know of no such research, and none is cited.

And so on. Many of the suggestions sound good. They may even be helpful. But they are not based on scientific knowledge; they have not been tried and shown to work. Instead some group of psychiatrists, deciding on their own, based on their personal intuitions, beliefs, tastes, and perhaps experience, have chosen to tell parents what to do. It is unscientific pop psychology. Trust it no more than you would trust your Aunt Sally or Uncle Fred or the nice neighbour or, for that matter, yourself.

Then there is the group that represents my field – the American Psychological Association. Psychologists are trained to do and interpret research; the whole focus of their graduate education is research; they are required to do a research thesis. Most of the relevant research was done by psychologists and published in psychology journals. Surely APA can be trusted.

Think again. The APA is probably the worst offender in this whole story, not because its statements are any worse than the others, but because it should know better. The APA has taken the lead in the battle against media violence. It has issued many press statements and policy positions and has testified often in front of the U.S. Congress. Lest I be accused of being unfair to American psychologists, let me add that the Canadian Psychological Association has been just as bad, though less active. If the psychologists had taken careful, principled positions thoroughly supported by systematic research, this would be cause for applause. As it happens, this is a sad chapter in the organization's history, since it is probably the case that most of the other organizations have based their stands on what the psychologists have had to say.

The APA published a report called *Violence and Youth* that deals with the effects of media violence. It states in no uncertain terms that viewing media violence has all sorts of negative effects. Consider this extract, published in bold type in the report: 'There is absolutely no doubt that higher levels of viewing violence on television are correlated with increased acceptance of aggressive attitudes and increased aggressive behavior.' And this one: 'In addition, prolonged viewing of media violence can lead to emotional desensitization toward violence.' In support of these definitive statements, the report refers to three major national studies: the Surgeon General's Commission report of 1972, the National Institute of Mental Health ten-year follow-up of 1982 (which I'll discuss in detail below), and its own Committee on Media in Society of 1992. The APA says that these groups 'reviewed hundreds of studies to arrive at the irrefutable conclusion that viewing violence increases violence.'

There are many inaccuracies and misstatements in these few statements. First, none of these reviews looked at 'hundreds' of studies, because there are not that many studies now, and there certainly were not that many when these reviews were done. This is mere puffing to inflate the numbers to make the reviews sound more impressive. The psychologists do not claim 'over 1000,' like the pediatricians do, but they are still inflating (unless, I suppose, what they mean is 'two hundreds,' since that is about the right number). Second, the first two reviews were done by other groups, and presumably the psychologists should only make a pronouncement if they have looked at the research themselves. Third, although there is pious talk of a thorough review by the APA committee, this committee did not conduct the kind of open hearings that might have allowed people with divergent views to appear. In any case, this committee released a statement but never released an actual review. In sum, the APA's bold report is not based on an independent review of the research, or if they did conduct such a review they have never released it for public consumption, comment, and – God forbid – criticism.

In addition, the APA makes serious factual errors. Let me put aside for now the question whether the research shows that media violence has an effect on violence – that, after all, is what this book is about. The APA says that viewing violence is associated with increased acceptance of aggressive attitudes. Now that's a new one. Not even the other organizations mentioned that, and it appears more or less out of the blue. Yes, it has been the subject of speculation, but there has been almost no research on changes in attitudes due to viewing violence. It may be true, but surely the APA does not know it is true – so why do they say there is 'no doubt' about it?

Then the report mentions emotional desensitization toward violence. Again, there has been speculation about this, and a few relevant studies have been done. But there is no reason for the APA to believe that this effect of media violence has been demonstrated definitively. As we shall see, my review shows that it is probably not true. For now the important point is that so little research has been done that no serious scientist could have faith in the existence or non-existence of the effect. So why does the APA mention it?

This lack of concern with actual research was evident again in testimony given for the APA to the U.S. Senate Subcommittee on Juvenile Justice. John Murray, speaking for the APA, was slightly more careful than the APA report. In answer to his own question 'Does televised violence produce aggressive behavior?' he said that 'the answer seems to be yes.' Not 'yes'; not 'proven beyond a doubt'; but 'seems to be yes.' Good for him. Unfortunately, the rest of his testimony had the effect of changing the 'seems' into 'does.'

Perhaps the most interesting part of his testimony – and, incidentally, of the report issued by the APA committee described earlier – was the research he mentioned. Both Murray and the report offered very few references to studies. Yet both referred to a study in which preschool children were shown various types of programs. Indeed, this study by Friedrich and Stein (1973) is often cited as showing the harmful effects of violent television. Now remember, of all of the studies that could have been cited, this is one of the very few that the APA chose to mention in its report and in its presentation to Congress. Presumably it was chosen because it produced such clear, unambiguous, and powerful results.

Here is the way Murray described it to the Senate committee: 'They found that the youngsters who watched the Batman and Superman cartoons were more likely to hit their playmates, start arguments, disobey the teacher and be more impatient.' This description is similar to the one in the report of the committee on violence.

Yet it is just plain wrong. That is not what the study found. The study used four basic measures of aggression and one additional, computed measure that combined two of the others. It found no difference between children who watched the aggressive cartoons and those who watched *Mister Rogers* (the prosocial program) on any of these measures. That is, just to make this perfectly clear, there was no difference on physical aggression, verbal aggression, object aggression, fantasy aggression, or interpersonal aggression (which combined physical and verbal). Those who watched the cartoons were *not* more likely to hit their playmates or start arguments. (They were also *not* more likely to disobey or be impatient, but this review is not about those effects so I will not focus on them.) There was a complex, marginally significant relationship between initial levels of aggression and type of film, but even this did not show any increase in aggression due to the 'violent' cartoons. In other words, Murray was wrong and the APA committee was wrong to cite this study as showing an increase in physical aggression due to watching Batman and Superman cartoons. There was no such effect.

Several years ago I debated this issue at a conference at the Hoffstra Law School. Murray was also there. In arguing that media violence is harmful, he cited this same study. When it was my turn to talk, I happened to have figures that proved he was wrong – the study did not show what he said it showed. His response to this was that you could always poke holes in any particular study. This surely is a classic instance of *chutzpah*. As I said to him, 'You picked the study, I didn't pick it. You chose it to make your point and you were wrong.'

Think about it. In testimony to Congress and in its report, the APA claimed that the scientific research definitively shows that exposure to media violence causes aggression, and it cited a study to support this assertion. *And that study is wrong – it does not show what the APA said it shows.* It could have chosen any study it wanted to mention; it could have picked one that *did* show an effect, because there are some. But no, it picked one that did not show an effect of media violence. I hope this makes people doubt the APA's assertion, since if it was wrong on this, why think it is correct in its more sweeping statements? That the APA selected this study shows just how sloppy that group is, and how little concerned with ensuring it has the science right. Embarrassing!

Thus the APA – the organization that represents many psychologists in the United States and around the world – pronounced that media violence causes aggression without doing a thorough review of the literature, without consulting those who disagree with this conclusion, without any hearings, and apparently with little concern for scientific accuracy. Perhaps the APA was worried about its public image. It knew that the public was concerned about media violence. Maybe the APA worried that if it took a more moderate stand or did not take a stand, the public would be upset. A more likely explanation is that the APA was worried about the reaction in Congress. The APA knew that many members of Congress were blaming television violence for the increase in crime rates. It also knew that psychologists depended on Congress for funding and for all sorts of other issues. Maybe its strong stand against media violence was to appease Congress. Or maybe it was simply that some psychologists believe in the causal effect and convinced the rest to go along with them. Whatever the reason, the APA failed to be scientific.

Surely the National Institute of Mental Health would be more careful. This is a huge organization with a vast budget. Its mandate is to promote and protect mental health. With its almost unlimited resources and its vital mandate, one would have thought it would be in a position to do a thorough, objective review of this issue. Perhaps the APA and the other professional organizations do not have the resources to do this, but NIMH certainly does. Surely, before making a pronouncement on the effects of violent television, it would have done or commissioned an intensive, unbiased review of the research findings. There are several ways it could have done this. One would have been to ask two or more people with different points of view to do such a review and then have a group of unbiased scientists consider the reviews. Another would have been to ask a group of scientists representing all points of view to consider the findings together. Either way, NIMH would have had a review of the research and could then have evaluated it.

Before going on, it may be helpful to consider what a review of this sort entails. First, all of the relevant studies have to be located. I can tell you that this is a major undertaking all by itself. Computerized search engines are a big help, but they often miss important articles, and of course give you a great many that are not relevant. Then each article that is identified as relevant has to be found. Again, this is a substantial undertaking since the articles have appeared in dozens of different journals and a great many books. Once the articles are located, they have to be read carefully and critically. It does not do to read just the abstract or just the conclusions, because authors are not always entirely accurate in how they describe their findings and because a fair evaluation of the findings requires an analysis of both the method and the results. Finally, after all the articles have been read and evaluated, the results must be summarized. In other words, it's a big job. On the other hand, it's the only way to establish what the research shows.

This kind of review has been done with other issues, even controversial ones. For example, at the request of Congress the Institute of Medicine convened a panel of thirteen scientists to review the research on the effects of silicone breast implants. This group held public hearings, met in private, and evaluated more than 1,000 research reports. Later, Judge Sam C. Ponter Jr of the U.S. District Court in Alabama appointed a group of scientists to report to the court on what this research had found. If this can be done for breast implants, surely it could be done for media violence. I am not comparing the seriousness of the issues, but merely pointing out that they are both important social issues, that both potentially affect a great many people, and that both have been the subject of considerable scientific research as well as public controversy and concern.

One would have expected NIMH to understand that it would have to conduct a serious review of the research on media violence before drawing any conclusions. Obviously, there was no point assembling a panel of experts and devoting a great deal of time and money to the issue if NIMH was simply going to depend on what other people had done. If NIMH wanted to rely on reviews already done, there was no reason to make a big deal of it: all it had to do was restate the previous findings. But that was not the stated intention. NIMH was *supposed* to do a brand-new, thorough evaluation of the issue. For that it needed a comprehensive, thorough, unbiased review. Such a review would have taken many months or even years to complete. It would have considered every study, described the studies, stated how each had been evaluated by the reviewer, and then summarized the findings. The final report surely would have run to several hundred pages and would

have provided anyone who was interested with all of the details necessary to evaluate it. Best of all, it would have been entirely transparent,
in that readers would be able to see how each study was evaluated and
why it was evaluated that way. This would allow readers to decide
whether the evaluation was fair. That is what one might have expected
from NIMH.

Alas, as far as one can tell no such review was done. The impressive
committee and group of advisors certainly did not review the research
in this kind of detail. Instead, in dealing with the whole question of
television and society, it asked a number of people to review the work
relevant to particular issues. With respect to the issue of the relationship between violent television and aggression, it commissioned four
reports. One, by George Comstock (1982) was an overview of the issue;
a second one, by Signorelli, Gross, and Morgan (1982) was concerned
mainly with the presence of violence on television. Only two papers
dealt with the possible effects of violent television on aggression. But
one of these, by Milavsky and colleagues (1982) was simply a description of their own research – it was not in any way a review of the
literature.

That leaves a paper by Huesmann (1982), which was probably meant
to be a review of the literature. In one sense Huesmann was an excellent
choice to review this literature, in that he had devoted many years to
research on the issue. But he also was one of the most outspoken
believers in the causal hypothesis. One might go so far as to say that
he had based his whole career on showing that television violence
is harmful. So he would certainly have been inclined to evaluate the
findings in as favourable a way as possible for his own belief. He
would, in a sense, be the expert witness for one side of the issue –
he would certainly not be considered a disinterested or neutral party.
That would have been fine if NIMH had then commissioned someone
else – someone more neutral or even on the other side – to do a similar
review. At least NIMH would then have available two reviews from
people with different points of view. As has often been found in court,
this can sometimes be the best way of getting to the truth.

Sadly, NIMH did not commission any other review. At least in terms
of the published report, no review of the literature was done by anyone
else, and none seems to have been done by the board of experts. So at
the very best, NIMH had available to it a review done by someone who
was hardly neutral.

As it happens, NIMH did not even have that, because Huesmann did not to do a thorough review. I have no way of knowing what he was asked to do. Perhaps NIMH did not want a thorough review of the literature. In any case, Huesmann obviously did not see his role as providing such a review. In his paper he devoted a few pages to a cursory review and then spent the rest of his paper discussing his own research. In sum, NIMH did not have available any new review of the literature, and certainly not one that appeared in its publication.

Finally, to make matters still worse, the brief review done by Huesmann was inaccurate. In it, he argues that the issue is essentially settled and that a great deal of research had shown that exposure to media violence causes people to be more aggressive. He focused on the field research because many people were sceptical of the laboratory research. Cook and his colleagues wrote an analysis (1983) of the NIMH report in which they discussed Huesmann's review of the field research. They said that of the six field studies he cited, only four were said to support the causal hypothesis, but one of these did not show an effect, one showed a weak effect confined to a subgroup of children (and supposedly did not replicate), and the others were all done by one group and had problems. They concluded: 'In our view, the field experiments on television violence produce little consistent evidence of effects, despite claims to the contrary.' Those who wrote this criticism personally believed that television violence probably does cause aggression, but they acknowledged that the research findings are weak. In other words, the only review of the research commissioned and published by the NIMH study was brief, inaccurate, and almost dismissive of the notion that the issue might be controversial.

One can only speculate what NIMH had in mind. Perhaps the panel had already agreed that television violence is harmful and was merely going through the motions. Perhaps the panel actually spent lots of time reading the original research and therefore did have a review – albeit not one committed to paper. Perhaps there were heated debates within the panel and the final report came out of them. All we know is that the published papers were supposed to be the basis for the conclusions, that there was no independent, new review of the literature for this huge NIMH report, and that what does appear in the published papers could not possibly justify the conclusions reached by the panel. A great opportunity for a serious review was lost and the public was misled. What a shame.

It is a sad state of affairs when one cannot trust scientific and professional bodies to review the research carefully before making public pronouncements. It is likely that the APA and the rest have been influenced by public concerns and political considerations, and also presumably by the self-interest of those who have based their careers on demonstrating the harmful effects of media violence. Many of these people – perhaps most of them – are entirely sincere and mean well. They are worried about aggression and crime; they believe that media violence causes both; this makes sense to them. And they then make the dangerous leap from intuition to truth. They conclude that because they care and because it makes sense, it must be true. But this is not science, and it should not be passed off as science.

The real problem is that they are presenting views as scientific and proven when they are neither. Yet those views may have a direct effect on the public. People are extremely concerned about the effects of media violence. They base their concerns in part on their own intuitions, but also in large part on what they are told are the findings of scientific research. Because their intuitions are supported (or so they think) by hard science, they have no doubt that media violence is dangerous. This has led many people in the United States to believe that media violence is the major cause of violent crime in our society. With a few exceptions, even those scientists who are the most fervent believers in the causal hypothesis would not go this far. Rather, the conventional wisdom among these scientists is that media violence may account for about 10 per cent of aggression and crime. This is still a lot, but it is far from the major cause of crime. However, this view is rarely heard or publicized, perhaps because it is not exciting. So people are told that media violence causes aggression and crime, and that scientific research proves this, and they come to believe that reducing media violence will greatly reduce aggression and crime.

Given the public pronouncements from professional organizations and the strong recommendations to avoid exposure to media violence, people naturally worry about their children being exposed to it, and even more about other people's children being exposed to it. Some people are so upset about this that they devote their lives to trying to reduce media violence. Indeed, I heard one such person accuse a mother of child abuse because she let her children watch the 'Mighty Morphin Power Rangers'. This is admittedly an extreme view, but why shouldn't she think that? If she had accused the mother of child abuse for smoking in the room of her infant son, many might agree with her. Well, I have heard a social scientist tell a large audience that the effect of media violence on aggression is as strong as the effect of smoking on lung cancer. This is, of course, total nonsense, but that is what the public is hearing from the experts. Is it any wonder that people are concerned?

The public is also affected indirectly through the actions of the U.S. Congress. Many members of Congress strongly favour reducing media violence. They support their position by citing the scientific evidence. Presumably they have not read the research themselves, and we would not expect them to have the time or expertise to do so. Instead they rely on the APA, NIMH, and other scientific and quasi-scientific bodies to evaluate the evidence for them. When the APA and NIMH and all the other organizations state unequivocally that media violence causes all sorts of harm, it would be irresponsible for Congress not to do something about it.

The difficulty is that these organizations have not reviewed the research either. Everyone is trusting everyone else to do it for them. The public and Congress have not done it and probably are not equipped to do it; the psychiatrists and pediatricians also have not done it and also are probably ill-equipped to do it. Fine. These groups can and should rely on the experts. And the experts are the psychologists. They are trained to review scientific research of this kind, and in the context of the NIMH review, they had the time and the funding to do the review. But they also have not done it. The APA did not do it; NIMH did not do it nor did it ask anyone else to do it. Just what NIMH based its conclusions on is unclear, but at least in terms of the published report, there was no review of the literature that would serve as the basis for drawing any conclusions.

In short, every organization has avoided the job of reviewing the research in detail. If they had acknowledged this, it would not be so bad. The real difficulty is that they have acted as if they *had* reviewed it. They have made definitive, powerful statements about the findings of the scientific research when they had no solid, independent basis for making them. Instead, presumably they have relied on what other people said and on their own intuitions. Sad!

2

Method

The purpose of this review was to find out what the scientific research has discovered. I did not want to rely on what anyone else had said about it, because too many people have been basing their beliefs on what others have reported. I also did not want anyone else to have to rely on what I said. So my plan was to make the review totally transparent. Anyone reading the review would be able to see how I evaluated each study, what criticisms I offered about it, what decisions I made about what the results showed, and why I made those decisions. With this information, readers could then go back to the original articles and decide for themselves whether they agreed with my assessments. They would not have to trust my judgments – they could make their own. Naturally, few people would bother reading all the research. However, they could select a few articles to evaluate my review, and they could also see very easily how I dealt with any article they considered important. I expect that some people will disagree with some of my assessments, but I am confident that these disagreements will be few.

I wanted to consider every piece of published research that was relevant to the issue of media violence and aggression. As anyone who has attempted one of these reviews knows, there are two phases to the search. The first step is finding the references. To do this I resorted to Internet search engines, the reference sections of published articles, the reference sections of previous reviews, systematic searches of the indexes of relevant journals, word of mouth, and any other sources I could imagine. The next step was obtaining copies of the actual publications. This was easy if they were in standard journals or recently published books. It was much more difficult if the articles were in obscure journals, or in any journals that were not in the University of

Toronto libraries or other libraries in the vicinity. To get these articles I relied on interlibrary loans, the help of friends who had access to other libraries, e-mails to authors with pleas for help, and so on. Getting the relevant books was surprisingly difficult, because many of them – even the most important – were out of print. Sometimes I had to rely on searches done by bookstores and publishers (shopping by e-mail was remarkably helpful in this respect). In all of this, I was helped by So-Jin Kang, a student at the University of Toronto and now a graduate student. She spent many hours finding and duplicating articles for me. I am grateful to her for her enormous energy and perseverance.

I placed two limitations on the search. First, with a few exceptions, I did not deal with unpublished research. This is partly because it had not been peer reviewed and therefore was likely to be of lower quality than published work. A more important consideration was that finding unpublished research would necessarily depend to some extent on chance contacts, and the articles I found that way might constitute a biased sample. For example, it is likely that a higher proportion of unpublished than of published articles failed to obtain significant effects (this is typical). If so, the unpublished research would tend not to support the causal hypothesis. Had I included many unpublished studies, I would have left myself open to charges of bias against that hypothesis. Given that there was a substantial body of published research, it seemed wiser to exclude unpublished work. In the end, I included a few unpublished articles, because they were referred to often by others and because they seemed important.

Second, I reviewed only research that was available in English. I apologize to those whose articles appeared in other languages – no disrespect was meant. Sadly, I did not feel competent to read articles that were not written in English. Although this probably excluded some excellent studies, almost all of the research in this area was either published originally in English or was translated, so this restriction eliminated very few studies.

Overall, though I cannot guarantee that I have reviewed every single relevant study, I am confident that I have included the vast majority of them and all of those that are commonly cited in the literature. As you will see, it is not possible that a few more articles would have changed my conclusions appreciably.

Some may be surprised at the small number of articles included in this review. As I noted earlier, some professional organizations, in making statements about this issue, have referred to the existence of thousands of articles, as have the popular press and some writers on this topic. John Murray suggested at the conference at Hoffstra Law School that he may have inadvertently been the source of this misinformation. He said that when he was associated with the NIMH review of television, he estimated that at that time there were approximately 2,500 publications of all kinds that were relevant to the review. This included articles in the popular press and theoretical articles, as well as scientific research articles. Moreover, it included articles that were relevant to all aspects of the review, not just television violence and aggression. Dr Murray thought it quite amusing that people were tossing around this totally inappropriate figure. I agree, but I also find it somewhat disheartening that supposedly scientific organizations and supposedly careful journalists could be so careless.

Whatever the source of the reference to 'thousands' of studies, the figure is wildly inaccurate. The fact is that there are around 200 separate scientific studies that directly assess the effects of exposure to media violence on aggression or on desensitization (and fewer separate publications, since many articles and books describe more than one study). Paik and Comstock (1994) reviewed 217 studies – about the same number as are included in my review. The overlap is by no means perfect. Those two included articles that I did not think fit my criteria (mainly because they were unpublished), and I have included some articles that aren't in their review. However, it should be clear that there are not thousands or even hundreds of relevant articles. The roughly 200 studies included in this review constitute virtually all of the published studies that present original research on the topic.

Not a Meta-analysis

In assessing this body of literature, I did not rely on a meta-analysis. The meta-analysis is a sophisticated way of combining and assessing the results of a number of studies. When every study or almost every study gets the same results, one does not usually need any fancy statistics to know that there is or is not an effect. But when the studies do show an effect, it is often important to know how strong it is, and this is sometimes difficult to assess. Meta-analysis can provide the answer. For example, there have been quite a few investigations of the relationship between cigarette smoking and lung cancer. Although the results have virtually always shown a relationship, the size of the effect has varied from study to study and for different kinds of cancer. A meta-analysis by Khuder (2001) combined the results of all the studies and concluded that smokers are between 4 and 38 times more likely than non-smokers to get lung cancer, depending on the particular type of cancer.

Meta-analysis is even more useful when the studies have produced inconsistent results – that is, when some show an effect, some show no effect, some show an effect under some conditions or with some populations but not others, and some even show an opposite effect. When this occurs, as it does in the research on media violence, it may be difficult to establish whether the overall results indicate that an effect exists. A meta-analysis can sometimes be used to reach sensible conclusions about whether there is an effect and, if there is one, how strong it is.

An example of this is a meta-analysis of studies that investigated the effect of treatment on juvenile offenders (Lipsey, 1992). A wide variety of treatments have been used, and a wide variety of outcome measures (e.g., repeat offending, school grades, self-esteem). Whichever outcome measure was used, the results also varied considerably. A few showed a strong positive effect; a few showed a strong negative effect; and most showed quite small effects, either positive or negative. However, a clear majority of the studies found positive effects: 64 per cent positive versus 30 per cent negative and 6 per cent no effect. This pattern of results suggests that there is generally an effect that is quite small, but without some kind of statistical test it is difficult to have much confidence in those conclusions. The meta-analysis comes to precisely those conclusions and thus reinforces the more subjective impression. If the breakdown of the results had been closer – if 55 per cent had been positive, 40 per cent negative, and 5 per cent no effect, subjective impressions would have been less clear, and the meta-analysis would have been even more helpful.

There is no question that meta-analysis is a powerful and useful technique, but it does have serious limitations. The standard procedure is to look at each study and extract the relevant result. In the lung cancer study, it was the odds ratio (OR) of how many got cancer in one condition compared to another. If 1 per cent of non-smokers and 15 per cent of smokers got lung cancer, the OR would be 15.0 (fifteen times as many smokers got cancer). In the juvenile delinquent treatment study the chief measure used was the difference between conditions in how many reoffended. As long as there is only one measure of the effect (or perhaps two) and the measures are straightforward, there are few problems at this stage.

The next step is to decide how many different tests of the effect were included in each study. If a study compares smokers with non-smokers and looks at how many got lung cancer, there is one test. If (as in the example given above) several different types of lung cancer are considered, there is still one overall effect (total lung cancers), but also several subeffects, one for each type of lung cancer. If a study looks at smoking and ten different diseases, there are ten different tests of the effect. This is important, because the more tests there are, the more likely it is that some will occur simply by chance. This does not matter much if the effects are powerful and consistent, but it matters a great deal if the effects are weak and inconsistent. So counting the number of tests is crucial.

Although all of this may sound straightforward, there are many difficult decisions to make. And the more complicated and varied the research, the more difficult these decisions become. These difficulties are especially apparent in the research on media violence, which involves complex research designs, small samples, incomplete presentation of the results, and multiple measures of often questionable validity.

Let me take a meta-analysis of the literature on television violence as an example of the difficulties. Wood, Young, and Chachere (1991) conducted a meta-analysis of experiments in which the measure was what they called 'unconstrained social interaction.' That is, they looked only at studies in which people were exposed to violent programs and their actual aggressive behaviour was observed in a natural setting. They included twenty-three studies, some of which were unpublished. This is a very small percentage of all of the research on this topic, and did not include quite a few studies that would seem to have met their criteria. Nevertheless, it was a serious albeit limited enterprise.

The first decision the authors had to make was which studies to include. They had resolved that the studies would have to observe aggression in a natural setting; now they further decided to exclude studies in which observers rated the behaviour at the end of some period rather than immediately. This excluded only a few studies, but among those was a study by Feshbach and Singer (1971) in which the main measure of aggression was based on ratings done at the end of the day by the students' teachers. This is admittedly a somewhat different measure than one based on direct observation, but there is no reason to think it is less accurate. Indeed, it may be more valid and accurate than measures based on observations taken immediately after the showing of a film. The authors are not clear about why they excluded it, and they may have had excellent reasons. But the fact is that if they had included it, the results of the meta-analysis would have been quite different. The Feshbach and Singer study was considerably more extensive than any of the studies they did use. It included seven related but separate experiments (i.e., the same experiment done in seven different institutions) that would have constituted a substantial percentage of all of the experiments included in the meta-analysis. Had those seven been added it would have brought the number to thirty, with the seven being almost one-quarter of the total. Moreover, three of the Feshbach and Singer experiments found a significant effect in the opposite direction from that predicted by the causal hypothesis, and none of the other four found any effect. So the decision to exclude this study, while perhaps justified, had a substantial impact on the analysis, shifting it considerably in the direction favouring the causal hypothesis.

The authors also decided to exclude studies that employed 'highly structured interaction contexts,' which they argued might underestimate or overestimate naturally occurring aggression. This justification is arguable, and given the small number of available experiments, one would have thought the authors would want to include as many as possible. In any case, this decision seems to have excluded just two studies, both conducted by Hapkiewicz and colleagues (Hapkiewicz & Roden, 1971; Hapkiewicz & Stone, 1974). Like the Feshbach and Singer experiments, these studies would have provided evidence against the causal hypothesis.

The Hapkiewicz experiments involved quite large groups of children – much larger than in most of the studies that *were* included in the analysis – and observed their aggression against other children. One study compared the effects of an aggressive cartoon with those of both a non-aggressive cartoon and no cartoon. It found that the cartoons had no significant effect on aggression for boys and girls combined, but that the boys were more aggressive in the no-cartoon condition. The measure for the sexes combined (which is all that the paper provided) indicates an effect size of –.7, which is larger than all but a few reported in the meta-analysis.

The second study compared an aggressive film with real people (*The Three Stooges*), an aggressive cartoon, and a non-aggressive film. The type of film had no effect on the girls' aggression. The boys were most aggressive after *The Three Stooges* and least aggressive after the aggressive cartoon. Again, the results generally failed to support the causal hypothesis. At best one could classify them as three failures (both comparisons for the girls, and the comparison aggressive cartoon to non-aggressive film for the boys) and one success (*The Three Stooges* versus non-aggressive film for the boys).

These two studies, with their large numbers of participants, provided results that would have changed the outcome of the meta-analysis. They consisted of mostly no effects, one slightly supportive effect, and one quite strong contradictory effect. I am not suggesting that these studies were deliberately omitted from the analysis. My only point is that the decisions the authors made about what studies to include substantially altered the results of their analysis.

Besides judgments about which studies to include, the meta-analysis required judgments about how each of the twenty-three studies was to be classified in terms of the number of tests and the effects found. In my opinion, some of those classifications were incorrect. Consider a study by Huston-Stein (Huston-Stein, Fox, Greer, Watkins, & Whitaker, 1981). The goal of this study was to compare and assess the impact of the amount of action in films and violence in films on aggression. This was similar to research on reducing blood pressure, in which some people are put on a low-fat diet and are given drugs, others are put on the diet and are not given drugs, and still others neither go on a diet nor take drugs. If blood pressure is reduced more with the diet plus drugs than with just the diet, then the drugs are effective. But if diet alone is as good as diet plus drugs, obviously the drugs do not work.

In the Huston-Stein study, some children watched films that were high in violence and also high in action, others watched films that were low in violence and high in action, and still others watched films that were low in both violence and action. Other children did not see a film. On the key measure of overt aggression, the type of film had no overall effect, and no two group were shown to differ significantly. Of particular importance, the high violence/high action group and low violence/high action groups were very similar in terms of their aggression (in fact, the former showed slightly less aggression). In other words, action without violence had about the same effect on aggression as action *with* violence – the violence was followed by no additional aggression and may even have reduced the effect. Since the main point of this study was to compare the effects of high action with the effects of high violence, clearly this result should be classified as showing either that the films had no effect or that it was the action that affected the aggression, not the violence. Instead of supporting the causal hypothesis, the result contradicted it. Accordingly, I see no justification for classifying the result as showing that violence increased aggression. Yet that is how the meta-analysis classified it. This is like a drug company claiming that a drug was effective even though diet alone had the same effect as the diet plus the drug. It is incorrect and clearly distorts – indeed reverses – the implication of the result.

The review also included the study by Friedrich and Stein (1973) that I mentioned earlier. I disagree with the authors of the meta-analysis on almost everything about this study except the number of participants. First, I believe there were five main measures of aggression, not one; and two comparisons for each of them (the violent group versus the prosocial group, and the violent group versus the neutral group) for a total of ten tests of the hypothesis. Moreover, measures were taken at several points in time, which provided at least two tests to compare to the baseline measure. I also believe that there was no significant difference on any of these tests – that is, the experimental group that saw violent films did not differ from either the neutral or the prosocial group on any of five measures of aggression. Thus, even ignoring the time element, I would have classified the results as ten failures as opposed to the two successes recorded in the paper. If one wanted to focus only on physical aggression, there would be two failures. The authors of the meta-analysis apparently ignored these basic tests that failed to support the hypothesis. Instead, following the lead of the article's authors, the meta-analysis focused on a complex and questionable statistical analysis that combined two measures, divided children into high and low aggression on the basis of their initial scores, and even then found only a marginally significant effect. There was no justification for basing the meta-analysis on this secondary analysis, but that is what Wood and colleagues did. As with the previous study, this reversed the classification of the results from not supporting the effect to supporting it.

A third study, by Josephson (1987), is difficult to classify. It is a complex study with very complicated results. I am confident that overall, these results do not show that exposure to media violence increases aggression. Rather, I would classify the study as showing at least two no effects, one strong reversal, and perhaps one effect.

I disagree with some of the other classifications in the meta-analysis, but it is not worth going through all the details. The point I am trying to make is that it is not always easy to classify results. Although I do not agree with Wood and colleagues in their classification of the Huston-

Stein and Josephson studies, I am not entirely sure how the results should be classified. A meta-analysis requires a simple classification – whether the results supported, did not support, or contradicted the effect, and how large the effect was. Yet often this kind of simple classification is not easy or even possible. In contrast, a more detailed description of the study does not require this kind of simple classification. As will be seen, it is possible to decide that its results were complicated, and perhaps supported the effect in one respect and contradicted it in another. Meta-analyses allow this type of classification, but they are rarely used.

It is interesting that those who especially like meta-analysis sometimes say they eliminate the possibility of bias. In contrast, reviews that describe studies in detail and try to make sense of them supposedly involve more judgment and therefore more chance for bias. As I hope I have made clear, this is a false distinction. With simple studies, little judgment is necessary and bias is unlikely to affect classification. With complex studies, considerable judgment is involved in classifying results, and bias can enter into the classification whether it is a meta-analysis or a more qualitative one. In particular, I believe that Wood and colleagues tended to err on the side of classifying the results as showing the effect and also on the side of minimizing the number of tests of the effect. Both proclivities tended to increase the apparent strength of the effect.

Since this analysis covers only a small percentage of the relevant studies, it is not worth debating whose analysis is correct. The point is that meta-analysis is no cure-all: one must still read critically and decide how to classify each study, how much weight to give it, and whether to accept the methodology and statistical analyses. These are, of course, matters of judgment, and people differ in the judgments they make. But ignoring this and using a 'blind' meta-analysis does not guarantee getting at the truth. Indeed, meta-analysis is useful only after one has made the judgments, difficult though they may be.

In 1994, Paik and Comstock conducted a much more extensive meta-analysis. Their conclusion: studies of all kinds – lab experiments, field research, and so on – indicate that media violence increases aggression. Furthermore, the effect was highly significant. For some reason, the published paper did not indicate at all how they classified the results, how many tests each study included, and so on. Since these details are crucial, it is impossible to evaluate their analysis. As we shall see, their conclusions differ markedly from mine, and frankly, I find it difficult to understand how they could have reached them. However, lacking the details, I cannot comment on what they did.

Although some are enamoured of meta-analysis, I hope I have made it clear why I do not think it is especially helpful with this literature. In conducting such an analysis, it is often very difficult to make judgments about the number of tests available, and to classify the results for each test. If these judgments and classifications are arbitrary or biased, the analysis will be incorrect. Also, one cannot simply accept the results of the research as presented by the authors: a review must assess each scientific study and decide how much weight to give it. Accepting the authors' descriptions of the results without an independent assessment can lead to false conclusions. Similarly, when unpublished studies are included that have been obtained without an exhaustive search, the result can easily be a biased selection of studies that tend to favour the position held by those doing the meta-analysis. Had I searched for unpublished articles, those I found would probably have been somewhat different from those found by Paik and Comstock or by Wood and colleagues. Since unpublished studies have not been peer reviewed and do not constitute a complete or even nearly complete set of all unpublished work, they should not be included. Finally, I should repeat that in doing a meta-analysis, it is essential to review all the studies in detail. Those who conduct meta-analyses may do this kind of review, but they do not publish the details. Yet only by knowing these details can a reader evaluate the findings and the quality of the meta-analysis.

It is precisely this kind of detailed review that I have undertaken. I believe that this complex literature is best assessed by an exhaustive review of the research combined with a count of the results of the studies. That is what I have carried out.

How the Review Was Done

In reviewing each article, I begin by summarizing the methods and results at 'face value.' I ignore any problems with the methods and any ambiguities in or difficulties with the results. This does not always mean that my presentation of the results is precisely the same as what the authors provide. It does mean that I describe the results as they are shown in the actual tables and graphs of the article, not as they are described in the abstract or the discussion section. In other words, I do not rely on what the authors say about the results; instead I describe the results as they appear in the results section.

After presenting the methods and results without criticism, I offer any criticisms that I think are appropriate. In particular, I offer these when I believe they concern how the results were interpreted. I acknowledge that I began this review being quite sceptical of the causal hypothesis and the research that supposedly supports it. While doing this review I was aware of my own scepticism and tried very hard to take a balanced approach to each study. Few studies are perfect, and it is almost always possible to find fault or limitations. I tried to focus on only those points that mattered, and I made a great effort to be equally critical regardless of the study's results. That being said, I spent much more time on those studies that purported to find significant effects (in either direction) than I did on those that failed to find effects. I believe this was justified, because it is the former studies that bear the brunt of the scientific argument. I also spent more time on those studies that have been widely cited, because again, they have been at the centre of this debate.

Having described and then criticized the studies, for each I draw a conclusion as to whether it supports the causal hypothesis, does not support it, or produced mixed results. For each type of research, I then summarize what the studies found. Finally, I present an overall summary that brings together all the individual summaries and reaches a conclusion about the current status of the causal hypothesis. In a shorter section I do the same for the desensitization hypothesis. Thus, this review of all or virtually all the relevant research will enable the reader to assess whether each of the key hypotheses is supported by the scientific research.

In terms of organization, the studies are divided into survey studies, laboratory experiments, field experiments, longitudinal studies, studies that assess aggression or crime when television is present or absent (I call these 'with and without' studies), a few studies using different methods, and studies that are relevant to the desensitization hypothesis. The summaries of the findings and conclusions are presented in a series of chapters dealing with the various kinds of research. This is followed by an overall summary and conclusions.

3

Survey Research: Are Exposure to Media Violence and Aggression Related?

The first question to be asked is whether exposure to violent media and aggression are related. Are children who watch more violent programs more aggressive than those who watch fewer? This is the first question because only if the answer is yes is there much reason to pursue the issue further. If, in the real world, there is an association between exposure to violent media and aggression, this raises the possibility that the former causes the latter. If there is no such association – if children who are exposed to lots of violent programs are no more aggressive than those who are exposed to fewer – it becomes exceedingly unlikely that violent programs affect aggression. So, the first step in studying the issue is to ascertain whether there is a correlation between exposure to violence and aggression.

The way to find out whether the two are related is simple in theory but quite difficult in practice. The idea is to find out how much media violence children are exposed to and also how aggressive these same children are, and then calculate whether the two measures are related. To do this all that is necessary is a measure of exposure, a measure of aggression, and a statistical calculation of the correlation between the two measures. All of this is straightforward. Similar studies have been done on hundreds of measures such as the relation between smoking and cancer, eating fat and heart disease, diet and height, and all sorts of personality measures. Scientists know the basic method and have been using it for decades. Unfortunately, it is easier said than done.

Problems with the Research

Doing the research well so that it provides meaningful results is very difficult. The first problem is obtaining information that will generalize to the general population. It is important to understand that these are descriptive studies. They are not trying to test a theory or assess the effect of one variable on another. Rather, they are trying to describe the relationship, if any, between exposure to media violence and aggression among real people in the real world. To do this they gather information on only a tiny percentage of all of the people in the world and hope that what the study finds will be an accurate reflection of not just the people included in the survey but all people, or at least all people in a particular area or country. Though it might be interesting to find out the association between exposure to violence and aggression in a group of forty six-year-olds in an élite private school in New Hampshire, no one would suggest that this finding should be generalized to the rest of New Hampshire, much less to the rest of the United States or the world. Yet that is what we care about. We want to know whether there is a relationship between exposure to media violence and aggression in all children in all countries.

To put this in perspective, it may be useful to think in terms of the polling that is done for presidential campaigns. The goal of these surveys is to get a sense of the opinions of potential and likely voters, and in the long run to predict the outcome of the election. Finding out how forty people in a small town in Kansas are planning to vote is not especially helpful. How the forty Kansans are likely to vote does not even tell you how the rest of the town will vote, because forty is too small a sample. After polling every voter in the town, you could be quite confident about how that town was going to vote, but even that poll would tell you very little about the rest of Kansas, and almost nothing about the rest of the country.

Pollsters need a large enough sample of voters to provide a reasonable estimate of the opinions of the rest of the population. However, a large sample is not sufficient, because it might tell you about only a limited portion of the population. To provide an accurate estimate for the whole population, the sample must include the same percentage of every type of person that the whole population contains. This is difficult to achieve, but that is the task of survey experts. Both criteria are crucial: the sample must be large enough, and it must also be representative enough to offer a chance of reflecting the opinions of all voters.

Sample size. The sample must be large, because with a small group there is too much chance of error due to all sorts of known and unknown factors. If you ask fifty people how they are planning to vote, purely by chance you may have selected more Democrats (or more Republicans) than there are in the population at large. You have no way of knowing this, but you can minimize the chance of error by asking enough people. The results of surveys are usually reported with some statement about the range of error and also the likelihood of error in that range. We hear all the time that the survey is accurate within 4 per cent 95 times out of a 100. What the 4 per cent figure means is that if the poll shows that one candidate has 55 per cent of the vote, you can be fairly confident that the true, underlying, actual preference of the population at that moment is 55 per cent plus or minus 4 per cent, or somewhere between 51 per cent and 59 per cent. What the 95 times out of 100 means is that the odds are 19 out of 20 (or 95 out of 100) that the true figure falls in the range from 51 per cent to 59 per cent. These kind of figures (4 per cent range 95 times out of 100) would be true only for quite a large sample of people. If you sampled only 100 people the range would be far greater, and any less than that and the figures would mean very little. To have any reasonable confidence that the survey accurately describes the population, you need a sample of several hundred, preferably close to 1,000. Surprisingly, the size of the sample you need does not increase much as the size of the population increases. To poll the opinions of all Americans you probably need a sample that is no larger than you would need to poll the opinions of all Canadians. The margin of error depends on the size of the sample, not the size of the population. The important point is that regardless of the size of the population, you need a pretty big sample.

Representative sample. The second and even more difficult requirement is that the sample be representative of the population of interest. If you are interested in opinions of students attending a particular university, you would want a sample that included students from all classes, all programs, both sexes, all ethnic and racial groups, all levels of ability, and so on. Only if you sample students from all groups, and sample them in proportion to their actual representation in the total population of students, can you have much confidence that your results will reflect the opinions of the whole school. The same is true whatever the population of concern. So to find out the opinions of those who live in Chicago, you need a representative sample of people in Chicago; to find out the opinions of those who live in California, you need a sample of Californians; and to find out the opinions of all

American voters, you need a representative sample of all voters in the country.

Those who do survey research are extremely good at getting representative samples. Using sophisticated techniques, they can be almost certain that they have obtained responses from approximately the right number of people from each of the groups they want. They know that if they do not have a representative sample, their findings will be flawed (i.e., will not reflect the opinions of the population). Thus they go to great lengths to get good samples. This is expensive and time consuming, but necessary if the results are to be meaningful.

Unfortunately, the research on our concern – exposure to media violence and aggression – has not generally obtained large enough samples, and samples that have been used have almost never been representative. A few studies had samples in the thousands, and some had samples in the hundreds, but many had samples of less than 100 (which makes the findings extremely unreliable). Also, and even more serious, only one study employed a national, representative sample. A few tried to obtain representative samples of particular communities or states, but most did not even try to use representative samples. This lack of representativeness is especially salient when one considers how small most sample were. For example, a study done in Israel reported some of the strongest relationships in the literature, yet it used a non-representative sample of only seventy-six children. The small size makes the results highly unreliable, and the lack of representativeness means that one cannot generalize from this result (even if it were reliable) to the population as a whole. Indeed, in this same study another sample, this one from another part of the country (a kibbutz rather than a city), found no relationship between exposure to media violence and aggression. Similar problems arise in many of the studies. Thus, there is no question that the studies in this group generally fail to meet the usual standard of survey research, and this makes it difficult to evaluate their results. Certainly, the findings do not merit the same level of confidence that one would have in research that did have large representative samples.

I should note that there are many good reasons why most of the studies did not attain the usual standards of survey research. The research we are interested in required that aggression and exposure to media violence both be measured. Both of these are complex variables that cannot easily be measured using the usual survey techniques. Also, large surveys are extremely expensive. There is a lot more money available to poll voting preferences and opinions about soft drinks than there is to study media violence. Although some of the studies described above were probably very expensive, most of them were not. Limited funds and specialized needs meant that the usual survey techniques were not well suited to collect the needed data. Therefore, my comments about small sample sizes and lack of representativeness of those samples are not meant as a criticism of the work, but merely an acknowledgment of its limitations.

Measurement problems. The other limitation of the research is the difficulty of obtaining reasonable measures of the two key variables. It is relatively easy to find out people's political preferences. When you ask them how they are likely to vote, and when you assure them that their answers are totally confidential and anonymous, most people are quite willing to tell you honestly. There is nothing embarrassing about being for either major candidate – or, for that matter, being for a minor candidate. The people have little reason to withhold an answer or to lie.

In contrast, when they are asked how much violent media they watch and how aggressive they are, people may be reluctant to give any answers, much less entirely honest ones. It is not that it is terribly embarrassing to like violent television, but most young people know that most adults would prefer them to watch less violent programs. More to the point, all young people know that it is considered wrong to be aggressive and very wrong to be violently aggressive. Even if their answers are entirely confidential, they may be reluctant to tell the whole truth; and if their answers are not confidential or they are not certain of confidentiality, they are more likely to distort the truth. Thus, more than with most variables, we cannot be entirely confident that the answers are honest.

Moreover, even if everyone is being as honest as possible, the measures of both variables have serious limitations. If someone asks you how many eggs you eat every week, and how often you eat cold cereal, you can probably give an extremely accurate answer. I eat almost no eggs and I eat cold cereal four or five times a week. Asking about media violence and aggression is far more difficult. You cannot simply ask people how much violent television they watch or how aggressive they are, because most people cannot give an intelligent, meaningful answer. Think about it – if you were asked how much media violence you are exposed to, would you find it easy to answer accurately? Certainly it would be hard for most people to answer in terms of a scale ranging from 'none' to 'a great deal.' Unless people never watch any violent programs, how are they to judge how much they watch? If the choices are in terms of the number of programs per week containing violence, it may be somewhat easier to answer; but this does not make a distinction between slightly violent programs and very violent ones. If the question asks for the person's four favourite programs, and the programs are then rated for violence, it will give some indication of exposure. But someone whose four favourites are all violent but whose next six favourites are not will be scored the same as someone whose ten favourites are all violent.

Measuring aggressiveness is probably even more difficult. When people rate themselves either in terms of overall aggressiveness or in terms of specific aggressive acts, they have all sorts of reasons not to tell the whole truth. Furthermore, it would be difficult for them to give accurate answers even if they wanted to. Indeed, even conceptually, it is not clear how we should rate people in terms of aggressiveness. Is someone who commits many minor aggressive acts more aggressive than someone who commits few, more serious aggressive acts? What about someone who is almost never in the least bit aggressive, but who once or twice has committed very serious acts of aggression? There are no easy answers to this, and no measure of aggression has succeeded in dealing with this issue.

Contamination. An especially serious problem is that the measures of exposure to violent media and aggression may not be entirely independent – that they may contaminate each other. This can happen for several reasons. First, it is possible and even likely that the answers to questions about the two behaviours affect each other. People who are willing to say they watch a lot of violent television may also be willing to say they engage in aggressive behaviour – or at least, they may be more willing to admit the latter if they are also willing to admit the former. In contrast, some people may not be willing to admit either. But these people may in fact be quite aggressive even though they do not watch much vioent television, or they may not be very aggressive even though they watch a lot of violent television. To the extent this is true, the two variables may seem more closely related than they really are. Other kinds of response biases can also inflate the correlation between the two variables.

Second, when other people do the ratings they may be influenced by their beliefs about how these variables are related. In several studies, mothers were the source of information about their children's viewing preferences. Their responses may have been influenced to some extent by their knowledge of their children's aggressiveness. A mother who knows that her son is very aggressive may assume that he likes violent programs. A similar effect can occur when peers do ratings of aggressiveness. If they know, for example, that a girl loves violent television, they may assume that she must be aggressive and rate her accordingly. Perhaps even more likely, if they know that a boy dislikes violent programs, they may think he is not aggressive and rate him low on aggression, even though in reality he is quite aggressive. We have no way of knowing how strong these effects are, but they are very likely to be present to some extent. Any such effects will produce an overestimation of the actual correlation. More to the point, they will tend to make the correlations positive even if the 'true' correlation is zero or negative.

Measurement errors. A different problem with this research is that all of the ratings are subject to various sources of error. However good the measures are, their accuracy depends heavily on those giving the answers. In much of this research, peers rate one another on aggressiveness. As I will discuss in another section, this may well be the best way to measure aggressiveness; after all, peers are familiar with one another, they have lots of time to observe one another's behaviour, and unlike teachers and parents, peers have an opportunity to observe one another when adults are not present. However, peers almost certainly make all sorts of mistakes in their ratings. Some of them will not take the task seriously and will even make deliberate mistakes. Some will make honest mistakes, confusing Fred with Frank or Helmut with Heinrich (this is especially likely when the ratings are done from memory). Others will have response tendencies that interfere with accurate ratings (some people avoid extreme ratings, others prefer them), and so on. All of these factors make the measures less good and less reliable. To the extent that the measures are unreliable, the correlations that are found tend to underestimate the true correlation.

In other words, the previously noted problems with the research tend to magnify the relationship between the two variables; in contrast, measurement problems tend to minimize the relationship. There is no way of knowing the net effect of these two opposite tendencies, but it should be clear that this research has not produced, and cannot produce, results in which we can place strong confidence. The research may exaggerate or understate the actual relationship between exposure and aggression. For now all we can do is describe the findings of the research and make an educated guess about the actual relationship.

Results

It may be helpful now to describe some of the findings. With a large representative sample of children in New York City, McCarthy and colleagues (1975) found no appreciable correlations between measures of preference for violent programs and aggression. Thornton and Voight (1984) reported correlations around .15 with the sexes combined (which tends to inflate the real correlation). Eron and colleagues (1971) used the entire third grade population of Columbia County in New York and computed a correlation of .31 for the boys but only .02 for the girls. McLeod, Atkin, and Chaffee (1972) found positive correlations for both boys and girls. Among sixth graders in Wisconsin the correlations were .12 for boys and .38 for girls. With a large probability sample – which is similar to but somewhat less good than a true representative sample – of junior and senior high school students in Maryland, Hartnagel and colleagues (1975) discovered an overall correlation of .12 between favourite programs and aggression. Greenberg (1974) reported a correlation around .15 for both boys and girls in London, England. Milavsky and colleagues (1982) found correlations that averaged .17 for boys and .30 for girls. With generally much smaller samples, the cross-national project (Huesmann & Eron, 1986) found considerable variation in correlations. In the United States (the largest sample) the correlations ranged from .13 to .29, in the Netherlands from .08 to .40, and in Finland from –.16 to .38. In Australia all correlations were small. In Israel the correlations were very high (.48 and .45) for the city sample, but zero for the kibbutz sample (all with very small samples).

The above results were for children under ten. With older children the correlations were typically smaller. Greenberg found correlations around .15. Milavsky and colleagues reported correlations for teenage boys ranging from .16 to .07. Using a large sample of teenagers that was to some extent representative, Hartnagel and colleagues found a correlation of .12. Eron and colleagues followed up their original sample ten years later (Lefkowitz et al., 1977), and reported that at the age of eighteen there were no positive correlations between preference for violent television and any measure of aggression for either sex. Surprisingly, the amount of television (not the amount of violence but total television viewing) was negatively correlated (–.19) with aggressiveness for boys.

Inconsistency. With all of the limitations of the work, it is not surprising that the studies produced highly variable results. Even if the measures of exposure and aggression were perfect (which, of course, they could not be), the lack of representative samples and the small size of the samples would be expected to produce highly variable results. Sure enough they do. As can be seen in the list of results, the correlations between exposure to (or preference for) violent television and aggression ranged considerably. The actual range was from negative (–.20) to strongly positive (.68). Indeed, even within the same studies, some samples found strong positive correlations while others found no relationship. Ignoring the results of the studies with very small samples, the range in correlations was still from about –.2 to +.4.

Moreover, even the pattern of results was inconsistent from study to study. For example, in their early study Eron and colleagues found a positive correlation for boys but not for girls; some years later, in their section of the cross-national study, the correlation for girls was higher than for boys. The authors went to considerable lengths to explain the lack of correlation for girls in the first study and the relatively strong correlation in the second study. Their explanation dealt with changing patterns of female aggression, the presence of aggressive women in television programs, and so on. Yet at almost the same time as Eron and colleagues did their first study, McLeod and colleagues found the opposite pattern – stronger correlations among girls than among boys. Thus, no complex explanation is necessary or even appropriate. Rather, it seems that this is just one more example of the lack of consistency in these results.

The lack of consistency is almost certainly due in large part to the small size of the samples. Also, some of the differences in the results may be due to the fact that the studies used quite different methods. Some studies based their measures of violence viewing on what parents said about their children's viewing preferences. As suggested by the finding that mothers and fathers differed considerably in their responses, this is probably not as good or reliable a method as asking the children themselves. In contrast, asking peers to rate one another's aggressiveness (a method developed by Eron et al.) is probably an excellent method – better than asking the children to rate themselves, and almost certainly better than asking their parents to do the ratings. Similarly, measuring exposure with a list of programs actually watched is better than simply asking for preferred programs without knowing how often they are seen. Given that some measures are better than others, and that some are quite unreliable, it is not surprising that the studies produced somewhat different results.

However, it should be clear that these variations cannot explain all the inconsistencies. All of the studies in the cross-national project used very similar methods and measures, but obtained correlations ranging from strongly positive (in the Israeli city sample) to essentially zero (in the Israeli kibbutz sample and in Australia). It is possible but highly unlikely that the underlying correlations are that different in different communities and different countries. Just why the studies obtained such diverse results is not clear, but that they are inconsistent certainly is.

Conclusions

Given this pattern of results, what conclusions can we draw from the findings? First, despite the inconsistencies, and despite the contamination of the measures, it seems likely that the underlying correlation is positive, at least for children under ten. True, there are a few negative correlations, but the vast majority are positive. Of greater importance, the best studies – those with the largest samples combined with the best measures – produced correlations that were quite consistently positive. And in those studies the correlations stayed about the same size from ages six to about ten, which suggests that there is an underlying positive correlation that is fairly constant. So, I think it is reasonable to conclude that the true correlation between exposure to violent media and aggression is positive for children up to about age ten.

On the other hand, it would be a mistake to overstate this. It has sometimes been asserted that the relationship between exposure to violent media and aggression is one of the most strongly and consistently supported findings about social behaviour. This is obviously not true. In fact, the evidence is weak and inconsistent. My conclusion that there is probably an underlying relationship is not based on strong evidence. If I had to bet, I would bet that a relationship exists, but I would not bet much, and I would not have much confidence that I would win. A plausible alternative view is that the contamination of the measures is sufficient to produce positive correlations and that therefore we have no idea whether the true correlation is positive. In a strict sense, this is correct. We cannot estimate the amount of contamination, nor can we estimate the effect it has. Since the correlations are generally quite low, they could have been produced entirely by contamination.

Despite the limitations of the research and the availability of alternative explanations for the positive correlations, I think the best guess is that the underlying correlation for children under ten is positive, and I shall proceed from that point of view. It would be extremely helpful if someone would conduct a study with a large representative sample that obtained measures of both exposure to media violence and aggressiveness so that for once we could say with some confidence that the two are or are not correlated. Absent that, the most we can conclude is that there probably is a relationship, but the scientific evidence for it is quite limited.

Second, it seems clear that the correlations are rather small. Contamination would magnify them; unreliability would reduce them. We cannot assess the relative strengths of these two factors, so I think it is best to ignore them both. While there is no solid basis for estimating the real correlation, I think the best guess is that the actual underlying correlation is in the range .1 to .2.

Some have described the correlations as being around .3. There is no scientific foundation for that assertion. As noted earlier, some studies have found correlations that high or higher, but most have not. The underlying correlation could be as high as .3, but it seems unlikely, especially given that some of the best studies, with the largest number of subjects, found smaller correlations.

The difference between a correlation between .1 and .2 and one of .3 may not seem of great consequence, but it is substantial. A correlation between .1 and .2 means that the association of the two variables accounts for between 1 and 4 per cent of the variance. If one picked the mid-point of .15, it would explain just over 2 per cent of the variance. To put this differently, knowing the exposure score allows one to predict about 2 per cent of the aggression score, and vice versa. This is not a strong association. In contrast, the highest conceivable correlation of .3 would explain 9 per cent of the variation – more than four times as much. This is still not an enormous relationship, but it is substantial. Whatever the actual number, it seems likely that there is some positive relationship between the variables. This leaves open the crucial question whether there is any causal relationship. That is what the bulk of this review will attempt to answer.

A Note on Correlations and Causality

In reading the rest of the review, it is important to keep in mind how difficult it is to establish the causes of complex human behaviour. As difficult as it is to obtain accurate, precise descriptions of human behaviour, it is a far greater challenge to pinpoint causality. The difference between description and causal conclusions is especially evident when we are dealing with correlations. A correlation exists when two factors or variables are associated with each other in the sense that when one is present, so is the other and when one is absent, so is the other. More generally, a correlation exists when as one variable increases, the other variable tends to increase, and vice versa for decreasing. As a simple example, children's age and height are correlated – older children tend to be taller than younger children. This is a very strong correlation and is due, of course, to the fact that children grow from birth to adolescence. Correlations can be positive (as one increases so does the other) or negative (as one increases the other decreases); and they range in magnitude from –1.0 to +1.0. A correlation of 1.0 means that there is an absolute and total association – as one variable increases, so does the other at precisely the same rate (or decreases at the same rate). Correlations of less than 1.0 mean that the association is weaker.

Correlations do not indicate causality. What makes correlations both interesting and tricky is that we all have an inclination to assume that when two things are correlated, one must cause the other. Scientists know this is not true, but even they are tempted to believe it is. This can produce a great deal of confusion and false conclusions because correlations do not indicate causality – they may raise the possibility that one factor causes the other, but whether it actually does is an open question.

Let me use a medical example. Imagine that eating carrots and the incidence of heart disease are negatively correlated – the more carrots people eat, the less likely they are to get heart disease. This has actually been reported a number of times, as have similar associations between diet and other medical conditions. Assuming the research has been done well, we start with the knowledge that carrots is correlated with lower rates of heart disease. This sounds interesting. When this is reported, it is often suggested that carrots must reduce the chances of having a heart attack, and that people should therefore eat lots of carrots. Now it may well be true that carrots are good for your health and do help prevent heart attacks, but the correlation does not prove that.

If carrots do not prevent heart attacks, why is there a correlation? With most correlations, there are three logical possibilities regarding causality: factor A can affect factor B; factor B can affect A; and some other factor or factors can affect both A and B although A and B have no effect on each other. Consider our carrots. The usual conclusion people jump to is that A causes B – that eating carrots prevents heart attacks. An alternative is that B causes A, that somehow heart attacks make people eat fewer carrots. Although perhaps we could think of how this would work, in this case it seems pretty implausible – not impossible but unlikely. But – and this must always be considered – there is the third possibility that some other factor makes people eat lots of carrots and also reduces the risk of heart attack. An obvious third factor would be that some people take better care of their health than others – that they exercise, get enough sleep, take vacations, avoid too much alcohol, don't smoke, and eat healthy foods. These people are healthier than most people and are less likely to have heart conditions; these people also tend to eat more carrots (they also eat more vegetables in general, less fat, more fish, and so on). In other words, carrots have nothing much to do with a lower risk of heart attack – the correlation is caused by healthy lifestyles, which lead to both more carrots and fewer heart attacks. Carrots by themselves may have had absolutely no effect on heart attacks.

The problem for scientists, and for all of us, is to decide whether either of the factors in a correlation causes the other. This is not easy, but it is the crux of the scientific discussion and the core of a great deal of research. Forgive me for repeating this, but it is absolutely crucial in understanding this review: that two variables are correlated does not mean one causes the other – they may have no effect on each other. Only research can tell us if there is any causal connection.

To bring us to the current inquiry, we are fairly confident that children who watch a lot of media violence – or perhaps only prefer violent programs – tend to be more aggressive than children who watch less media violence. However, this is not the end of the inquiry but rather the beginning of it. This correlation raises the possibility that exposure to media violence causes children to be aggressive, but it is *only* a possibility. Most of the research in this field is devoted to trying to establish a causal link between media violence and aggression.

Some very knowledgeable experts believe that only experiments can demonstrate causality. Although there is no question that experiments are the best way to do this, there are times when the perfect experiment is not possible. Then we must rely on non-experimental research (correlational research) to try to demonstrate causality. I agree that only experiments can prove causality, but I believe that it is possible to make a case for causality using non-experimental methods. This is difficult, and we can almost never have the same degree of confidence in the result. Nevertheless, when the appropriate experiments cannot be done, I do not think we should give up. We can try to gather evidence that is consistent with a causal effect and that is inconsistent with or less likely to be consistent with a non-causal effect. The lines of reasoning are difficult and require considerable ingenuity, but the right arguments and the right results can provide evidence that can be quite convincing – not definitive as with experiments, but sufficient to make most people accept that a causal connection is highly likely. In reading the rest of this review, it is essential to keep in mind that correlations do not prove causation.

To repeat my earlier conclusion: the results of this review of the survey research seem to indicate – despite some inconsistency in the results – that exposure to or preference for media violence is related to aggressiveness. The correlation is small, probably between .10 and .20, which would explain only 1 to 4 per cent of the variance. It might conceivably be as large as .3, which would explain 9 per cent of the variance. The important question is whether this rather weak relationship is due to a causal effect of media violence on aggression.

4

Laboratory Experiments: Controlled Research in the Laboratory

The scientific experiment is a marvellous device. Unlike other methods of inquiry, an experiment can tell you with great certainty that an action caused something to happen. As discussed in the previous chapter, when two factors or two events tend to go together, we often assume that one causes the other. People who eat carrots are less likely to have heart attacks than those who do not, so we assume that carrots prevent heart attacks. Someone tends to get migraines in warm weather, so assumes that the heat causes the headaches. Children who watch a lot of media violence tend to be more aggressive, so we assume that the violent programs cause the aggression. I suppose it is human nature to make these assumptions, and they are often correct. But they are also often wrong. Carrots do not prevent heart attacks; that association is probably caused by the lifestyles of those who eat carrots compared to those who do not. Warm weather does not cause migraines; that association (if there is one) is probably caused by the larger amounts of pollen and other pollutants in warm weather. For the moment, let us leave media violence and aggression except to say that the association by itself is not evidence of a causal relationship. Only additional research will tell us whether there is a causal relationship.

The best possible type of research for this purpose is the experiment. The great benefit of an experiment is that when you get an effect, you can be sure the experimental variation caused it. Suppose you give some children with earaches drug A and give other children with earaches a placebo (a pill with no active ingredients), but in every other respect you treat the children identically. Also suppose that the children are randomly assigned to the two conditions. Otherwise, there is the chance that those given the placebo were sicker to begin with. If you find that those given drug A got better quicker, you can be sure that the difference was due to the difference between the drug and the placebo, and that drug A is effective against earaches.

The same method can be applied to almost any question concerning how one factor affects another. As long as you can control the factors and measure the outcomes, and as long as the research is ethical, legal, and practical, you can do an experiment to test your hypothesis. Since we are almost always concerned with causation, and since experiments are by far the best way of assessing causation, modern science has been founded mainly on the experimental method.

Problems with Experiments

When we draw firm conclusions about causation from an experiment, we are assuming that everything has been done correctly. But science is not easy. Doing perfect experiments is often very difficult if not impossible. Even in the relatively simple experiment just described there are many possible pitfalls. First, it is essential that the experimental groups be as similar to each other as possible, with the exception of the factor of interest. It would be a mistake to compare a group given the drug with a group given nothing, because taking a pill is quite different from not taking one. There is the possibility that just taking the pill will make you feel better (the well-known placebo effect), or that if the child is not given a pill, the parent will take other measures to treat the condition. If all the children take pills and the only difference is that some contain a drug and others do not, you avoid these confusing possibilities.

Second, it is important that no one knows which children are taking the drug and which are taking the placebo. If the children know they are getting the drug, they may feel better due to the placebo effect; if their parents know, they may treat the child differently; and either of these could make these children get better sooner. Also, and this may be less obvious, the doctors giving the pills should not know, because they may treat the children differently in subtle ways. More important, the doctors' assessment of how a given child is recovering could be influenced by the knowledge that the child got or did not get the drug. If the doctors believe the drug works – and they probably do, otherwise they should not be giving it to patients – this could make them expect to see more improvement in those who got the drug than in those who did not. Since what we see is often influenced by what we expect, this expectation could distort the actual effects. Therefore, almost all drug research of this kind is done in what is called a 'double-blind' fashion, which means that neither those getting the drugs nor those giving them know who is getting what. Of course, there is a code somewhere that can be used to define the two groups, but you use that only after the experiment is concluded. That way, nobody's expectations or knowledge can possibly affect the results so as to produce an effect when one is not there.

With drug research it is possible to keep those in the study ignorant of their experimental condition. With other kinds of research this is rarely possible. If you ask people to vary their diets, obviously they are going to know what they are eating. If you give them a training program to help them stop smoking, they are going to know they are getting the training. More generally, if you expose people to a stimulus in order to compare it to some other stimulus, they are going to be aware of the stimulus.

This produces an extremely serious problem: knowledge of the stimulus can itself have an effect. In the case of diet, people who believe they are eating a healthy diet may be encouraged to take other steps to be healthy: 'Since I am already eating all of this healthy stuff that I don't really like very much, I might as well also exercise and drink less.' These other steps can reduce the risk of heart attack. If you find that those on the healthy diet have fewer heart attacks, you cannot know if it is due to the diet itself, or to other steps taken by the subjects, or to some combination of the two. Or maybe those on the diet decide that this will make them so healthy they don't have to exercise or take other measures to preserve their health. This may cause them to have more heart attacks than those not on the diet, which is also a distortion of the actual effect of the diet. Another possibility is that knowing they are eating a good diet may make the people feel happier and more satisfied. There is some evidence that a good mood reduces the risk of heart attack. So again, if there is a difference in heart attacks, it may be due to the diet or to the mood of the subjects.

Experimenter demand. When people are aware of their experimental condition, it is possible they will be affected by experimenter demand. This refers to the direct effect the experimenter or the experimental situation has on the person's behaviour (as opposed to the effect of the stimulus itself). It occurs when the stimulus to which they are exposed causes them to make assumptions about what the experimenter wants or believes or expects. Suppose an experimenter is interested in the effect of different kinds of music on children's behaviour. To study this, children are brought into a laboratory room in which music is playing. For some children the music is a classical string quartet; for others it is heavy metal. The children are observed in terms of how courteously they behave and how much noise they make. The hypothesis is that the heavy metal will make them less courteous and louder, and that is what is found. However, there is a strong possibility that it was not the music itself that produced the effect. When the adult chooses to play heavy metal to the children, it sends a clear message that this adult is 'with it,' is not stodgy, and is probably not very formal. From the point of view of the children, any adult who chooses this kind of music is not likely to expect them to behave perfectly or to be quiet. In contrast, the adult who plays a string quartet is stodgy and formal and will expect them to behave perfectly and to be quiet. That the children are entirely wrong – that these inferences are not at all correct – does not change the effect. They are reasonable inferences, and most children would make them.

The effect will be even more extreme if the dependent measure is more closely related to the music. Suppose the hypothesis is that the type of music played will affect the kind of music the children like. The experimenter hypothesizes that exposing children to classical music will make them like it, while exposing them to heavy metal will make them like that. So the children are exposed to the two kinds of music and are then asked to indicate the kinds of music they like. Sure enough, although all of the children prefer popular music, those who heard the quartet rate classical music higher than do those who heard the other music. The experimenter is delighted and concludes that the hypothesis is supported.

This is unjustified, because the effect is almost certainly due at least in part to experimenter demand. When classical music is played, the children assume the experimenter likes that kind of music, and similarly for heavy metal. When the experimenter then asks the children about their preferences, they will tend to want to please the experimenter (adults do the same). Thus, they will show some preference for the kind of music they assume the experimenter likes. The effect is due not to any direct effect of the type of music, but to the children wanting to please the experimenter. Moreover, the effect is not a real one in the sense that their preferences have actually been changed – all that has happened is that they have responded so as to please the experimenter. Their actual preferences have not been affected.

In designing experiments, careful scientists go to great lengths to avoid these demand problems. The double-blind procedure in drug research is one way to do it. When that is not possible, experimenters attempt to distance themselves from the choice of the stimulus. For example, in exposing the children to the music, instead of playing in the room, the experimenter could have it coming from outside the room and could comment that it is coming from across the street. Assuming this was plausible, it would prevent the children from making any inferences about the experimenter's tastes or expectations based on the music, since the experimenter did not choose it. Although it is often very difficult to remove demand factors entirely, it is essential that they be minimized so that any effects that are found can be attributed with confidence to the direct effect of the experimental variable.

What caused the effect? Another problem in interpreting experiments is that it is not always easy to decide which aspect of the experimental variation caused the effect. If the variable is getting or not getting a particular drug, and everything else is identical, one can be sure that any effect is due to the drug. If the experimental treatment is a drug plus diet compared to neither, any effect can be due to the drug, or to the diet, or to the combination of the two. One cannot conclude that the drug was effective unless it is compared to the condition of diet but no drug.

Deciding what produced the effect becomes much more difficult as the complexity of the stimulus or treatment increases. Consider the two types of music. If the research is done perfectly, there will be no demand effects. If the groups differ in their behaviour, one may want to conclude that the effects were due to the difference between classical music and heavy metal. But even under these ideal circumstances, that conclusion cannot be justified. You can conclude that the effect on their behaviour was due to the differences between the conditions, but you cannot know which differences were crucial.

There are many candidates. If the heavy metal was played louder, the crucial difference could simply be the difference between loud and soft music (although it would have been very sloppy not to have equated the music on loudness). If the children liked the heavy metal more than the classical, it could simply be the effect of liking or not liking the music. When they liked the music, they felt freer and more relaxed, so they were less formal and less quiet. A very likely and almost ubiquitous possibility is that the children were more aroused by the heavy metal than by the classical. It is well known that arousal has many effects on behaviour and is likely to make children louder and less well behaved. If the effect was due to arousal, it tells us nothing about the effect of the music itself.

Choice of stimulus. A related and especially difficult issue in this kind of research is how to select the stimuli to represent the two conditions. The children were exposed to heavy metal and classical music. True. On the other hand, they were not exposed to all instances of either – far from it. Instead, they were necessarily exposed to a very small, specific sample of these types of music – a heavy metal number and a string quartet. While these are representative of the two types of music, obviously one cannot generalize from these instances to all such music. Maybe an awful quartet was chosen and a terrific heavy metal number, or vice versa. Similarly, children may find string quartets especially hard to enjoy, though they might quite like symphonic or operatic music. Any effect would then be due to differences in the quality or likeability of the two selections rather than to the actual types of music.

Although all of these constitute serious difficulties in experimental research, the experiment is still by far the best method of establishing causality. Experiments must be done very carefully, with great pains taken to eliminate potential problems. With some questions, experiments cannot be done perfectly and so will have only limited use. Yet despite everything, this type of research remains extremely important and must always be taken seriously.

Media Violence and Experimental Research

The ideal way to test the effects of violent media on aggression would be a long-term experiment in natural settings. It would consist of randomly assigning a large group of very young children to various diets of television and films. Some would watch a great deal of violent programs and movies, some would watch a moderate amount, some would watch little, and some would watch none. They would do this for many years, during which their aggressive behaviour would be assessed at regular intervals. Later, their behaviour as adults would be assessed in terms of both aggressiveness and criminality. If those who were exposed to more violence were also more aggressive and more likely to commit crimes, the causal hypothesis would be supported. If this did not occur, it would not be supported. This experiment, done correctly with sufficient numbers of children, with great attention to detail, and with excellent measures, would end the debate.

This experiment cannot be done. For all sorts of ethical, legal, and practical reasons, we cannot assign children to these conditions, and we could not enforce the assignment even if we were willing to do it. We do not and should not have that kind of control over the lives of others. As with most questions concerning childrearing, parenting, and other complex social issues, the ideal experiment is not possible. Instead we must rely on experiments that are less than ideal. In this chapter we are dealing with laboratory experiments; in the next chapter I shall discuss experiments done in more natural settings.

When it comes to the topic of media violence, there are far more laboratory experiments than any other type of research. This is partly because psychologists favour laboratory research, and also because it is easier, quicker, and more efficient to do this kind of research than any of the other kinds we will describe. The typical laboratory experiment brings children or adults into the laboratory, shows them violent or nonviolent films, and obtains some measure of aggression. In some experiments the programs are shown outside the laboratory but aggression is measured in the laboratory, or vice versa. When either exposure to the violence or the measurement of aggression was done in the laboratory, I have treated it as a laboratory experiment.

The causal hypothesis predicts that those shown violent programs will be more aggressive than those shown non-violent ones. If there is significantly more aggression after a violent program than after a non-violent program or after no program, the hypothesis is supported; if there is not a significant difference, it is not supported.

Although all this seems straightforward, classifying results was not always simple. In deciding whether the results of an experiment support the hypothesis, it is important to take into account the number of possible tests of the hypothesis. If there is one violent film, one non-violent film, and one measure of aggression, the experiment provides only one test of the hypothesis. If there is a significant difference on the measure of aggression between those exposed to violent and non-violent programs, obviously the result is consistent with and supports the causal hypothesis; if there is a substantial but not significant difference, it is still consistent with the hypothesis and provides some support for it; if there is no appreciable difference or if the difference is in the opposite direction (i.e., less aggression after the violent program), it is inconsistent with and does not support the causal hypothesis. These decisions are straightforward.

The situation is a little more complicated if there is one violent and one non-violent film and two or more measures of aggression. This allows several tests of the hypothesis (one for each measure). If there is a significant difference on all of them, the hypothesis is supported; if there is no appreciable difference in the predicted direction on any of them, the hypothesis is not supported. However, if there is a significant difference on one measure but not on the others, or if the results go in opposite directions on the measures, the result is less clear.

Assessing the meaning of the results was even more difficult in the more complex experiments. Classification was especially difficult when there was more than one violent program condition, when there was more than one measure of aggression, and when some other variable was being manipulated. If there were three types of violent films (or only one violent film but three ways of introducing it, or any other variation) and one non-violent film, this allowed three tests of the hypothesis. If there were three types of violent films and two non-violent films, this allowed six tests of the hypothesis (each violent film compared to each of the non-violent ones). And so on. Moreover, if there was more than one measure of aggression, each of these allowed a separate test of the hypothesis for each of the other conditions. So, for example, an experiment that had two violent film conditions, two non-violent film conditions, and two measures of aggression provided eight tests of the hypothesis.

Previous reviews have sometimes counted a study as supporting the causal hypothesis if any measure showed the effect for any comparison of violent and non-violent programs. This seems inappropriate. It seems clear that the number of tests must be taken into account when assessing the results. If there are many tests and only a few get the predicted effect, it is a very different pattern from having only one test getting the effect, or having many tests and most or all getting the effect. In the extreme, if a study has twenty possible tests and only one shows the effect, you must consider this not as supporting the hypothesis but as *failing* to support it. Therefore, when there were several possible tests, and some obtained the predicted effect and some did not, I classified the result in terms of the pattern shown by the results.

Another issue is whether the results have to be statistically significant to count as supportive. If the group shown a violent film is slightly more aggressive than one shown a non-violent film, statistical analysis is necessary to see if this result should be taken seriously. If such an analysis indicates that the result is significant, this means that it is reliable, that it is likely to occur again if the study were repeated, and that we can therefore have confidence in the result. If it is not significant, it means it is not reliable, is unlikely to occur again, and we cannot have confidence in it. Although non-significant results are usually not given much weight in scientific journals, I did not require that the results be significant. Instead, as with the direction of the results, I based my classifications on the pattern of results.

In one sense, how I classified the results is less important than the details of the studies themselves. With the other kinds of research, I will be discussing all of the studies in some detail in this book. However, because there have been so many laboratory experiments, I have been compelled to summarize them. Readers can find more detailed information in the actual articles, but I understand that most people will not bother reading all the details. Therefore, how I classified the results is extremely important here, so let me be as specific as possible. In classifying the studies in terms of patterns of results, I applied some simple rules.

Supportive: I classified a study as supportive if it met any of the following criteria: (1) all of the results significantly supported the causal effect; (2) at least one result significantly supported the effect, and all or most of the others were in the same direction; (3) no result significantly supported the effect, but all or most were in that direction and at least some were close to significant; (4) if the best measure or measures supported the effect, I considered it supportive even if many of the others did not.

Non-supportive: I classified a study as non-supportive if it met any of the following criteria: (1) none of the results significantly supported the causal effect, and none or only a few of many were in that direction and appreciable; (2) one result significantly supported the causal effect, but many others did not. For example, if there were ten tests of the effect, and one was significant but the rest were not and were not close to significant, I considered it non-supportive.

Mixed: I classified a study as mixed if it met any of the following criteria: (1) one or more results significantly or close to significantly supported the effect, but others to the same degree showed an opposite effect; (2) the effect was supported but under only limited conditions, with the effect not being supported or being contradicted under other conditions.

Despite these fairly straightforward criteria, I must acknowledge that this is a large body of research with many variations and complexities. I confess that no matter how carefully I read some of the studies, the

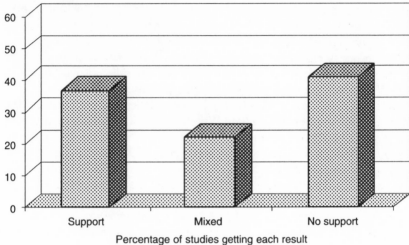

Figure 4.1. Results of laboratory experiments

results were not entirely straightforward. Especially with those studies that included many measures and many tests of the effect, the results were often not fully reported. Relying on the information that was provided, I have tried to be fair in my classifications. People may disagree with some of my decisions, but I am quite certain that our overall tallies would be quite similar.

Supportive and Non-supportive Results

I found eighty-seven laboratory experiments that provided a test of the causal hypothesis. That is, some people were exposed to a violent program, others were not, and there was some measure of aggression. Because there are so many studies, I do not describe all of them here. However, Table 4.1 provides the complete list of studies and how I classified them. As can be seen in the table and as shown in figure 4.1, of the eighty-seven experiments, I classified 37 per cent as supporting the causal hypothesis; 22 per cent as getting mixed results (some support but also some non-support), and 41 per cent as not supporting the hypothesis. Although a simple count such as this is a rather superficial way of summarizing a body of complex research, it is nonetheless striking how different this pattern of results is from the way this research is usually described. Fewer than half the experiments provided

Table 4.1 Classification of Laboratory Experiments

Supportive results

With children as subjects – 19
Akins, 1983; Bandura, Ross & Ross, 1961; Boyatzis, 1995; Drabman & Thomas, 1977; Ellis & Sekyra, 1972; Fechter, 1971; Hanratty et al., 1969; Hicks, 1965; Kniveton, 1973; Kniveton & Stephenson, 1970, 1973; Liebert & Baron, 1972; McHan, 1985; Musson & Rutherford, 1961; Savitsky et al., 1971; Steuer et al., 1971; Talkington & Altman, 1973; Walters & Willows, 1968

With adults as subjects – 13
Bushman, 1995, 1998 (2); Bushman & Geen, 1990 (2); Doob & Climie, 1972; Hartmann, 1969; Leyens & Dunand, 1991; Leyens & Parke, 1975; Meyer, 1972b; Thomas & Tell, 1974; Wilkins et al., 1974; Worchel et al., 1976

Non-supportive results

With children as subjects – 22
Albert, 1957; Collins, 1973; Collins & Getz, 1976; Gadow et al., 1987 (2); Hapkiewicz & Roden, 1971; Hapkiewicz & Stone, 1974; Huston-Stein et al., 1981; Josephson, 1987; Kniveton & Stephenson, 1975; Leyens et al., 1982; Liss et al., 1983 (2); Lovaas, 1961 (2); Parke et al., 1977 (2); Potts et al., 1986; Sawin, 1981; Siegel, 1956; Sprafkin et al., 1987, 1988

With adults as subjects – 14
Anderson, 1997; Berkowitz & Alioto, 1973; Donnerstein et al., 1976; Feshbach, 1961; Geen & Berkowitz, 1967; Geen & O'Neal, 1969; Lando & Donnerstein, 1978; Linz et al., 1988; Manning & Taylor, 1975; Mueller & Donnerstein, 1983; Mueller et al., 1983; Thomas, 1982; Zillmann, 1971; Zillmann & Johnson, 1973

Mixed results

With children as subjects – 9
Bandura, Ross & Ross, 1963b; Day & Ghandour, 1984; Dubanoski & Parton, 1971; Gadow & Sprafkin, 1987; Hall & Cairns, 1984; Hanratty et al., 1972; Kuhn et al., 1967; Lovaas, 1961; Sanson & Di Muccio, 1993

With adults as subjects – 10
Anderson, 1997; Berkowitz et al., 1963, 1974; Berkowitz & Geen, 1966; 1967; Buvinic & Berkowitz, 1976; Geen & Berkowitz, 1966; Meyer, 1972a; Walters & Thomas, 1963; Zillmann & Weaver, 1999

clear-cut support for the causal hypothesis, and just as many found either no support at all or results that directly contradicted the hypothesis. This is far from the 'overwhelming' support that is typically claimed for the causal hypothesis.

This was an extremely surprising outcome. I had been sceptical of the strength of the evidence in favour of the causal hypothesis, but I had always believed that the laboratory experiments (as opposed to the other research) provided fairly consistent support. When I reviewed the research on television violence in 1984, at the journal editor's insistence I included only non-laboratory studies. Although I did not think they meant much (for reasons I will discuss at length later), I was convinced then that the laboratory experiments offered reasonably good support for the causal hypothesis. At the time, I had not read all of the research. I had read some of the experiments, and they did not produce as consistent results as I had been led to expect from the way they were usually described. Nevertheless, I assumed that the findings were quite supportive. They had consistently been described as virtually all providing support for the hypothesis. Even taking that with a grain of salt, I assumed they were generally supportive. After reviewing all of the laboratory experiments in detail, I was, frankly, astounded at the inconsistency of the findings. Because my assessment of the results runs counter to what has always been said and to my own previous belief, let me give some examples to make the case more clearly. Some of these examples will help explain how the conventional wisdom about these results is so different from the actual findings.

Examples of non-supportive research. One of the earliest laboratory experiments was conducted by Lovaas (1961). The paper describes three experiments, with twelve children in the first, twenty in the second, and the same twenty in the third. The subjects watched either an aggressive or a non-aggressive cartoon and were then given the opportunity to behave aggressively. Although these experiments have regularly been cited as showing that exposure to violent media causes aggression, none of the three experiments found a significant difference as a function of type of film. The third study found a difference that was appreciable but not significant. These studies did not support the causal hypothesis; if anything, they failed to do so. However, I decided to count the third study as partly supportive.

In an earlier chapter I mentioned two experiments conducted by Hapkiewicz and colleagues. These studies involved relatively large numbers of subjects. One experiment had 60 children, the other 180. The children watched various films that were either aggressive or non-aggressive or, in experiment 1, did not watch any film. The measures of aggression were better than in most studies since they were based on actual behaviour in free-play situations. The first study (Hapkiewicz &

Roden, 1971) produced no significant effect for type of program; in fact, among the boys the greatest amount of aggression was exhibited by those who did not watch any film (the opposite of what would be expected by the causal hypothesis). In the second experiment (Hapkiewicz & Stone, 1974), the type of film had no overall effect. There was no effect at all on the girls' behaviour. The boys were most aggressive after watching a Three Stooges film and least aggressive after watching an aggressive cartoon (with those who watched a nonaggressive film falling in the middle). Again, these results were contrary to the predictions of the causal hypothesis. These two experiments, with large numbers of subjects, with better-than-average measures of aggression, and done with considerable care, clearly failed to confirm the causal hypothesis and could be considered evidence against it. These papers are rarely if ever cited in reviews of the literature.

As I discussed earlier, Huston-Stein and colleagues (1981) showed young children programs that varied in level of violence and level of action. Then their interpersonal behaviour was observed and rated for aggression. There was no difference between those shown violent programs and those shown non-violent programs. The major finding was that programs that were high in action, with or without violence, seemed to be followed by more aggression. The authors interpreted their results as supporting the idea that effects arise from observing action, not observing violence per se. Obviously, the findings do not support the causal hypothesis. This paper too is rarely if ever cited.

Two experiments conducted by Donnerstein and colleagues failed to support the causal hypothesis. In one (Mueller, Donnerstein, & Hallam, 1983), subjects watched either a violent film or a non-violent film and then were given opportunities to be aggressive and to be helpful. Those who saw the violent film were no more aggressive than those who saw the non-violent film. Moreover, under some conditions, those exposed to the violent film were actually more prosocial than those who saw the other film. Clearly, these results contradict the causal hypothesis. In the paper reporting on this study, the lack of effect on aggression is mentioned in precisely one sentence, and is not even included in the abstract. In the other study (Mueller & Donnerstein, 1983), subjects watched an aggressive, humorous, or neutral film and then were given an opportunity to act aggressively. Those who saw the aggressive or the humorous film were more aggressive than those who saw the neutral film. Since the aggressive and humorous films did not differ in their effects on aggression, the result fails to support the causal hypothesis.

The authors interpreted the finding as supporting an arousal explanation. I should note that since these experiments were published, Donnerstein has reversed his position and is now one of the most enthusiastic advocates of the causal hypothesis. I should also note that neither he nor any other supporter of the causal hypothesis tends to mention either of these experiments when they discuss the research on the effects of violent media.

These are just some of the many studies that failed to support the causal hypothesis. Of course, there are others that do support it. The point is that the studies described here were conducted at least as well and carefully as most of the experiments in this group. They did not support the hypothesis, and they are almost never mentioned in reviews of this literature. Given that the non-supportive studies tend not to be cited, whereas the supportive studies *are* cited, it is hardly surprising that most of us have been given the impression that the results are consistently supportive. If all of the studies were cited, or if a representative group were cited, we would not have received this false impression.

Detailed Analyses of the Findings

Fewer than half the experiments provided support for the causal hypothesis. However, as noted above, a simple count of the successes and failures is not a sufficient indication of the overall results. It is important to analyze the results in more detail to get a better sense of just what was found and what was not.

Questionable measures. One of the difficulties in laboratory research on aggression is finding an adequate dependent measure. For ethical and practical reasons, one cannot allow people to engage in really aggressive behaviour in the laboratory. Experimenters cannot stand by while children beat each other up, nor can they let adults punch or kick each other. Even if this were possible, adults would rarely if ever engage in physical aggression in the formal setting of a psychology laboratory. Children do sometimes behave aggressively toward one another, and they can be allowed to as long as the behaviour does no harm to anyone. However, using their actual aggressive behaviour as a measure is fairly complicated and requires a great deal of time training observers to make accurate ratings.

For these reasons, most of the laboratory experiments did not observe actual aggression; instead they have relied on what might be called analogues of aggression. Several merely measured people's thoughts and associations after watching different kinds of films. If after seeing a violent film they had violent thoughts, this was the measure of aggression. In these studies there was no indication that the people were made more aggressive or that their behaviour was affected. It is entirely possible that they had thoughts of violence but that these thoughts made them *less* likely rather than more likely to be aggressive. Surely after watching a serious film about warfare or racial conflict most people would be thinking about violence, but most would probably be having negative thoughts about violence. Seeing the film would make them think of violence but also make them less likely rather than more likely to behave violently themselves. Thus, while relevant to the general discussion and perhaps to the processes underlying any effects, studies using these measures are not really relevant to the causal hypothesis.

Similarly, many of the experiments with children defined aggression in terms of behaviours that are so remote from actual aggression that they are highly questionable or even laughable as measures of aggression. Probably the most extreme instance was an experiment (Mussen & Rutherford, 1961) in which the measure of aggression was to ask a child whether he would pop a balloon if one were present. Not only is this totally hypothetical, but it is really ridiculous to think that popping a balloon when you are allowed to is an aggressive act. Quite a few studies with children defined aggression as hitting or kicking a Bobo doll or some other equivalent toy. Bobo dolls (which are apparently called Bozo dolls in England) are inflatable plastic dolls in the shape of a clown. As anyone who has owned one knows, Bobo dolls are designed to be hit. When you hit a Bobo doll, it falls down and then bounces back up. You are supposed to hit it and it is supposed to fall down and then bounce back up. There is little reason to have a Bobo doll if you do not hit it. Calling punching a Bobo doll aggressive is like calling kicking a football aggressive. Bobos are meant to punched; footballs are meant to be kicked. No harm is intended and none is done. The behaviour is entirely appropriate and is not aggressive. Therefore, it is difficult to understand why anyone would think this is a measure of aggression.

I realize that some people disagree with this position. Many of those who conducted studies using Bobo dolls and other such toys presumably felt that they were studying aggression. That is why I included these studies in the overall analysis of the results. However, it seems clear to me that no aggression is involved. In these studies, typically some children watch a movie in which an adult or a child punches a Bobo doll and performs other similar behaviours, while other children watch a film in which the adult or child does not punch the doll but instead hugs it and performs other similar behaviours. The children are then given a chance to play with the Bobo doll, their behaviour is observed, and punching and kicking are considered aggressive acts. The children who watched the adult punching the doll tend to imitate the adult – they have presumably learned what one is supposed to do with a Bobo doll; those who have not seen the adult punch the doll tend to punch it less, presumably because they are less sure how one is supposed to treat Bobo. Thus, the research tells us quite a lot about imitation, but in my opinion nothing about aggression, because none occurs.

This position is supported by some of the researchers in the area. Kniveton and colleagues conducted several experiments on the effects of media violence on aggression. In three studies (Kniveton, 1973; Kniveton & Stephenson, 1970; Kniveton & Stephenson, 1973) they used the treatment of a Bozo doll as the measure of aggression and found that the aggressive film increased aggression. In their last experiment (Kniveton & Stephenson, 1975) they used a measure based on interpersonal behaviour and found non-supportive results. The authors were obviously impressed by the contrast between the findings using the two measures. In their paper, the authors comment: 'This limited effect of the film in itself is an important finding, and undermines somewhat the position of recent commentators who base their alarmist conclusions largely on the results of experiments portraying doll-directed attacks.'

The tabulation of results given earlier included all the relevant studies. However, by including studies that used measures that may have little or nothing to do with aggression, I risked giving the wrong impression of the findings. Accordingly, I conducted a second analysis that eliminated experiments that used doubtful measures of aggression. The point of this was to get some sense of what the results showed when the measures of aggression seemed reasonable and were likely to capture at least some aspect of what we really mean by aggression. As shown in Figure 4.2, when the most doubtful measures of aggression are eliminated, the results look even less supportive of the causal hypothesis. Of the remaining studies – all of which used relatively good measures of aggression – only 28 per cent were supportive, 16 per cent

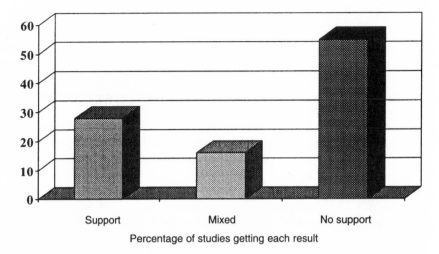

Figure 4.2. Results of laboratory experiments: No Bobo dolls, no thoughts

were mixed, and 55 per cent were non-supportive. In other words, just to make this perfectly clear, among those experiments that employed measures of aggression that seem reasonable, fewer than one-third supported the causal hypothesis, and a majority did not support it.

Children versus adults. It is sometimes asserted that the effects of exposure to media violence are stronger for young children than for adults. This is not what these experiments show. With children, 38 per cent of the experiments obtained supportive results and 46 per cent obtained non-supportive results, compared to 37 per cent supportive and 40 per cent non-supportive when adults were involved – virtually identical numbers. When the questionable measures are removed, only 29 per cent of the experiments with children supported the causal hypothesis, whereas 58 per cent were non-supportive; the comparable figures for adults (i.e., questionable measures removed) were 29 per cent supportive and 50 per cent non-supportive – slightly better than for the experiments with children. Thus, there is no indication from the laboratory research that children are more susceptible than adults to the effects of media violence.

Of course, it should be understood that quite different methods were used for adults and children. Entirely different films and programs were used for the two age groups. Children were shown cartoons, slapstick comedy such as *The Three Stooges*, or, quite often, a short film in which actors behaved 'aggressively' toward inanimate objects or occasionally toward people. With a few exceptions, these programs contained at most moderate violence. In contrast, adults were shown segments from actual movies or television programs, and these often contained a great deal of violence. One film used for the adults was a short segment from *The Champion*. This movie is a serious, critically acclaimed work, and the piece selected portrayed one boxer beating another mercilessly. Clearly, the violent programs chosen for the adults were considerably more violent than those chosen for the children.

Another major difference among the experiments related to the measures of aggression employed. As noted earlier, some used measures that were so remote from real aggression that one can only wonder whether they were studying aggression at all. Even setting those aside, there was a great diversity of measures. The experiments with children tended to rely much more on their behaviour in relatively natural settings. Many allowed the children to play together, with a confederate, or with an inanimate object. The children's behaviour was observed and rated for aggression. While some of these ratings probably did not involve actual aggression, at least the measure was based on fairly free and spontaneous actions by the children. In contrast, almost all of the experiments with adults used artificial measures, by which I mean that they were based on reactions to a procedure that was designed specifically for the experiment and that did not exist in the world outside the laboratory. The most common test involved giving subjects the opportunity to deliver electric shocks or loud noises in what was supposedly a learning situation (of course, the shocks and noises were not actually given). In this situation, the person supposedly getting the shocks was not visible to the person giving them. Moreover, the subject was given explicit permission to give the shocks – indeed, it was their job in the experiment to give them. The measure of aggression was how many shocks or how intense the shocks the subject chose to give. This may be related to aggression, but it is surely more remote than the actual behaviour exhibited by the children.

Thus, it is possible that the adult experiments showed somewhat stronger effects because the films showed more violence and the measures used were less closely linked to real aggression. This is pure speculation, but given the considerable differences in the methods used for the two age groups, I would not draw any conclusions regarding differences between children and adults in susceptibility to the effects of media violence. Of course, let me repeat that neither set of experiments found consistent effects. With both children and adults, fewer than half the experiments produced results supportive of the causal hypothesis.

Differences between the Supportive and Non-supportive Experiments

When the results of experiments differ markedly, it is always important to ask whether there are systematic differences between the experiments that produced the two kinds of results. Accordingly, I attempted to find any factors that differentiated the supportive and non-supportive experiments. One obvious possibility was that it was mainly a matter of sample size, with the non-supportive studies failing to get effects because they used very few subjects. This was not the case with the studies involving adults. Few of the studies had fewer than fifty participants, and most had many more than that. There was no apparent difference in size between those that got supportive results and those that did not. Thus the size of the samples cannot explain the inconsistencies in the findings for adults.

The research with children, on the other hand, did point to a clear relationship between the size of the samples and the direction of the results. However, it was exactly the opposite of what one would expect if the causal hypothesis were correct and failures to find effects were due to small sample sizes. The experiments that obtained supportive results were considerably smaller on average than those that failed to support the hypothesis. As shown in Figure 4.3, the experiments that found supporting results had an average of 51.6 children, those that got mixed results had an average of 63, and those that did not support the hypothesis had an average of 100.8. Considering only those experiments with the better measures of aggression, the corresponding numbers are 37.4 for supporting experiments, 48.7 for those with mixed results, and 98.6 for the non-supporting experiments. Rather than failing to get an effect because of small numbers, this pattern makes it possible that some experiments obtained an effect due to chance or to other factors involved with very small samples. Whether or not this is true, one way of considering this pattern is that among those experiments that used plausible measures of aggression, support for the causal hypothesis comes from the data of 337 children, whereas lack of support comes from the data of 1,578 children.

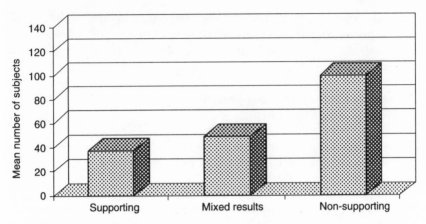

Figure 4.3. Number of subjects and results of experiments

Another possible explanation for the inconsistency in results is that the studies differed in quality. If an experiment is not designed well or is conducted sloppily, it may not obtain the result that would have been obtained with better design and more careful procedures. Alternatively, poor design and sloppy procedures sometimes produce an effect when better research will not. So it is important to consider whether differences in quality could explain the differences in results.

It is not easy to judge overall quality. Certainly, some of the studies were designed better than others. The better ones took at least some steps to reduce experimenter demand. They also tried to make the situation realistic for the subjects, and they employed relatively good measures. Also, it seems that some experiments were conducted with greater attention to detail than others, although this is even harder to judge. With all this in mind, I tried to assess whether the supportive and non-supportive studies differed in quality.

I found no evidence that they did, and not a hint that the better studies obtained supportive results whereas the less good ones did not. Some of the supportive studies appeared in the top journals in the field (*Child Development* and *Journal of Personality and Social Psychology*), but some of the non-supportive studies appeared in the same journals. Some carefully done studies by well-known and respected psychologists obtained supportive results, some did not. Some studies that had obvious methodological problems obtained supportive results, some did not. One problem that occurred with some regularity was that improper statistics were used. This was typically because the subjects were observed interacting in groups yet the analyses were based on individuals. This is almost always inappropriate and tends to inflate any effects that occur. Generally, I ignored this problem in classifying the results, even though ordinarily it would be serious enough to disqualify the research. In any case, some of the experiments that had this problem produced supportive results and some produced non-supportive results. Since the error tends to inflate the effects, keeping these experiments in the list overstates to some extent the number of supportive results. It is also interesting that even the same experimenters often obtained supportive results in one study and non-supportive results in another. Sometimes the same research team conducted a number of studies and used essentially the same methods in all of them, yet found inconsistent results across the studies.

Considering all of the experiments, the only factors that I could find that differentiated them were that studies with questionable measures of aggression were more likely to get effects than those with more reasonable measures. Also, with children but not with adults, experiments with larger samples were less likely to support the hypothesis.

Inconsistent Findings

In scientific research, inconsistent findings should not be ignored. If one carefully done experiment obtains one result, and another equally good experiment obtains another result, there is obviously a problem. A scientist must deal with these problems, because both results cannot be correct. Only after the reasons for the inconsistency can be specified is there any sense that one understands the process. Besides the major inconsistency in the results regarding the effect of media violence on aggression, there are other inconsistencies in these findings. These inconsistencies do not just reduce our confidence in the findings; they also relate to the theoretical underpinnings of much of this research. Because of this, it is disheartening that in this body of research so little attention has been paid to the inconsistencies, even when they appear in research done by the same people. Indeed, the inconsistencies are rarely if ever even mentioned. They have generally been totally ignored. Yet I would have thought that they strike at the very essence of the causal hypothesis. Let me describe some of the more important and pervasive inconsistencies.

The Role of Frustration/Anger/Arousal

In some studies subjects were frustrated or angered before obtaining the measure of aggression, while in others the subjects were not frustrated or angered. There are three issues related to this variable. First, there should be more aggression when people are angered (or frustrated) than when they are not. When this does not occur (as it often does not in this literature), one must question whether the behaviour should be considered aggressive. Second, there seems to be a general assumption that the effect of exposure to media violence will be greater when the subjects are angry. This is plausible, although it has rarely been discussed in detail. Sure enough, in some studies the effect of a violent program was greater when the subjects were first angered. But in other studies, there was no difference between angered and not angered subjects. Third, some studies found an effect of exposure only when subjects were deliberately angered, and no effect in the no-anger condition. Yet other studies that did not anger the subjects sometimes found an effect of exposure.

This inconsistent set of findings leaves us confused about various theoretical issues. Those who favour the causal hypothesis sometimes argue that violent programs cause viewers to learn behaviours or scripts involving aggression. When they are then angered – these scripts influence their behaviour, causing them to be more aggressive than if they did not have the scripts. If they are not angered – if they have no reason to behave aggressively – there should be no effect of the learning or scripts. According to this notion of the mechanism, violent programs should increase aggression only when the subjects are angry or frustrated or provoked.

An alternative view is that viewers learn the behaviours they observe, and whether they actually express them depends on whether the behaviours had been rewarded or punished. This view, proposed especially by Bandura, is based on a fairly strict social learning model. If those who act aggressively in the film suffer negative consequences, their aggressive behaviour should not be imitated; if they have positive consequences, it should be imitated. According to this mechanism, violent programs should cause more aggression if the model in the film was rewarded, and should not cause aggressive behaviour if the model was punished. Frustration or anger should play little or no role except perhaps to increase the overall level of aggression.

A third mechanism is considerably more complex. Berkowitz (e.g.,

Berkowitz and Green, 1966) proposed that the key element is whether the environment contains a cue that relates to the aggression that was seen in the film. I think the idea is similar to the first one – namely that viewers learn scripts that tend to elicit aggression. The additional factor is that the aggression will be elicited only or perhaps especially when a cue triggers the aggressive behaviour and, probably, when the subjects are angry or frustrated, making aggression a likely response. According to this theory, viewing media violence should not increase aggression unless subjects are angry and there is an appropriate cue, but should when both factors are present.

There are probably other plausible mechanisms to explain why exposure to violent programs would increase aggression, but these seem to be the most prominent. One difficulty is that none of these mechanisms has been described in sufficient detail to make very strong predictions. The predictions I have provided at the end of each model seem reasonable given the model, but the authors of the models are not entirely clear on what they expect. Nevertheless, it seems obvious that the models must lead to predictions about the roles played by anger or frustration (crucial in models 1, important in model 3, not present in model 2), outcomes of the viewed aggression (crucial in 2, not in the others), and cues (crucial in 3, not in the others). Many of the experiments were designed to test these three models, and thus the results should provide some indication whether each is supported.

Unfortunately, remarkably little attention has been paid to the detailed results from the relevant research, and virtually no attention to whether the results have been consistent. Consider the role of anger or frustration. Almost any model – even the second one – should predict that the effect of exposure to violence should be greater when the subjects are angry or frustrated. Even if anger is not a central element in the model, at the very least, anger would be expected to increase aggression and should therefore increase the effect. In fact, little or no real aggression should be expected in the absence of anger, so the effect should be seen largely or entirely when anger is aroused.

As it happens, the results regarding the role of anger have been extremely inconsistent. Some studies that aroused anger obtained effects, some did not; some studies that did not arouse anger got effects, some did not. In other studies some subjects were made angry and others were not made angry, thus providing a direct comparison of the two conditions and of the effect of anger. Yet some of these studies found effects only when anger was aroused, whereas others found no difference between anger and no anger conditions. This pattern of results makes little sense and, I believe, casts doubt on almost any interpretation of the studies. Yet those who have conducted the research have not tried to explain the inconsistencies, and generally do not refer to them even when they arise in their own studies.

A similar state of confusion exists regarding the role played by cues to aggression. There seems to be a reasonable amount of evidence that the presence of appropriate cues will lead to more aggression. However, it is not at all clear that the presence of such cues is necessary for or even increases the effect of exposure to violent media. Most of the relevant research had been conducted by Berkowitz and colleagues. One procedure they have employed is to show subjects an excerpt from the film *The Champion*, in which Kirk Douglas plays a fighter who is badly beaten by another fighter. In some conditions the confederate is also named Kirk, in others he is not named Kirk. Other variations are also used, but the basic idea is that when the name of the confederate is the same as the name of the person in the film or the actor playing that role, the effect of the film should be greater. In some studies the predicted effect occurs; in others the trend is as predicted but it is not significant; in still others there is no interaction of condition with name of confederate. In other words, even within this set of studies, the results are far from consistent.

Of perhaps greater importance, almost all the laboratory experiments conducted by others researchers used methods in which the confederate was not named and there was no manipulation of the presence or absence of cues to aggression. Yet some of these other studies got an effect of media violence and some did not. If cues are necessary, there should be no effects without them. Thus, though cues may increase aggression in some circumstances, it seems clear that they are neither necessary nor sufficient to find an effect of media violence on aggression.

The point of discussing the role of frustration/anger and cues is not to reach any conclusions about these two factors. Rather, the point is that these factors – which some authors consider very important – have produced inconsistent results. Frustration and anger sometimes increase scores on the measure of aggression, sometimes not; sometimes they increase the media violence effect, sometimes not. The effect is obtained both with and without anger or frustration; and is not obtained both with and without anger or frustration. Similarly, cues to aggression sometimes increase the media violence effect, sometimes not; sometimes they are necessary for the effect to appear, sometimes not. Research that focused on these inconsistencies might have helped resolve them and given us a better understanding of the processes involved. Yet the experimenters seem not to have noticed the inconsistencies and to have made no attempt to resolve them. This is bad science and has left this area of research in a considerable muddle. As I discuss below, the lack of attention to these issues means that the body of findings is open to alternative explanations that have little interest and that are not consistent with the causal hypothesis.

The Role of Justified versus Unjustified Violence

It has been suggested that media violence that is seen as justified has a greater effect on aggression than media violence seen as unjustified. The idea is that subjects shown the justified violence are more likely to imitate it. I must admit that I do not understand why this should be so: one could easily make a plausible argument for the reverse. If the violence in the film or television program is perceived as justified, the message may be that one can act aggressively only if aggression is justified. In contrast, when the violence in the film is not justified, the message may be that one can act aggressively even when it is not justified. By this reasoning, unjustified media violence should have a greater effect on aggression than justified media violence. Personally, I doubt that this factor matters at all. My only point is that the logic underlying the idea that justified violence has a greater effect is unclear.

In any case, the research findings have been mixed – sometimes there is a difference between justified and unjustified, sometimes not. Most of the research does not deliberately vary the degree of justification, and it seems obvious that most of the media violence that has been used in this research is not described as or perceived as justified. In other words, almost all of the work has involved unjustified violence. The few studies that varied this factor produced inconsistent results. Apparently, those who did the research on this issue some time ago lost interest when the effects were inconsistent. As a result, there has been no resolution of this issue, and no clear pattern of results that would allow us to accept or reject the idea that justification matters. Nevertheless, we still hear psychologists talk about the dangers of justified violence as being greater than those of unjustified violence. It should be clear that there is no scientific support for this notion.

Portraying the Consequences of Violence

A relatively new idea in this field is that media violence in which the consequences of the violence are not shown has more harmful effects than if the consequences are shown. Cartoons in which characters are squashed, blown up, dropped off cliffs, and so on yet emerge healthy soon after are prime instances of the presumably worst kind of violence. In contrast, a movie such as *The Champion*, in which one fighter is beaten to a bloody pulp by the other, is an example of the less harmful kind of violent media. The experimental research has not generally explored this issue. Almost all of the research with children used violent programs in which consequences were not shown; whereas at least some of the research with adults used programs in which the consequences were shown. Yet experiments using both kinds of programs produced results that sometimes showed an increase in aggression after the violent programs and sometimes did not. Probably the most violent portrayal of violence that has been used in this research is the excerpt from *The Champion*. It is realistic, vivid, and very well done. The consequences are shown in great detail, and they are devastating. Yet this film, which has been used more than any other, has sometimes produced increases in aggression, sometimes not. There is certainly not the slightest indication that it reduced the aggressive responses shown by the subjects. One study (Zillmann, Johnson, & Hanrahan, 1973) deliberately varied the ending of a violent film, adding either a happy ending or not, and found less aggression with the happy ending. Though this is not precisely the same as showing the immediate consequences of violence, it is related, and the result was in the opposite direction from what would have been predicted.

Those who are concerned that violent media do not show the consequences of violence seem to focus on the lack of injury it often produces. The critics argue that this gives children the wrong impression about the effects of violence and that it therefore encourages them to act aggressively. This idea is repeated often, and is prominent in the National Television Violence Study (1995). The executive summary states in the text and in a highlighted box in the margin that: 'showing the negative consequence of television violence can serve to reduce the risk that viewers will imitate such portrayals' (16). This seems to have become one of the standard messages of those who are concerned about the effects of media violence. I have heard serious psychologists stating categorically that media violence that does not show consequences is more harmful than if the consequences are shown. This may be true. But there is not the slightest scientific evidence to support this assertion. There has been little systematic research on the issue, and the results of the laboratory experiments offer no support for it. In fact, this body of research suggests that this is not an important factor one way or the other.

Then there is the related issue of whether aggression was rewarded or punished. There has been little systematic research on this question, and what research has been done has not produced any consistent effects. In my opinion the most interesting relevant research was done by Bandura and colleagues. They conducted two experiments in which children watched films of adults behaving aggressively toward other adults. This is unusual; rarely are children shown actual aggression. In one condition in the first study (Bandura, Ross, & Ross, 1963b), one man acted aggressively toward another, and the second one attempted to retaliate but was overpowered. The one who started the aggression clearly won. This was considered the aggression-rewarded condition. In the aggression-punished condition, the film began the same way, but the second adult turned the tables, sats on the first adult, and spanked him. In a third condition, two adults played together (non-aggressive condition). The result of this experiment was that the children who watched the aggression-rewarded condition engaged in more imitative aggression than those who did not. The aggression-punished condition did not differ from the non-aggression condition, or from a no-film condition. In a second experiment (Bandura, 1965), an adult was seen 'attacking' a Bobo doll. He was then either rewarded by a second adult, or punished by that second adult, who ended up sitting on him and spanking him, or there were no consequences. In this study there was no more aggression after the rewarded condition than after the control condition, but there was less in the punishment condition.

There are two points to make about this pattern of results. First, the findings are inconsistent. In the first study, rewarded aggression was followed by more aggression than in a control condition; in the second study, rewarded aggression did not increase aggression compared to a control. In other words, positive reinforcement did not increase aggression consistently compared to a condition without any exposure to aggression.

There is, however, a more general point to be made here, which depends on an appreciation of what the adults were doing in the film. In study 1, an adult started a fight, the other retaliated, and the first adult either won or lost. Bandura considered the first adult the aggressor, and it is on the consequences of his behaviour that Bandura focuses. This ignores the fact that the second adult also behaved aggressively, especially when he won. He did not start the fight, but he also was aggressive, and in some instances he won. It seems to me that the condition in which the adult who started the fight lost has the element of most violent movies and television programs. A 'bad guy' starts a fight; a 'good guy' responds aggressively; and eventually the good guy wins. To win he resorts to aggression himself – sometimes even more so than the bad guy. This is classic, formula programming, both in the movies and on television, especially in children's programs. This is what Batman does; this is what the Power Rangers do; this is what Dirty Harry, John McClain, the Roadrunner, and every other hero does. They do not start the fight, but once it has started, they are even stronger and more violent than the bad guys, and the good guys win. This is the type of program that has been attacked as especially harmful, presumably because it teaches children that the way to deal with problems is to use violence. Yet in this classic study that has been cited over and over as showing the bad effects of media violence, those children who watched the 'good guy' use violence and win were no more aggressive than those who watched a non-aggressive film or did not watch a film. And in study 2, children who watched the bad guy get punished by the good guy – who used more violence than the bad guy – actually were less aggressive than those who saw aggression with no consequences.

How should these findings be interpreted? They seem to show that typical plots in violent films and television either have no effect on aggression or even reduce it. There is no evidence that the children learned it was acceptable to be aggressive because the good guy eventually came out on top. If one were to accept this result as indicative of the true state of affairs, it would mean that we should stop worrying about the Power Rangers and Batman and other heroes' aggressive behaviour. As long as the hero behaves aggressively only after a bad guy starts the fight, and as long as the hero wins, children will not learn to be aggressive. This kind of violent program seems to trouble many people, but the research provides no evidence that it is especially harmful – or harmful at all, for that matter. Frankly, I would not put much faith in these two studies, but certainly that is what they show. More generally, the important point is that there is no scientific justification for claiming that programs in which violence is rewarded have more negative effects than those in which violence is punished or in which the outcome is uncertain.

Conclusion

This body of literature obtained inconsistent results. Some experiments found the effect predicted by the causal hypothesis; some found mixed results that partly supported and partly contradicted the hypothesis; and some found no supportive results. Contrary to the way this literature has often been described, the results are not overwhelmingly in favour of the hypothesis. In fact, there are more experiments which do not support it than there are that do, and with regard to the research on children, those experiments which do not support the causal hypothesis involved many more children on average and in total than those which do support it. Overall, this pattern of results should be discouraging for the hypothesis. When more studies fail to get the expected results than do get them, obviously the hypothesis is not well supported, to put it mildly. Ordinarily, a hypothesis that achieved so little support would be either abandoned as incorrect or modified in such a way that more support could be found. I conclude that the laboratory experiments do not support the causal hypothesis.

Why Did the Supportive Results Occur?

One the other hand, I do not think we can simply dismiss the supportive results. These studies are experiments, and experiments have a unique place in scientific research. The non-experimental studies that I will describe in later sections cannot prove causality. Even when they produce significant findings, they can at most build a case for causality. No single result can provide much support for a causal connection – it requires a series of results, all pointing in the same direction, to provide a convincing argument for causality. This means that with non-experimental research, the consistency of the findings is absolutely crucial. In contrast, every experiment provides evidence for causality. When the experiment is conducted properly, any significant difference between two conditions must be due to the experimental manipulation. One or two results may be due to chance, but not a large number of significant results. Whenever there are significant results from experiments, as long as chance and procedural errors can be ruled out we *must* take the findings seriously.

Despite the weakness and inconsistency of the results of the laboratory experiments, there is no question that some of them have found significant effects in the predicted direction. The meta-analysis reported by Paik and Comstock (1994) concluded that the laboratory experiments showed a significant effect of exposure to violent media. Because the paper did not provide any of the details of their classifications, I cannot evaluate its accuracy. Nevertheless, there is no need for a meta-analysis or other kinds of statistics to know that given the right conditions and procedures, it is possible to find higher scores on some measure of aggression after exposure to a violent program than after a non-violent program. Accordingly, we have to ask why so many experiments – fewer than half, but still a substantial number – did find increased aggression after exposure to violent programs. To put this somewhat differently, if the causal hypothesis is not correct, if exposure to media violence does not cause increased aggression, why did any of the experiments find an increase in aggression after exposure to violent programs? There is no definitive answer to this question, but a likely possibility is that various aspects of the experiments other than the violent content of the films may have led to an increase in aggression. There are two especially plausible explanations for this.

Arousal

In any experiment it is essential that the conditions being varied be as similar as possible except for the factor being studied. Otherwise, any effects that are found may be due to differences other than the factor of concern. In the research on the effects of media violence, the hypothesis being tested is that seeing a violent film increases aggression compared to seeing a non-violent film. It is the violence in the film that is of concern, not any other factor. This means that in order to conclude that it was the violent content that produced the effect, the violent and non-violent films or television programs or live models must be as similar as possible. Ideally, they will be identical films except that one has violence and the other not. Since this is not possible, every attempt must be made to minimize any other differences between them.

If the goal is to specify causality, it is essential that the two conditions differ in only one way. Yet because any two movies differ in many different ways, specifying the cause of an effect (assuming there is one) is impossible. This is especially true if the films differ in ways other than the amount of violence that could plausibly affect aggression. An example of this is a study involving trainees at the New York City Police Academy (Atkins, Hilton, Neigher, & Bahr, 1972). In this experiment some of the trainees watched films of the 1968 Democratic Convention in Chicago in which there were violent confrontations between police and demonstrators; other trainees watched standard training films that contained no violence. In addition – and this is obviously crucial – the violent films also contained narratives that accused the police of misbehaviour, whereas the standard films did not. The difficulty, of course, is that this combines exposure to violence with exposure to accusations against colleagues of the subjects. The accusations could reasonably be expected to make many if not all of the trainees angry. Sure enough, after the films, those who saw the violent films described themselves as more angry. They also showed a greater preference for boxing as opposed to a less aggressive activity. Clearly, one cannot attribute any of the effects to the presence of violence in the films. Rather, it seems highly likely that the effects were due to the accusations against the police.

Similarly, if the violent film in an experiment is extremely unpleasant and the non-violent one is very pleasant, any difference in aggression may be due to the pleasantness of the films rather than their violent content. If the violent film is more upsetting – that is, if it makes the subjects more uncomfortable or more nervous – this could produce the difference. People who are bothered by having to watch an unpleasant film, who are upset by the content of a film, or who are angry because of the content of a film or because they were made to watch a film they did not want to watch, may all be more aggressive. Their aggression would be caused not by the violence in the film, but rather by these other characteristics of the film or by their reactions to the film.

Few experiments have used films that differed as dramatically and obviously as the one in the police academy study. However, almost all the films in these experiments differed in one particular way that is of great importance: the violent film tended to be more exciting and arousing than the non-violent one. Violence tends to be exciting on its own. Also, it is often combined with other factors that cause arousal. A typical violent film shows competition between good guys and bad guys, threats, scary themes, chase scenes and other strong action, exciting music, and so on. Because of all this, it is very difficult to equate violent and non-violent films in terms of excitement and arousal. Many of the experiments did not even try. In some experiments violent programs were compared with no program of any kind. For example, one experiment involved showing some children a twenty-two-minute episode of the Power Rangers while showing other children nothing (Boyatzis, Matillo, & Nesbitt, 1995). In others, violent films were compared with films that were unlikely to be the least bit arousing. Perhaps the most extreme was a study that compared the effect of a film of a violent, bloody prizefight with that of a film about canal boats in England (Berkowitz, Corwin, & Heironimus, 1963). One wonders what the authors had in mind when they chose the canal boat film. They certainly were not worrying about trying to equate the films in terms of interest or arousal. In some experiments an attempt was made to equate the programs. Several experiments employed non-violent sporting events as the non-violent stimuli. Without seeing and rating the actual films, it is impossible to compare them. But the likelihood is that watching a running race, without knowing the runners or having anyone to cheer for, was less exciting than watching a prizefight.

A difference in arousal between the aggressive and non-aggressive programs is also found in those experiments in which children saw a film of a model behaving 'aggressively' or 'non-aggressively' toward a Bobo doll or another person. Watching a model play gently with a Bobo or another person is unlikely to be especially novel or interesting or arousing. In contrast, watching a model punch and kick a Bobo doll, or (even more so) punch another person, is extremely novel (indeed, in many of these experiments the aggressive film was designed to be novel). Watching the aggressive model would be very interesting, possibly upsetting, certainly arousing – almost certainly more so than watching the non-aggressive model.

While it is difficult to equate aggressive/violent films with non-aggressive/non-violent ones in terms of arousal, it is not impossible. One can imagine a cartoon or movie with lots of action, chases, close calls, and escapes that involves no aggression or violence but is very exciting and arousing. The typical disaster film has little or no interpersonal violence but is surely exciting. Many adventure films are exciting but non-violent. The people in the non-aggressive films made for children could be shown running around and engaging in high-action activities so that the films were exciting and interesting without containing any violence. Using films of this sort as the non-violent films would have made them more similar in arousal to the violent films; to some extent this would have eliminated arousal as an explanation of any effects of the violent film. Unfortunately, this was not done.

In general, the laboratory experiments did not make much effort to equate the aggressive and non-aggressive films in terms of action or excitement. There is little question that almost always, the aggressive programs were more arousing than the non-aggressive ones. Because of this, we can be quite certain that in most if not all of the experiments, the subjects who were shown the violent film were more aroused than those shown the non-violent film or no film.

This is extremely important, because it is well known that when people are aroused, they tend to act more forcefully and strongly. Given an opportunity to act aggressively, they will be more aggressive than if they were less aroused. If the violent films are generally more arousing, those who watch them will be more aroused than those who watch the other films, and this by itself can cause them to commit more aggressive acts. The increase in aggression will have been caused not by the violence in the films, but by the arousal they produced. In fact, several experimenters have argued just this – that it is the arousal that is crucial, not the violence. The one study that attempted to compare the effect of action with that of violence found that it was the action – presumably the arousal caused by the action – that affected aggression, not the violence itself. Since no systematic research has ruled out this possibility, it remains a plausible explanation of why some studies obtained the effects.

Indeed, many of the experimenters attributed the effects they found to differences in arousal rather than to the presence of violence in the films. This was the conclusion reached by Doob and Climie (1972), Donnerstein et al. (1976), and Zillmann (1971). Zillmann in particular has argued for the importance of arousal in explaining the effects (although he may have changed his mind about this in recent years). In fact, Zillmann and Johnson (1973) point out that unlike most of the materials used in laboratory experiments, violent films and television programs usually contain many non-aggressive episodes. Because of this, the authors go so far as to suggest that typical aggressive films 'may well produce salutary effects.' They also comment: 'It should also be recognized that, with aggressive episodes of considerable duration, arousal is likely to decay because of fatigue and exhaustion, which again would yield a reduction of subsequent aggression.'

Let me be clear: if it is arousal that produced the increase in aggression after violent films, the result does not support the causal hypothesis. That hypothesis states that exposure to violence causes an increase in aggression. The idea is that the person learns to be aggressive or is motivated to be aggressive. The hypothesis requires that the increase be caused specifically by the violent content, not by anything else. If any kind of arousal can produce the effect – if a non-violent but exciting film can produce it as well, if a funny film can produce it as well, if an erotic film can produce it as well, the causal hypothesis is not supported. It must be the violence itself, not arousal associated with it, that causes the aggression. Otherwise, the causal hypothesis is not supported. Therefore, to the extent that the increases in aggression after exposure to media violence have been due to arousal, the causal hypothesis is not supported. The differential arousal caused by the violent and non-violent programs thus provides a plausible, indeed almost unavoidable explanation for the differences in aggressive responses that have sometimes been found.

Experimenter and Situational Demand

Almost all of the laboratory experiments involved demand characteristics. As explained earlier, whenever some aspect of the situation or some action of the experimenter suggests to the participants that they are expected or allowed to act in a particular way, there is the possibility that this will cause them to act that way. People are almost always influenced by what they perceive as the expectations of those around them. Imagine that young Fred, eight years old, goes to dinner at Sally's house. Fred's parents are very formal at dinner – they expect him to sit quietly, to eat carefully, and generally to behave in a very grown-up, serious manner. At Sally's house, in contrast, everything is pretty loose. There are several children, and they come and go during dinner, eat with their fingers occasionally, talk while others are talking, and generally do not behave in a very grown-up, serious manner. Would anyone be surprised if Fred, influenced by the obvious expectations of Sally's household, behaves the same as the rest of the children? And if Sally eats at Fred's house, surely she will be influenced by what is expected there and will behave much more formally and seriously than she does at home. The children have not learned that it is right to be formal or right to be informal. They are merely responding to the demands and expectations of the situation.

Now imagine the typical laboratory experiment on media violence and aggression. The participants are shown a brief film and then given an opportunity to behave aggressively. Those who are shown an excerpt from a travel film or track film probably infer nothing about aggressive behaviour. The program they have been shown is not very powerful, is not unusual, and therefore carries no particular message. In contrast, those shown an excerpt from a violent fight film, or from a film of a model vigorously attacking a doll or another person, must wonder why this program was chosen. They are rarely given any explanation, so we must not be surprised if they make the connection between the film and the measure of aggression. They may very well say to themselves, 'The experimenter expects me to act aggressively (just like in the film) – maybe he even *wants* me to act aggressively. Why else would he show that film?' In a sense, they have been given permission to act aggressively or even instructed to act aggressively. Having been given permission or instructions to act aggressively, it is not surprising that at least sometimes they do what they are told. After the non-aggressive films (permission denied), they are less aggressive than after the aggressive films (permission granted). Thus, the effect of type of film may be due not to social learning or imitation or even arousal, but merely to the message implicit in the choice of films.

This is especially true in experiments in which young children are shown films of people interacting with Bobo dolls or other such toys. In these studies, usually the children are told nothing about why they are watching the films. They watch a film of an adult kicking or hugging a Bobo doll in a room that contains various other toys, and they are then taken to the very same room, which still contains the Bobo doll and the other toys. Surely even quite young children will infer that they were shown the film as an indication of how they should behave in the room. What other possible reason could there be? So when they find themselves in the room, they 'know' that they are supposed to kick the doll (if that's what the adult did) or hug it (if that's what the adult did). They have not learned to be aggressive – they have merely learned what is expected of them in this situation.

This interpretation is supported by the fact that there is no evidence that children who have seen the 'aggressive' adult, engage in more non-imitative aggression than children who have seen the non-aggressive adult. If they have learned to be aggressive, one would expect them to behave aggressively in general, not just with respect to the specific actions they have witnessed. On the other hand, if they have merely learned that they are expected to do what the adult did, they should engage in more of those behaviours but not in more aggression of other kinds. Since that is what is found, the evidence favours the explanation in terms of demand.

Given the importance of demand factors, good experimental design requires that a great deal of attention be paid to explaining to the subjects why the films are being shown and why these particular ones have been chosen. The subjects must not think that the experimenters chose the films because they liked them or wanted the subjects to model them or thought they were appropriate. If the subjects draw any of these inferences, it could affect their behaviour. In Bobo doll studies the film must show adults interacting with other objects (not just the Bobo doll). Also, the room should be entirely different from the one used by the children, who should be given some plausible reason why they are seeing the film. Every effort must be made to minimize the possibility that the children will draw the inference that the film is being shown to teach them how they are expected to behave toward the Bobo doll.

One way to do this is to separate the choice of films from the experimenters. If the experimenters have not chosen them, no inferences can be drawn – at least not about the experimenters' opinions or wishes. Alternatively, the subjects can be given a detailed explanation about why these films are being shown, but an explanation that does not allow an inference about the experimenters' opinions. Admittedly, neither of these is easy to accomplish. It would take some ingenuity and creativity to think of a story that would explain why someone else chose these films or why only these films are available. Similarly, it is difficult to think of a good reason why the experimenter is using the films that does not carry with it some message about the content of the films. However, good experimentation involves solving these kinds of problems, which I do not think are insurmountable.

Yet almost no study bothered giving the participants any plausible explanation of why a particular film was being shown. Most of the experiments provided no explanation at all. Children were rarely told anything about why they were in the experiment, what it concerned, or why the film were being shown (this would not be acceptable today, but was more or less standard when most of these studies were conducted). Adults were usually given a minimal explanation of why they were there and what they would be doing. The explanation for the films was usually that it was a filler between tasks, or that the experimenters were interested in their reactions, or some such minimal account. For this reason, when there were effects on aggression, it is possible that they were due to demand factors rather than to a direct effect of the aggressive film.

A study by Leyens and Dunand (1991) directly supports this explanation. In this experiment, adult subjects were led to expect to see either a violent movie or a non-violent movie. However, the subjects did not actually see any movie – they simply expected to see one. When they were then given an opportunity to deliver electric shocks, those who anticipated the violent movie were more aggressive than those who anticipated the non-violent movie. Obviously the difference between the two conditions could not have been due to the effect of the actual content of the films, since no films were ever shown. Instead, the effect was due to the atmosphere or environment or demand created by the knowledge that the experimenters were going to show a violent film. The most plausible explanation is that knowing that a violent film had been chosen caused the subjects to infer that violence was more acceptable or even expected, especially since they were then given a chance to behave aggressively. In other words, demand factors produced the effect – no actual films, violent or otherwise, were involved. If merely anticipating a violent film can produce demand pressure that increases aggression, it seems likely that actually watching a violent film can do the same.

As with the explanation in terms of differences between the films, this explanation in terms of demand factors is not at all far-fetched. All careful experimenters know that demand factors are always of great concern in laboratory experiments. Well-designed studies devote a great deal of attention to eliminating or minimizing demand factors. If this is not done, any results of the studies are suspect, because the effects may have been caused by demand factors rather than the variable of interest. Yet for some reason the laboratory experiments on media violence have generally ignored this problem entirely. Most of them have been infested with strong and obvious demand factors; thus, any effects they obtained could have been caused by demand rather than by exposure to media violence.

In summary, demand factors and differences between violent and non-violent films (especially differences in arousal) could well account for the increases in aggression found in some of the laboratory experiments. So I would not give much weight to the fact that some of the experiments found more aggression after violent films. These effects do not demonstrate that exposure to media violence increases aggression.

All they may show is that when other factors are not well controlled, aggression may increase due to factors other than the violent content of the programs.

Final Conclusions

First, the laboratory experiments do not provide much support for the causal hypothesis. Fewer than half the experiments produced support-ive results, and when questionable measures of aggression are elimi-nated, the results are even weaker. One could easily interpret the results as disproving the hypothesis – surely they do not support it.

Second, because of problems in equating programs, and because of the presence of strong demand factors (as well as other reasons), the laboratory experiments should carry less weight than research outside the laboratory. Even if the laboratory experiments had found strong support for the causal hypothesis, it would still have to be demon-strated that these effects exist in the more natural settings outside the laboratory. The effect of a brief excerpt containing only violent scenes may be entirely different from the effect of a full-length movie or television program containing all sorts of material other than violence. And the effect of exposure to one violent program may be entirely different from long-term exposure to a complex and varied diet of programs. There is no way of knowing whether brief exposures in the controlled setting of the laboratory maximize or minimize the effects – one could make an argument for either side. Therefore, the laboratory research tells us relatively little about the actual effects of exposure to violence. That the laboratory experiments produced such weak support is surely discouraging for the causal hypothesis. Nevertheless, the hypothesis must stand or fall mainly on the results of other kinds of research. The rest of this review deals with these other sources of evidence.

5

Field Experiments

Experiments conducted in psychology laboratories have various weaknesses, which I have already discussed. Though there is disagreement about the importance of these problems, I believe there is general agreement about the value of experiments done in more natural settings, sometimes called field experiments. It should be noted that the distinction between laboratory and 'field' is somewhat arbitrary. My own feeling is that to qualify as a field experiment, the research should be more natural than lab research in as many ways as possible. Showing films in class or in the cottages where the subjects live is quite natural; taking them from class to another room in the school for the purpose of showing them films is less natural, unless this happens often at the school; taking them from class to a different building is less natural still, again unless this happens regularly. In other words, in terms of the independent variable in this research (exposure to programs), studies in which subjects are exposed in their own homes or classes, or in settings in which they expect to watch programs, qualify as field experiments. In terms of the dependent variable (aggressive or criminal behaviour, or prosocial behaviour), observing this in school playgrounds or the equivalent, or in natural settings of any kind, qualifies as field observation. In deciding which studies to include in this section I have generally accepted the authors' own descriptions of their work – if they think it is a field experiment, I have treated it as one.

Field experiments have several advantages over laboratory experiments. First, because they are more natural than laboratory experiments, they avoid some of the problems of experimenter demand. When someone is brought into a psychology laboratory and shown a film, it is reasonable for the person to wonder why that film was chosen. If the film shows violence, the subject may well decide that the experimenter approves of violence, or expects violent behaviour or at least allows such behaviour. In a field setting these effects, while not entirely absent in most cases, are considerably weaker. The extent to which they are weakened depends on the reasons subjects are given for why the films are being shown, and probably on a variety of other details.

In the perfect field experiment, demand pressures would be entirely absent. Imagine that students at a school – or maybe, more realistically, at a summer camp – go to a local movie theatre once a week and watch whatever is being shown there (assume only one movie is shown). Imagine also that an experimenter arranges with the theatre to show violent films and non-violent films on alternate weeks (having convinced the school or camp to agree to this). Finally, imagine that the teachers or counsellors keep track of any aggressive acts committed during the week after each movie is shown. All of this would allow us to compare the amount of aggression following a violent movie with the amount following a non-violent movie. The youths would not know that the films had been deliberately chosen, and there would be no reason to think that any demand pressures were affecting their behaviour. If they were more aggressive in the week after seeing the violent movie than in the week after seeing the non-violent movie, it would support the causal hypothesis and the result would not be open to the criticism that it was due to demand factors. The study would have some other limitations, and it could probably be improved, but at least it would go a long way toward eliminating demand problems.

As it happens, no such experiment has been conducted. Every field experiment that has been conducted probably involves demand pressures to some extent. Nevertheless, these pressures are almost certainly less obvious and less serious than in virtually all laboratory experiments. Thus, one great advantage of field experiments is that they reduce the effects of demand pressures.

Second, field experiments allow one to assess the effects of longer-term exposure and also to assess how long those effects last. Most laboratory experiments involve very brief exposure to violent and non-violent materials. A typical laboratory experiment shows children or adults a brief film – sometimes as short as three minutes, rarely longer than ten minutes. This is obviously unrealistic in that it is so different from what people watch in the real world. Such brief films – especially the ones chosen as the violent ones – have little or no plot, and no character development, and are nothing like the films and television programs people usually see. Then, with very few exceptions, the effects are assessed almost immediately. In contrast, field experiments have involved exposures and observations for as long as many weeks. This is an extremely important difference, because presumably we are concerned mainly with the long-term effects of media violence. Six-year-olds do not generally commit serious acts of aggression or any violent crimes. If watching a violent program makes them a little more aggressive, it is probably not terribly serious. But if watching violent programs for years makes them more aggressive when they become teenagers and makes them more likely to commit crimes when they are adults, that is very serious. So although we would all prefer our young children not to be aggressive, I think most people's main concern about media violence is that it has effects that show up when our children have grown up. Laboratory research cannot address this concern. Field experiments are also quite limited in this respect, but they are much better than laboratory research.

Third, field experiments involve observing real behaviour in a natural setting. Some laboratory experiments use observations, but most do not. Even when they do observe behaviour, they suffer from the fact that the settings in which the behaviour occurs are less natural. Field experiments look at people's behaviour in their actual schools or residences. Also, the behaviour is not performance on some psychological test or pressing a button that supposedly gives an electric shock or punching a Bobo doll, but real aggression with real people. Some of the field studies on media violence have failed to make the crucial distinction between real aggression (hurting or trying to hurt another person) and play aggression (fooling around but not trying to hurt someone), but at least they have involved real behaviour rather than behaviour in artificial situations.

Probably the most important limitation of field experiments is that they cannot solve the problem of equating programs on dimensions other than violence. As we discussed in the context of laboratory experiments, movies and television programs that differ in amount of violence also differ in many other respects. Violent programs tend to be more exciting and active than non-violent ones. This need not be true, but it often is. Only if programs are equated on these dimensions can any effects be attributed to the violence rather than to arousal. Also, violent programs are sometimes more enjoyable than non-violent ones. This certainly need not be, but again, if they are not equated on this dimension, any effects may be due to this factor rather than to the violence. Field experiments have not done much better than laboratory experiments in dealing with this problem. On the other hand, in this context one great advantage of field experiments is that they usually involve the showing of entire programs or movies, not just short clips. This does not solve the problem of equating the programs on action, but at least they are real programs that real people have been exposed to rather than selected segments chosen to make a point. Thus, any results that are found are more likely to reflect the effect of programs in the real world.

For all these reasons, field experiments constitute a better test than laboratory experiments of the effect that viewing violence actually has in the real world. The situation is very similar with other kinds of research, such as the testing of new drugs: the work may begin in the laboratory, but the real test is in the world outside the laboratory. No matter how promising the laboratory results are, they must be confirmed by field studies with real people in real settings. If the laboratory results are not replicated in the real world, the drugs are not approved. Similarly, even if the laboratory experiments on the effects of violent media had produced consistent results supporting the causal hypothesis – which, of course, they did not – the real test of the effects would still be the results of research in the real world. Indeed, this is implicitly acknowledged by those who favour the causal hypothesis – it is they who have conducted most of the real world research.

Moreover, field experiments are extremely important for the simple reason that they *are* experiments. Only experimental research can provide an unambiguous, rigorous test of the hypothesis that media violence causes aggression. Indeed, this is true of almost any hypothesis. When an experiment obtains an effect, one can be certain that it was due to the difference between the experimental conditions. If field experiments find that those exposed to violent media are more aggressive than those exposed to non-violent media, we can be certain that the effect is due to the differences between the two types of programs. It may not be due to the presence of violence (as noted earlier, it could be due to the amount of action or to any other difference in the programs), but it will have to be due to the type of program. In contrast, any field research that is not experimental is always open to all sorts of alternative explanations. That is why modern science is based mainly on the experimental method. Thus, although there have been various other types of studies on this issue, many of which are quite interesting and important, field experiments are clearly the best way to assess the effect of media violence. If this research consistently supports the causal hypothesis, it constitutes a powerful argument in its favour.

THE STUDIES

Feshbach and Singer (1971)

This is the grandfather of experimental field research on media violence. Although it has been criticized mercilessly by those who do not like its conclusions, and although I agree with some of those criticisms, I still think it is an important study. It began with a marvellous concept: boys in seven residential schools were randomly assigned to watch either only violent television programs or only non-violent programs for six weeks. During that time all of the boys were observed and their aggressiveness was rated by adults who knew them well and saw them every day. The strengths of this idea were that the boys watched real television, they watched it for a fairly long time, and their behaviour was observed in their natural environment. It was a major undertaking, and three decades after being published it remains probably the best field experiment on this issue.

Method. The settings were seven residential institutions in southern California and New York City. Four of these were homes for boys whose parents were unable or unfit to care for them or for boys who needed special care and treatment; three were private schools for boys. I will refer to them as the 'homes' and the 'private schools,' although some of the homes were also schools. There were originally 625 participants, although not all took part in all phases of the study.

Some of the boys were randomly assigned to watch only non-aggressive programs; others were assigned to watch only relatively aggressive, violent programs. Each group was required to watch only programs on their list. The boys could watch as much television as they wanted as long as they watched at least six hours a week. The authors were concerned that the boys might have negative reactions to the restrictions on what they could view. To minimize this possibility they made it clear that anyone who wanted to could drop out of the study at any time. There was no differential drop-out rate for the two experimental conditions. However, at three of the institutions those in the non-violent group objected because 'Batman' was not on the list, so it was added for those groups. This meant that for these non-violent subjects, the acceptable list contained this one relatively violent program. No other changes of this kind were made.

The main measure of aggression was based on ratings done by the adult (i.e., the teacher, house parent, supervisor, or proctor) who knew the child best. The adult indicated whether the child had engaged in any of nineteen aggressive acts, whether these acts were provoked or not, and whether they were mild or moderate to strong acts of aggression. There were separate scores for aggression toward peers and toward authority. There were various other measures of aggression, but these were less important and produced less clear results.

Results. Over the period of the study, those who watched violent television committed *fewer* aggressive acts than those who watched non-violent television. The difference was substantial (151.6 to 81.1) and statistically significant. Various other analyses and subanalyses produced essentially the same result. Moreover, the difference between the experimental groups was consistent across almost every particular type of aggressive act (e.g., fistfighting, pushing, destroying property), as well as for verbal aggression. Clearly, these results directly contradict the causal hypothesis.

Although the study was designed as one experiment, it is reasonable to look at the effect separately for each of the seven institutions. The effect on aggression toward peers was significant in three of the 'homes' and close to significant in the fourth. In the three private schools the level of aggression was generally lower and there were no significant effects of television viewing.

Discussion. Feshbach and Singer argued that the results were due to a catharsis effect – that is, watching violent programs reduced children's aggressive feelings, gave them a vicarious outlet for their feelings, and thus reduced their aggressiveness. Although I agree that the results are consistent with this catharsis explanation, most other research has not found a catharsis effect. Accordingly, I do not accept this account. That being said, what is important for the present review is that the results are clearly inconsistent with the causal hypothesis. Indeed, they are precisely the opposite of what the hypothesis would predict – rather than increasing aggression, violent television decreased it.

As many others have pointed out, one of the crucial difficulties with the experiment is that the boys in the 'non-violent' group were deprived of many of their favourite programs, whereas those in the 'violent' group were deprived of fewer. This suggests that the former group may have been frustrated and angry, and that this is what produced their aggressive behaviour. I agree that this is a plausible alternative explanation for the results: that the programs probably differed in how much they were enjoyed is definitely a flaw in the experiment. It makes the results less convincing and important than they would have been had the programs been equally liked.

However, this is not a flaw for which the authors should bear much blame, because there is no clear way to fix it. The same problem exists whenever subjects are exposed to different programs. When full-length real programs (TV shows or movies) are used, the experimenter is faced with the virtually impossible task of finding programs that will be equally enjoyable. Especially when the subjects are boys, as in the present study, it is extremely hard to find non-violent programs that they will like as much as violent programs. One could get around this by choosing very poor violent programs and very good non-violent programs, but then the level of violence and the quality of the programs would be confounded. Perhaps there are some non-violent programs that the boys would like a great deal – as much as they like the violent programs. But this would entail choosing very few non-violent programs, since few would be able to compete with a large number of violent programs. Probably most important, violent programs are almost always more exciting and arousing than non-violent ones. Perhaps this difference could be eliminated by choosing relatively unexciting violent programs and relatively exciting non-violent ones. But then one would be selecting unusual and perhaps less good examples of both kinds of programs. So I think we must acknowledge that there is no realistic way to equate violent and non-violent programs in terms of liking, excitement, and probably various other dimensions. Indeed, as I have noted before and will note throughout this section, none of the research studies have equated the violent and non-violent programs; this problem is present in every field experiment and in most other research on this issue.

That being said, when diets of real programs are employed – not brief excerpts from programs, as in many of the laboratory experiments, and not just a few programs but a full diet – this is not necessarily a fatal flaw. In the real world children are in fact exposed to various diets of television programs and movies. A study that modifies those diets but uses existing programs is essentially asking how various diets of existing programs affect the children. It is necessary to accept the variations in the existing programs because they are part of reality.

From this perspective, one interpretation of the Feshbach and Singer study could be that boys prefer violent television, and don't like it when they have to watch only non-violent programs, and this makes them more aggressive. According to this interpretation the study shows a frustration effect, not a catharsis effect. Of course, even this interpretation provides no support for the causal hypothesis, because there is no hint that exposure to a diet of only violent programs made the boys more aggressive. That is, forcing the boys in the violent television condition to increase their exposure to violent television (since almost all of them previously watched a combination of violent and non-violent television) did not increase their aggressiveness.

Conclusions. This is not a perfect study. Others have pointed out a number of problems with it that we must take into account in interpreting the results. I am most concerned about the non-comparability of the violent and non-violent programs, the inconsistency in results across the various measures of aggression, and the lack of effect in the private schools. Nevertheless, I think this is an important study, because it made a serious attempt to do an experiment in a natural setting, using diets of regular television programs, over a reasonably long period of time. The results are straightforward: those watching only non-violent television were more aggressive than those watching only violent television. For the purposes of this review the most important point is that whatever interpretation of this result one favours, the experiment produced no evidence in support of the causal hypothesis. There was not the slightest indication that exposure to violent programs increased aggression – indeed, almost all of the evidence showed the opposite.

Wells (1973)

Several authors referred to a study by Wells (1973), which they described as a replication of the study by Feshbach and Singer. According to Comstock and Fisher (1975) the study by Wells involved 567 boys in the seventh to ninth grades in ten residential schools. The boys were exposed to diets of either violent or non-violent programs for seven weeks, and measures of aggression were obtained before and after this period. Wells found that those exposed to the non-violent programs became more verbally aggressive, whereas those exposed to the violent diet became more physically aggressive. Comstock and Fisher note, however, that both trends were of low magnitude. They do not mention whether any of the differences were significant. I assume they were not, since none of the references to this study seem to consider it supportive of the causal hypothesis. In discussing this experiment, Liebert, Sprafkin, and Davidson (1982) wrote that it eliminated the problem of non-comparability of the violent and non-violent programs faced by Feshbach and Singer. Liebert and colleagues do not explain what Wells did to make the non-violent and violent programs equally enjoyable. It would be very useful to know how this was done, since it is difficult to imagine how one would manage it. Perhaps Liebert and colleagues were wrong, since Comstock does not mention this very important improvement. In fact, Comstock says that Wells interpreted his results as being due in part to the fact that the boys in the non-violent group were frustrated at being denied access to their preferred violent entertainment; this seems to indicate that the violent programs were more enjoyable than the others.

Even if it did not solve the problem of comparability of programs, this would be an important and useful study. Apparently it did not find any great increase in aggressiveness in the violent group or decrease in the non-violent group. If so, its results do not support the causal hypothesis. On the other hand, it did not find that the 'non-violent' group was more aggressive, and in that regard it did not replicate the results of Feshbach and Singer.

Conclusions. Assuming that the descriptions are accurate, this study provided no evidence in support of the causal hypothesis.

de Konig, Conradie, and Neil (1980)

I have not seen this report and cannot vouch for the accuracy of the description below. I am including it because it is mentioned by Liebert and colleagues (1982) and is clearly relevant. This is how they describe the research.

Two provinces in South Africa were just introducing television. Three diets were constructed, each comprising eighteen American television programs. One diet had aggressive programs, one had prosocial programs, and one had neutral programs. Approximately 700 children five to thirteen were assigned to these diets. They watched programs from the assigned diet for one hour every day for four weeks. Their behaviour, both aggressive and prosocial, was rated before and after the viewing periods.

The results were minimal, with few effects being significant. In terms of aggression there was some tendency for the neutral diet to decrease aggression against peers and for the prosocial diet to increase aggression toward authority, perhaps because the children disliked the prosocial programs and reacted negatively to them. The aggressive diet produced no changes. None of the diets affected prosocial behaviour.

Liebert and colleagues suggest various reasons why there were so few effects: the measures may have been insensitive, the children may have been temporarily overwhelmed by the novelty of television programs, the programs may have been differentially liked, and so on. I have no way of evaluating these suggestions, but they are all plausible. Nevertheless, assuming that the description of the study is accurate, this large and innovative study failed to produce any evidence that watching violent television increases aggression, or that watching prosocial television increases prosocial behaviour.

Conclusion. There is no support for the causal hypothesis, and perhaps some evidence against it.

Gorney, Loye, and Steele (1977)

This study attempted to observe the effects of varying diets of television on adult males. The authors recruited 725 husband–wife couples. The men were assigned to one of five conditions. These consisted of five diets of television programs: high in prosocial content, high in violence or hurtful content, neutral, mixed, and natural (what they usually watched). Before and after each program, the men rated their moods. They also rated their reactions to each program, including their emotional arousal. In addition, the wives served as observers of their husbands and provided daily reports of their helpful and hurtful behaviour.

Results. In terms of aggressive mood, the violent television group showed no change over the week, the prosocial group showed an appreciable decrease, and the other groups showed slight decreases. The overall effect was not significant, nor was the difference in scores between the violent group and any of the other groups. In terms of anxiety, the neutral and mixed groups became less anxious, and the violent and prosocial groups showed no change. All of the groups showed declines in terms of positive moods.

There were no significant differences among groups in helpful behaviour. For hurtful behaviour, the authors report that it was lowest in the prosocial and neutral groups, higher in the violent group, and highest in the natural group. The violent group did not differ significantly from any of the others.

Summary. Although this study has sometimes been cited as supporting the causal hypothesis, it provides no such support. The group watching only violent programs did not differ significantly from any other group on any measure, and was rated as engaging in less hurtful behaviour than the natural group. This difference was not significant, but the point is that even the direction of the differences is not what would be predicted by the causal hypothesis. There are so many problems with this study that I would not give it much weight. Nevertheless, it is clear that the results do not support the causal hypothesis.

Milgram and Shotland (1973)

This book reports a series of eight experiments in which people saw a film or television program that contained a scene in which a crime was committed, or did not contain that scene. They were then given a chance to commit the same crime or a similar one. The experiments were considerably more realistic than most of the research in this area, and involved many more subjects (almost 800 in total). Also, the programs the subjects watched were made as similar as possible, with the only difference being whether the criminal act was included. Although the behaviour in question in this research was a criminal act and not aggression, this body of work bears closely on whether viewing violence causes people to commit violence.

In one of the studies – the others are quite similar – people watched a program in a theatre and were promised a reward for their help. For half of them the program showed someone breaking into a charity box; for the other half this scene was not included. They then went to another building to get their reward. There was no one present in the room to which they were sent, but there was a message saying that the radios they had been promised were no longer available. There was also a charity box in the room with money clearly visible, and a dollar bill hanging on the outside of the box. The measure was whether the person took the bill and/or broke into the box.

Results. None of the studies found any effect of exposure to the illegal act, nor were there any trends. Those who saw the act in the televised or filmed program were no more likely to engage in that act than were those who did not see it in a program.

Discussion. These were imaginative studies conducted in a realistic setting. Since the particular acts being studied did not involve aggression, this body of research tells us little directly about the effect of media violence on aggression. Nevertheless, the fact that there was no imitation of the observed act suggests that imitation of what is seen on television may occur less often than is sometimes suggested.

The contrast with some of the laboratory findings is striking. In laboratory studies, watching a violent film sometimes causes subjects to score higher on some test of aggressiveness. The explanation offered is that the subjects imitate what they see or that they are taught that aggressiveness is acceptable. These studies are mostly quite contrived, and as noted at length earlier, many alternative explanations of the effects are possible. The Milgram–Shotland studies were conducted in much more realistic settings, and in some instances the participants did not even know that the films had been altered by the experimenters (which removed demand pressures). Also, the behaviour of concern was observed away from the location of the study and in a natural context. In these more realistic situations, with much less possibility of experimenter demand, there were no effects of the content of the programs. This suggests that the results of the laboratory experiments on television violence are due not to some general phenomenon such as social learning, but to more specific factors present in these unrealistic situations. If the kinds of acts studied in the Milgram and Shotland experiments are not imitated – if watching them occur in a program does not cause people to commit them – why should other kinds of acts such as aggressive acts be more likely to be imitated?

Conclusion. Although the behaviour studied was somewhat different from aggression, this series of studies, with a large number of subjects and relatively realistic settings, provides some evidence against the causal hypothesis. If viewing violence causes people to be aggressive, it is difficult to understand why viewing illegal acts does not have the same effect on illegal behaviour. That it does not suggests that the causal hypothesis is wrong.

Black and Bevan (1992)

Adults were approached either before or after they had watched a film at a commercial theatre. Some were attending the film *Missing in Action*, in which an American soldier returns to enemy territory to rescue prisoners of war (violent film); the others were attending *Passage to India* (non-violent film). All were given a questionnaire that is supposed to measure feelings of hostility.

Results. Those at the violent film scored higher in hostility than those at the non-violent film, both before and after the viewing. Also, the hostility scores of those at the violent movie increased significantly from before to after the movie; the scores of those at the non-violent movie did not change.

Discussion. This was not an experimental study, because people were not randomly assigned to conditions. Also, there was no measure of actual behaviour, which is a serious limitation: saying you feel hostile is quite different from acting aggressively. I have included it in this group because the authors seem to think it was an experiment and because it does not fit neatly into any other group. Taking the result at face value, it is consistent with the causal hypothesis. However, this study should be given little weight because of the absence of any behavioural effect.

On the other hand, this study does provide a striking example of the possible importance of the particular films chosen to represent violent and non-violent programs. I do not know why the authors chose these particular two films, but they could hardly have chosen two that were more different. *Missing in Action* is undoubtedly violent. It is also patriotic, arousing, and exciting. It is a B movie with little redeeming value other than the action. *Passage to India* is thoughtful, slow, profound, and moving, but not exciting. It was also one of the most highly acclaimed movies of the 1990s, with outstanding acting, direction, and cinematography. One might wonder why the authors chose movies of such different quality to represent violent and non-violent films instead of trying to match them in this respect. The two movies are so different that it's hard to determine what caused the difference in responses to the questionnaire. Perhaps people generally increase their scores when aroused (so arousal explains the effect); perhaps they generally increase them after an entertaining movie, but not if the movie is really serious (so it is the seriousness of the non-violent movie that is producing the difference); and so on. It is also possible that the content of the movies made no difference, but that those who attended the non-violent movie were sleepier than the others since it is a very long movie. The point is not that any of these explanations is necessarily correct, but that without controlling these other factors, there is no way to know whether it was the violent content or something else that made the difference.

Despite these problems, I count these results as providing some (very slight) support for the causal hypothesis.

Friedrich and Stein (1973)

Children in a nursery school ranging in age from 3.8 to 5.5 were shown violent, prosocial, or neutral films. The violent programs were six Batman and six Superman cartoons; the prosocial programs were twelve episodes of Mister Rogers Neighborhood; and the neutral programs were selected to contain no violence and little prosocial content. Trained observers noted each child's aggressive and prosocial behaviour at various times during the day in school.

Results. There were no effects of type of program on the children's physical, verbal, object or fantasy aggression nor on a measure called interpersonal aggression, which combined physical and verbal aggression. In short, viewing violent programs did not increase aggressiveness.

After failing to obtain the results they predicted, the authors conducted a complex internal analysis. The boys and girls were divided into those who were high in aggression, and those who were initially low in aggression and their interpersonal aggression scores were compared for the various film conditions. Those who were low in aggression initially tended to become somewhat more aggressive regardless of what programs they watched; those who were initially high in aggression tended to become less aggressive, again regardless of type of program. Both of these are obvious regression effects: if you select people who are high on almost any factor that can change, they will tend to get lower on that factor; if you select people who are low on the factor, they will tend to get higher. This is not due to any effect of an experimental manipulation, because it will occur without any intervention.

Besides this regression effect, there were differential effects of the type of program. Those who were initially low in aggression and who saw the neutral programs increased more in aggressiveness than those who saw the prosocial programs; and those who saw the prosocial programs increased more (very slightly) in aggressiveness than those who saw the violent programs. Similarly, those who were initially high in aggression and who saw the neutral programs decreased more in aggressiveness than those who saw the prosocial programs, who in turn decreased more in aggressiveness than those who saw the violent programs. In other words, the neutral programs produced both the largest increases in aggressiveness and the largest decreases in aggressiveness; the violent programs produced the smallest changes. To put it another way, the only possible negative effect of the violent programs was that after watching them, those who were high in aggression initially decreased less in aggressiveness than did those who watched neutral programs.

Conclusion. Taken at face value and at their very best, these results provide no evidence that watching violent programs increases aggression. The only significant result for aggressiveness was that among initially low aggressive children, those who watched the violent programs increased less in a measure that combined physical and verbal aggression than did those who watched prosocial or neutral programs; among initially high aggressive children, those who watched the violent programs decreased the least in aggressiveness. This is hardly an indication that filmed violence causes aggression (especially since there was no effect at all on physical aggression by itself).

Moreover, there were no main effects of type of film on any measure of aggression, including the combined measure of physical and verbal aggression. The significant effect appeared only after the usual analyses had been conducted, two measures had been combined, and the subjects had been divided into high and low on the basis of initial scores. Even if this division is appropriate, it is obvious that the best the authors could report was one marginally significant effect out of many analyses.

This study is repeatedly cited as showing that watching violent programs causes aggression. Yet it does no such thing. The results provide no evidence that exposure to violent programs increases aggression. If anything, they constitute a failure to find these effects, and thus provide evidence against the causal hypothesis.

Parke, Berkowitz, Leyens, West, and Sebastian (1977) and Leyens, Camino, Parke, and Berkowitz (1975)

These three field experiments are often cited as among the most important studies demonstrating that exposure to violent programs increases aggressive behaviour. They used similar methods, which involved presenting violent or non-violent movies to boys at residential homes. For convenience I will refer to the studies as the Leyens study and as Parke 1 and Parke 2.

LEYENS

This study was conducted in four cottages at a Belgian residential institution for boys who had legal problems or who did not have adequate care at home. The institution allowed very little television viewing, and what was allowed was strictly regulated and generally limited to news, sports, and a few musical shows. The experiment consisted of showing each cottage movies for one week, with two cottages being shown five movies containing violence and two cottages being shown five movies containing no violence. The aggressive behaviour of the boys was observed when they were not engaged in any organized activities. In scoring their behaviour, the observers were instructed to ignore the intent of the action (I shall return to this below).

Results. Although the results were not entirely consistent, in general those shown the aggressive films became more aggressive immediately after the films were shown. During the mid-day period the day after the films were shown, and the mid-day period the week after the films were shown, there were no consistent effects of the films on aggression. Taken at face value, these results offer some support for the notion that exposure to violent films increases aggression.

It is important to remember that even though the films were shown for five days, there was no carryover of an effect to the day after each film was shown, nor any cumulative effect that could be seen the week after the boys were exposed to the films. Thus, the results offer no indication that exposure to violent material had any lasting effect on the boys' behaviour. Rather, the results are consistent only with an immediate effect on aggression.

Discussion. There are a number of serious problems with this study that make its results almost impossible to interpret and that greatly reduce any support they might offer for the causal hypothesis. First, the statistical tests that deal with the effects of the films are all inappropriate. The boys in each cottage were treated as if they were independent when obviously they were not. The authors acknowledge this in a footnote: 'We based our analyses on individual scores that are clearly not independent' (351). It is good that they understood this, but they did not seem to realize the seriousness of the problem. The bottom line is that the significance tests they did have no scientific meaning: we have no way of knowing whether the change scores for the cottages are reliable, and therefore no way of knowing whether they should be taken seriously.

Second, it was a mistake to instruct the observers to ignore the intent of the actions. Developmental psychologists who study children's aggression have long made a distinction between real aggression and play aggression, which they sometimes call 'rough and tumble play.' Many boys are physically and verbally rough with each other. That is, they engage in wrestling, mock punching, mock fighting, and so on. When they behave in this way, they do not intend to hurt the other person and do not expect to get hurt themselves. By the usual definition and conception of aggression, they are not being aggressive. Combining these playful acts with real aggression risks greatly distorting our picture of the boys' behaviour. Since these two different behaviours were combined, we have no way of knowing whether there were many acts of aggression, or very few, or even none. For this reason, even if we leave aside the statistical problem, the results are impossible to interpret.

This is especially important, because it is possible that the somewhat higher scores for aggression in the violent film group occurred because the boys were acting out what they had just seen in the movie. Perhaps the boys were simply playing and their play was to some extent modelled on what they had just seen in the movie. If the movie had fighting, the boys engaged in play fighting; if the movie had comedy or romance, the boys engaged in activities that are closer to those. Perhaps after seeing *The Dirty Dozen*, one of the movies that was shown, the boys engaged in hand-to-hand fighting similar to that in the movie. Serious fighting (i.e., trying to hurt each other) would have indicated that the movie led to increased aggression. But merely fooling around, and playing in a way that resembled what was shown in the movie, would not indicate that the movie had any effect on aggression. There is a world of difference between these alternatives. The raters did not distinguish between real and play aggression, so we have no way of knowing which alternative to accept. This is a recurrent problem in this literature.

Third, it may be that the boys were more aroused by the violent movies than by the non-violent ones. The paper reports that the types of movies did not differ significantly in terms of excitement. However, the violent movies were rated more exciting, and the statistical test that was not significant did not directly compare the two types of movies. In fact, it is almost impossible to equate violent and non-violent movies in terms of excitement – not impossible, but very difficult – and doing so requires a very careful selection of both types of movies. If the boys were more excited by the violent movies, this by itself could explain the increase in aggressive behaviour, especially given that play and real fighting were scored the same. Moreover, this explanation would account for the fact that the effects did not last even until the next day and were not cumulative. If the boys were merely more aroused and excited and then went out and played rougher, the arousal would not be expected to last for long, and the effects would be expected to disappear a few hours later.

Conclusions. Although this study had admirable intentions, it suffers from so many problems that it is difficult to have any confidence in the findings. At the most, accepting them all at face value, there is some evidence that violent films resulted in a short-lived increase in aggression. However, this effect could be explained in terms of differential arousal, rather than any direct effect of the violence itself. The lack of appropriate statistics and the confusing of real and play aggression make even this weak interpretation problematic. In sum, for its time this was not a bad study; but unfortunately it offers little reliable information for our purposes. Despite all of this, I shall consider the results as providing some slight support for the causal hypothesis.

PARKE 1

This study was conducted in two cottages at an American institution for juvenile offenders ranging in age from fourteen to eighteen. The boys in one cottage were shown violent films, and those in another cottage were shown non-violent films – one per day for five days for each cottage. The measure of aggression was similar to that used in the Leyens study.

Results. Unfortunately, the boys in the violent movie condition were initially more aggressive than those in the non-violent movie condition. The authors attempted to deal with this by dividing each cottage into high and low aggressive boys and treating them as different groups. The results indicate increased aggression during the movie week for three groups – the two shown violent movies and the low-aggressive boys shown non-violent movies. The effect seemed especially large for the low-aggressive boys who watched the violent movies. The movies had no cumulative effect: the effects were the same early in the week as they were later in the week. During the post-movie period, most of the effects disappeared. At face value, the results provides some support for the causal hypothesis.

Discussion. This study suffers from all of the problems of the first one. The statistics are even more inappropriate because there was only one cottage in each condition. As with the first study, the lack of distinction between real and play aggression is a serious error, and makes it impossible for us to interpret the results, since we do not know whether the boys were being more aggressive or merely engaging in more aggressive play. Also, as the authors note, the violent and non-violent films differed in many ways, including arousal level and how enjoyable the boys found them. Thus, any effects might have been due to arousal.

Conclusion. Taken at face value, the results indicate that after watching violent movies, the boys scored higher in aggression than they did before the movies. But the movies had no cumulative effect of the sort that would have been expected from almost any account in terms of a causal effect of media violence on aggression. In any case, for all of the reasons given above, the results are difficult if not impossible to interpret. Even so, I would consider the results, at the descriptive level, as providing some slight support for the causal hypothesis.

PARKE 2

This study was very similar to Parke 1. One cottage was shown five violent movies, another five non-violent movies. But this time two other cottages were included, with one being shown only one violent movie and the other only one non-violent movie. Because in the previous study the boys found the violent films more enjoyable and more exciting than the non-violent films, in this study different neutral films were used in an effort to make them more equivalent to the violent films. The effort was apparently successful for the five-movie groups, who rated the two types of films equally exciting and enjoyable; it was less successful for the one-movie groups, who rated the violent film more exciting than the non-violent one.

Results. Unfortunately, once again the violent film cottage was initially more aggressive than the non-violent film cottage. It is too bad that having had this problem in the earlier study, the authors did not make sure that the less aggressive cottages were in the violent film condition. This would not have solved the problem, but at least the initial difference would have been in a different direction from that predicted after the films. Instead, once again, the boys in each cottage were divided into those who were high and those who were low in initial aggressiveness. The authors described the results this way: 'Boys who watched the five violent movies were more aggressive than those who saw the five non-violent films as measured by the general aggression index.' However, since the violent movie cottage was more aggressive to begin with, the fact that it continued to be more aggressive tells us nothing about the effect of the movies. Since the cottages differed in aggressiveness, the crucial data are the changes from the pre-movie week to the movie week. These data do not lend much support to the causal hypothesis. The high-aggressive boys did not change appreciably in aggressiveness regardless of the movies they saw (actually, those who watched the violent movies became slightly *less* aggressive and those who watched the non-violent movies became slightly *more* aggressive). In contrast, the low-aggressive boys became more aggressive regardless of which movies they saw. The change was larger for those who watched the violent movies, but was substantial for both groups. In other words, as far as one can tell from the figure (and no other data are given), there was no differential effect of exposure to five violent or five non-violent movies. The data for the one-movie conditions are not shown, but it seems clear that there was no effect of type of movie.

Conclusions. Even taken entirely at face value, these results provide little evidence that violent films have an effect on aggression. The high-aggressive boys did not change their aggressive behaviour after watching either type of film, and the low-aggressive boys became more aggressive after both types of films. The only hint of an effect is that the change for the low-aggressive boys was somewhat larger after violent than after non-violent films. There was apparently no effect on changes in aggression in the one-film condition. I conclude that this study provides no support for the causal hypothesis, and could be considered evidence against it.

Summary of the Results

- *Black and Bevan (1992).* Some slight evidence that watching a violent movie increases hostility, but no behavioural measure and no control on differences between the two movies.
- *de Konig et al. (1980).* No evidence that viewing violent television increases aggression; some evidence against it.
- *Feshbach and Singer (1971).* No evidence that viewing violent television increases aggression. In fact, the results of three of the seven experiments show the opposite – that viewing violent programs *decreases* aggression. This may be because the non-violent programs were less popular. Whatever the reason, no support for the causal hypothesis.
- *Wells (1973).* Unpublished study cited by others. Did not replicate the reverse effect found by Feshbach and Singer, but also did not find that viewing violent programs increases aggression. Again, no support for the causal hypothesis.
- *Friedrich and Stein (1973).* One marginally significant effect consistent with the causal hypothesis, but a great many analyses that found no effects on either aggression or prosocial behaviour. Overall, no support for the causal hypothesis; could be considered evidence against it.
- *Loye et al. (1977).* No support for the causal hypothesis.
- *Milgram and Shotland (1973).* Looked at effects on criminal behaviour rather than on aggression. In eight separate experiments, viewing a criminal act being committed did not increase the likelihood that people would commit the act themselves. No support for the concept behind the causal hypothesis and none for the hypothesis itself.
- *Parke/Leyens (1975/1977).* These three field studies have more serious problems than most of the research in this group. Also, the statistical analyses are almost all inappropriate. Two of the field studies provide limited support for the causal hypothesis (ignoring the

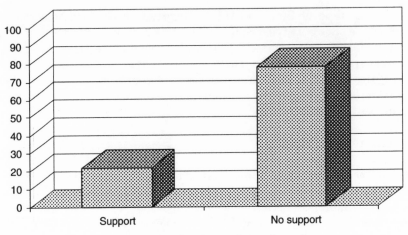

Percentage of studies getting each result

Figure 5.1. Results of field experiments

statistical problems); the third field study offers no support for it. None of the studies demonstrates a cumulative effect of viewing violent programs. Overall, the results of these three field studies provide only the weakest support for the causal hypothesis.

I hesitate merely to count the outcomes of studies, because such a count can be quite misleading. However, doing so does provide a simple measure of the consistency of the results. Only three of the ten studies obtained even slightly supportive results, and two of those used inappropriate statistics while the third did not have a measure of behaviour. The rest showed either no effect of media violence on aggression, a reverse effect, or a mixture of effects with most being inconsistent with the causal hypothesis.

However, this approach to tabulating the results gives a more favourable picture than is justified. It is important to remember that several of the studies that failed to find effects actually consisted of many separate studies. Feshbach and Singer conducted their study in seven schools and each should be considered an independent study; Wells apparently included ten schools; and Milgram and Shotland conducted eight entirely independent experiments. I do not know the results in the various schools used by Wells, but I assume that none of them showed a significant effect. Ignoring that study for lack of detailed information, we could count the other two projects as a total of fifteen experiments that failed to find support for the causal hypothesis. This alternative way of counting the results (see Figure 5.1) indicates that three experiments found some support, and twenty did not.

Finally, the studies differed greatly in the size of the samples used. The three experiments that obtained supportive results all had small samples. In fact, as pointed out earlier, the Leyens study had only two independent groups in each condition, while Parke 1 had only one. In contrast, at least some of the experiments that obtained non-supportive results had quite large samples, in the hundreds. Though it would be a mistake to have confidence in results merely because of large samples, it is justifiable to be cautious about studies involving very small samples, especially if they employ inappropriate statistics.

Conclusions

These studies were serious attempts to study a complex problem in real world settings. None of them was perfect in design or execution. Because of their various difficulties and limitations, they do not and could not provide definitive evidence for or against the causal hypothesis. Nevertheless, it should be clear that this body of work provides little or no support for the causal hypothesis. Not one of the studies produced unambiguous, consistent evidence that exposure to violent programs increases aggression; and most of them – a strong and clear majority – produced no supportive evidence. Accordingly, I believe it fair to conclude that taken as a whole these field experiments provide evidence *against* the causal hypothesis.

It may be valuable to compare these findings with those from the laboratory experiments. Although the lab experiments produced highly inconsistent results, quite a few of them did find increased scores on some measure of aggression after exposure to a violent program. But was this effect a direct effect of viewing media violence, or was it due to various other factors such as demand pressures or differential arousal? The field experiments could be seen as a way of testing the various interpretations. That the field experiments produced such negative results for the causal hypothesis is a strong indication that the laboratory results were not due to the direct effect of the violent media. A plausible interpretation of the results of the field experiments is that once some of the problems with laboratory experiments are removed, there is no longer any effect of viewing violent programs on aggression.

6

Longitudinal Studies: The Effect of Early Exposure to Violent Media on Later Aggression

Longitudinal research is one of the most important and revealing methods of investigating the effects of viewing media violence. With the exception of the survey studies, the goal of all of the research we have been reviewing is to test the hypothesis that exposure to violent media causes aggression. The ideal method of demonstrating causality is the experiment. However, as we have seen, the experimental work has serious limitations. The laboratory experiments are short-term, involve brief exposures, use measures that are often questionable, and are conducted in the artificial environment of the laboratory. They are also prone to problems such as the non-equivalence of the films in terms of arousal, and strong demand factors; both of these allow alternative and uninteresting explanations of any effects that are found. The field experiments are a little better but are still short-term and involve relatively few people. Longitudinal studies attempt to answer the question of causality, while solving many of the problems inherent in the experimental work.

Longitudinal research on media violence starts with the results of the survey studies described earlier. That research found that those who watch a lot of violent television tend to be more aggressive. The association was not strong, or even consistent across all of the research. Nevertheless, it seems likely that this relationship does exist. However, the mere existence of the association provides no information about the possible causal links between the two behaviours. As discussed earlier, that two variables are correlated does not mean or even imply that one causes the other. That exposure to or preference for violent television is correlated with aggressiveness raises the possibility that the former causes the latter, but it doesn't prove it. One reason for the association could be the one proposed by the causal hypothesis – namely, that viewing media violence causes an increase in aggressiveness. Another possible explanation is that aggressiveness causes people to prefer violent television (in fact, some of those who favour the causal hypothesis have suggested that this reverse effect also occurs). As with all correlations, a third possibility is that some other variable causes people to watch more violent television *and also* to be more aggressive. If this third explanation is correct, there is no causal connection between violent television and aggression. Longitudinal research begins with the belief that exposure to media violence and aggression are associated, and with the knowledge that this could be caused by any of the factors just described. Longitudinal work is meant to provide evidence that will help establish whether there is a causal effect of media violence on aggression.

There have been relatively few longitudinal studies. Most were extremely ambitious, costly, and impressive pieces of work. Before we consider the results, let me provide brief descriptions of the actual studies to suggest some of the complexity and scale of the research.

1. *The twenty-two-year study* (Eron, Walder, & Lefkowitz, 1971; Lefkowitz, Eron, Walder, & Huesmann, 1977; Huesmann, Lefkowitz, Eron, & Walder, 1984; Huesmann, 1986). Eron and his colleagues obtained data on the entire third grade of Columbia County in New York. Initially, they interviewed the children, their parents, and their teachers. Ten years later they interviewed many of the children again. And remarkably, they interviewed them still again twelve years after that. During this last phase they also obtained information about the subjects' arrests for criminal activity and for driving violations. The results of this study have been reported in books and numerous articles. It is probably the most widely cited and most influential study on this topic.

2. *The cross-national study* (Huesmann & Eron, 1986; Wiegman & Kuttschreuter, 1992; Wiegman, Kuttschreuter, & Baarda, 1986). This was actually six separate though related studies. Some years after beginning the Columbia County study, Eron and Huesmann organized a study in six countries. The idea was to use the same measures and methods in Australia, Finland, Israel, the Netherlands, Poland, and the United States. This would provide evidence regarding the universality of the effects, and at the same time allow six replications that would be an excellent test of the causal hypoth-

esis. The methods were similar to those used in the twenty-two-year study but were somewhat refined and improved. However, the samples in each of the six studies were generally rather small.

3. *Multiwave study* (Milavsky, Stipp, Kessler, & Rubens, 1982). This was the largest and most carefully conducted study in the group. It involved large samples of girls and boys in grade school, and a separate sample of teenage boys. To provide a measure of the effects of varying intervals, the younger children were interviewed in six waves, with the intervals between them ranging from three months to three years. The teenagers were interviewed in five waves, with intervals ranging from five months to three years. The measures were based on and similar to those used by Eron. The statistical analyses were by far the most complete, thorough, and sophisticated of those used in this kind of research.

4. *Manhattan study* (McCarthy, Langner, Gersten, Eisenberg, & Orzeck, 1975). This study collected information on a large sample of subjects in Manhattan. The sample was a random cross-section of youths in that borough between six and eighteen. The information was collected at two times separated by five years. All of the measures were based on interviews with the parents rather than with the subjects themselves.

5. *Nursery school study* (Singer & Singer, 1981; Singer, Singer, & Rapaczynski, 1984). This study collected a great deal of information about a small number of children in nursery schools. They were observed four times over a one-year period, with their aggressive behaviour being noted. Basing the measure of aggression on actual observations had strengths and weaknesses. The strength was that there was less chance of any contamination by knowledge of other aspects of the child's behaviour, and also less chance of distortions due to efforts to give a good impression. The weaknesses were that the observation of each child was so brief that it was unreliable, and that the ratings did not distinguish well between real and play aggression. Also, some behaviours that were rated as aggressive did not involve other people. Tearing up a poster and knocking down blocks do not fit the usual definition of aggression.

Information on television viewing was obtained from both the children and their parents. Exposure was scored according to type of program, based on categories that included, among others, cartoons, action-adventure, sports, and news.

A second wave of the study obtained information on some of the children two, three, and four years later.

6. *Parental mediation study* (Singer, Singer, Desmond, Hirsch, & Nicol, 1988). The authors of the nursery school study and their colleagues obtained information about the aggressiveness and television viewing of children from six to eight. There was no measure of exposure to violent media, only total viewing time, so the study is only tangentially relevant to our concerns.

7. *Netherlands study* (Van der Voort, 1986). Children in grades three to six were followed for one year. They provided detailed reports of their television viewing and preferences at the beginning of the study, but there was no measure of aggression at this point. A year later, peers, teachers, and the children themselves gave information about the children's aggressiveness. This study differed from the others in that exposure was measured only at time 1, and aggression only at time 2. Even so, it provides some interesting and useful data that is relevant to our concerns.

8. *Finnish study* (Viemero, 1986; 1996). This study began as part of the cross-national study described earlier. The first phase, which was included in the cross-national discussion, obtained information on children over a two-year period. The study continued and obtained information about some of the original sample six, eight, and seventeen years after the first interviews. The type of information gathered varied at the different points. At year seventeen the subjects were not interviewed, but data were obtained from police files about criminal acts and traffic violations.

Methods. In most of these studies, the basic method was to gather data on viewing habits and aggressiveness (and any other variables that seem relevant) more than once over some period of time. The typical study obtained these data when subjects were in the lower grades in school (age six to eight) and then again a year or more later. Some studies measured the key variables several times over the course of a few years, some only once a year. The maximum interval between the first and last measurements was generally two or three years, but two studies followed the subjects for many years – one for twenty-two, the other for seventeen.

Measures of exposure and aggression. The measures relating to media violence were quite varied. All of the studies obtained some information about television viewing; some also obtained information about exposure to and preference for films. The better measures concerned actual viewing of violent programs. Typically, the subjects or sometimes their parents were asked to indicate which shows they (the children) watched from a list of shows, or to name their four favourite programs. In some but not all of the studies they also indicated how often they watched each of the shows. Independent adult raters gave each program and film a score for violent content. For programs, this was done for the television series, not for any particular show; for films it was done individually. The subjects were assigned media violence scores based on the total or average violence of the programs and films they listed, and also usually a score of total violence viewing that weighted the programs by how often they were watched. Somewhat less valid measures simply asked for favourite shows without asking how often they were watched (if ever); this provided a measure of preference but not necessarily of exposure. In addition, most studies obtained measures of total time spent watching television.

The source of the information also varied. Some of the studies asked parents about their children's viewing preferences instead of asking the children themselves. Though parents can be very valuable sources of information about their children, it is likely that children describe their own preferences more accurately than their parents. This was obvious in one study, which asked both parents about their children's preferences and found that the mothers and fathers differed substantially in their responses. The study decided to rely mainly on what the mothers said, which was presumably the right choice; however, the disagreements should make one wonder whether either is very accurate. Most studies asked the children themselves and probably obtained more reliable and accurate information.

Aggression was also measured in various ways. The most common method was the peer nomination procedure: the subjects were asked to name others in their class who engaged in specific aggressive acts. The subjects were then assigned scores based on the number of times they were named, divided by the number of people doing the naming. Other measures included self-reports, reports by teachers and parents, scores on various standard tests, observations of the subjects' behaviour, and (for older subjects) police records of arrests for driving violations and criminal acts.

None of these measures is perfect. Peer nomination by classmates may give a good indication of how the children behave toward one another in and around school, but it provides little information about how they behave at home and in other settings. The opposite is true of ratings by parents. Self-reports have limited value because some people will hesitate to describe themselves as aggressive, whereas others will boast about it. Nevertheless, taken together these measures of aggression are quite good, and there is evidence from the research that they are fairly reliable. Measures of criminal behaviour based on police records seem impressive but are limited in that, naturally, they include only crimes for which people were arrested. Moreover, records of arrests (without convictions) may not indicate any criminal behaviour and, more important, are subject to bias in that police are more likely to arrest some kinds of people than others. Driving violations may be an indication of antisocial behaviour, but are not a measure of aggression in the usual sense of the term.

Summary of Results

These studies provide a great deal of immensely valuable information about how children's viewing habits relate to their aggressiveness, and how a wide variety of social, economic, and family factors relate to both. For the purposes of this review, however, I will not deal with the effects of these other factors, even though it is clear from some of the studies that they play an important role in both viewing of media violence and aggression. Instead I will discuss only the measures of exposure to media violence and aggression. The data from these studies are relevant to three issues.

Is Exposure to Violent Media Related to Aggression?

As noted in Chapter 3, these studies provide evidence of the relationship between exposure to media violence and aggression. These findings supplement the results of the survey research regarding the existence of a correlation between these two variables. The non-longitudinal survey studies have shown that they tend to be correlated, and the longitudinal studies also give estimates of the size of those correlations. I have already noted that the results of both kinds of research indicate a small relationship between the two behaviours.

Trends in the Size of Same-Age Correlations over Time

These studies also provide information about how the correlations change as people get older. If viewing violence causes aggressiveness, presumably the effect is cumulative – the longer the exposure, the greater the effect. Watching one violent program will have less effect than watching ten; watching violent programs for a week will have less effect than watching for a year. Almost any plausible model of how the media affect aggression would predict that the effects get larger and larger over a number of years up to some maximum.

One implication of this cumulative effect is that – assuming the causal hypothesis is correct – as children get older their exposure to media violence should play a larger and larger role in determining aggression. The reasoning is straightforward. Before children have seen any violent media, they may be aggressive. This aggressiveness would have been determined by all sorts of factors, including genetic predisposition, environmental stress, upbringing, and so on. It would not, of course, have been determined by or affected by media violence, since they would not yet have been exposed to it. When they do begin to see violent programs, the effect on aggression is relatively weak, and the other factors continue to be the major determinants of aggression. At this point, since the effect of media violence is so much weaker than the effect of other factors, the correlation between exposure to violence and aggression will be small. However, as the children get older and watch more and more media violence, its effect on aggression increases and it becomes a more important determinant of aggression. Accordingly, the correlation between exposure to media violence and aggression should increase.

Therefore, if the causal hypothesis is correct – if exposure to media violence causes aggression – the same-age correlations between exposure and aggression should increase with age. It is possible to imagine a reason why they wouldn't even if the causal hypothesis is correct, but surely it is a very plausible prediction from the hypothesis. Obviously, if there is no causal effect of exposure to media violence on aggression – if the causal hypothesis is wrong – there will be no cumulative effect, and no reason for the correlations to increase with age. Accordingly, there is no doubt that if the correlations do increase with age, this would provide some support for the causal hypothesis; there is also no doubt that the absence of this pattern would offer no support for the hypothesis and some evidence against it.

Not all of the longitudinal studies provide the necessary information. The relevant data are provided by the early phases of the twenty-two-year study, the six studies in the cross-national study, the multiwave study, the nursery school study, and the Finnish study. The results can be summarized very quickly: there is no evidence that the same-age correlations increase over time. To begin, let me note that both the twenty-two-year study and the multiwave study found that correlations among teenagers were lower than among younger children. I do not think this is crucial, because so many other factors intervene after childhood. The only reason for mentioning this is to dispose of the possibility that a longer interval would have resulted in a clearer increase.

There is no indication that correlations increase over time during childhood. For example, the American and Finnish studies in the cross-national project obtained measures in grades one through five. In the United States, for boys, the correlations for one sample were .16, .20, and .15 from first to third grade; and for the other sample, .24, .18, and .20 from third to fifth grade. The comparable figures for the Finnish samples were .03, .27, and .09 and .04, .38, and .28. Clearly, there was no hint of a trend for the boys. The correlations for the American girls showed some slight tendency to increase. These correlations were .22, .25, and .28 and .14, .26, and .29. However, there was no such trend among the Finnish girls, with correlations of .14, .02, and .33 and .05, −.16, and .04. In the multiwave study the correlations for the six waves for boys were .13, .08, .11, .10, .10, .17, and for girls, .37, .30, .32, .27, .21, .30. The Finnish subjects were followed for several more years, but there was no sign of a trend. Similarly, in the nursery school study the correlations over a year for boys were .32, .26, .03, .23, and for girls .04, .26, .68, −.21.

Thus, the only data that offer even a hint of a trend are those for American girls in the cross-national study. The American boys, the Finnish boys and girls, the boys and girls in the multiwave study, and the boys and girls in the nursery school study showed no indication of a trend. It seems fair to conclude that there is no evidence that same-age correlations between any measure of preference for or exposure to violent television, and any measure of aggression, increase with age.

As noted earlier, the existence of a trend would have been consistent with and provided some evidence for the causal hypothesis. The absence of such a trend is inconsistent with and provides some evidence against the hypothesis. Various explanations for the lack of a trend are possible; one plausible explanation is that there is no causal effect of viewing violence on aggression. In any case, there is certainly no evidence from this source that supports the causal hypothesis.

Regression and Cross-Lagged Correlations as Indications of Causal Effects

The most important aspect of the longitudinal studies is the evidence they provide on the association between early television viewing and later aggression. Besides assessing the same-age relationship between television and aggression, most of these studies also assessed the stability of both variables over the length of the study. This was done by computing a correlation between aggression at time one and aggression at later times; and doing the same for measures of violence viewing. When this was done, the studies usually found that aggression at time one is strongly related to later aggression; and that violence viewing at time one is related to later violence viewing, but not very strongly.

In terms of providing information about causality, the next step is the crucial one: to assess whether there is any relationship between early viewing of television violence and later aggression once the stability of aggression has been taken into account. It is important to understand the reasoning behind this. We know that viewing violence and aggression are related at, say, age eight. We do not know why they are related, and we cannot easily decide whether one causes the other or whether they are both caused by some other factor. We also know that aggression is very stable over time. Children who are aggressive at age eight will also tend to be aggressive at age ten. That is, early aggression is strongly correlated with later aggression. Since early viewing is related to early aggression, and early aggression is related to later aggression, it follows that early viewing will also be related to later aggression. However, the existence of a correlation between early viewing and later aggression tells us nothing about causality, because this relationship may be due entirely to the relationship between viewing and aggression that existed at age eight. The mere fact that viewing violence at age eight is related to aggression at age ten tells us nothing about whether the former causes the latter.

The existence of a causal relationship requires a more complex analysis. It depends on a straightforward prediction from the causal hypothesis. If exposure to media violence causes aggression, children who are equally aggressive at age eight but watch different amounts of media violence should differ in aggression at a later age. The one who watches more violence than average should become more aggressive over time compared to the one who watches an average amount; whereas the one who watches less than average should become less aggressive compared to the one watches an average amount. This spreading apart in terms of aggressiveness (see Figure 6.1) is absolutely essential for the causal hypothesis to be correct. More generally, the amount of exposure to media violence at age eight should be positively related to aggression at the later age even after controlling for aggressiveness at age eight.

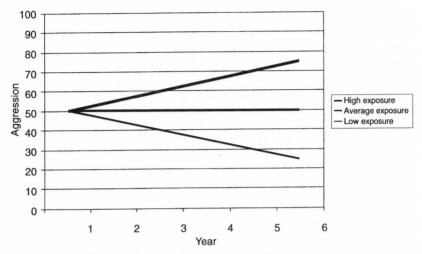

Figure 6.1. Predicted effect of exposure to media violence on aggression

This can be tested by a multiple regression analysis (or similar statistical analysis) that holds constant aggression at age eight and looks at the remaining relationship between violence exposure at age eight and aggression at the later age. If this relationship is positive and significant, it is consistent with and to some extent supports the causal hypothesis. If it is not significant, it is inconsistent with the causal hypothesis.

The same logic applies in testing whether a diet helps in losing weight. Obviously, you cannot judge the effect of the diet unless you take into account how much people weigh to begin with. One person may weigh 200 pounds and another only 150. This could be for all sorts of reasons, and the former is not necessarily fatter than the latter. If the 200-pound person goes on the diet and the other doesn't, a year later, the 200-pounder will presumably still be heavier. This is equivalent to the child who is more aggressive at age eight still being more aggressive at age ten. But taking into account initial weight, you should expect the person on the diet to become relatively thinner than the person not on the diet. In the same way, the aggressive child who watches a lot of violent media should become relatively more aggressive than a child who watches less. This spreading apart is the key test.

The great advantage to this approach is that it largely eliminates the need to explain the relationship between viewing violence and aggression at the earlier age. By including this as a control, the analyses remove the effect of whatever caused it. It does not matter if it was caused by television violence making children more aggressive or by some element in the children's lives making the children more likely to watch violent television and also to be aggressive. This effect is eliminated. Thus, if there is still a significant relationship (usually expressed as a coefficient), it is probably not due to the same factor that produced the correlation at age six. This leaves a causal effect of continued watching of violence as a likely explanation.

I should be clear, however, that this be only a 'likely' explanation. The evidence for it from this kind of analysis would not and could not be definitive. This is because an alternative explanation for a significant relationship could be the continuing operation of some factor that differentially affects violence viewing and aggression. If at age eight this factor has a strong effect on viewing and a weak effect on aggression, it would produce a small correlation between the two at that age. If the factor then had an increasingly strong effect on aggression, but no further effect on viewing, the statistical analyses would produce a significant coefficient between age eight viewing and age ten aggression. This might make it appear that viewing violence had caused the increase in aggression, when in fact the increase was due to the continuing operation of this same factor. I shall discuss this issue and some of the possibilities at the end of this section. For now, the important point is that the results of these regression analyses have generally been considered critical in evaluating the causal hypothesis, with significant coefficients being evidence for, and a lack of significant coefficients being evidence against the hypothesis.

Before summarizing the results, let me describe the individual findings in some detail.

1. The first two waves of the twenty-two-year study dealt with the relationship between preferences for violent television at age eight and aggression at age eighteen. For the boys, using the peer nomination measure of aggression, there was as strong a relationship between early preference for violent television and later aggression as there was for early aggression and later aggression. No such relationship was found for boys using two other measures, and there was none for the girls on any of the three measures of aggression.

Although the effect was only for the boys and only for one measure, it is a striking finding. That the boys' preference for violent television at age eight was so closely related to their aggressiveness ten years later is remarkable. Because this is probably the finding that is mentioned most often as supporting the causal hypothesis, it is important to discuss it in detail. This is especially true because for a variety of other reasons I consider the result to be of limited value.

In the first place, as noted earlier, the pattern held only for boys, not for girls. Indeed, the authors themselves state: 'The regression analysis ... indicates that viewing television violence may lead to *lessened* aggressiveness for some girls. While the effect is not strong, it is significantly different from zero ($p < .04$)' (italics in original). Although the authors presented plausible reasons for this, the fact remains that there was no hint that a preference for violent television caused the girls to become more aggressive – indeed, the evidence suggests that it may have the opposite effect. Getting an effect for half of the population is obviously less convincing than getting it for both sexes.

Second, even for boys the effect seems to appear for only one of several measures of aggression. At grade 13 there were two other measures of aggression: MMPI and self-ratings. It would have been much more impressive if a similar pattern had emerged for these measures, but the results for these measures are not presented. Yet there was no reason why the correlations could not have been computed between violence preference at grade 3 and all of the measures of aggression at grade 13. In fact, the authors do report those correlations, and they are small and not significant. They could also have computed a correlation between aggression at grade 3 as measured by peer nominations and aggression at grade 13 as measured by MMPI and self-report. Indeed, they do present correlations between all sorts of measures at grade 3 with these measures of aggression at grade 13; and they present a table showing that peer-nominated aggression at grade 3 is related to both measures of aggression at grade 13. It is apparent that the early violence preference measure does not correlate significantly with the other two later measures. Thus, the results for the other two measures do not repeat the result for the peer nomination measure and do not support the causal hypothesis. To be fair, the peer-nominated measure was the best of the three; even so, the fact remains that the other measures were obtained and were taken seriously by the authors. That results based on them do not support the causal hypothesis certainly casts some doubt on the one supportive result.

Third, as others (e.g., Kaplan & Singer, 1976) have pointed out, the peer nomination measure of aggression was phrased in the present tense at age eight but in the past tense at age nineteen. It is possible –

indeed, highly likely – that the responses given at age nineteen were based at least in part on the respondents' memories of how the other people acted many years ago. Since the subjects were no longer in school together, it is almost certainly not a pure measure of the person's behaviour at that time. What makes this potentially more damaging is that memories are less than perfect. There may be a tendency for the participants to sharpen the distinctions, so that aggressive children are remembered as even more aggressive than they were, and non-aggressive children as even less aggressive. This 'sharpening' would tend to inflate correlations with the earlier measures of both aggression and preferences for violent television. I have no way of knowing whether this occurred, but retrospective measures are almost always less reliable than concurrent ones, and are also prone to distortions of various kinds.

Fourth, the measure relating to violent television at grade three does not concern actual exposure but only preference. This is not to deny that preference is related to exposure. Given free choice, those who prefer violent television will watch more of it than do those who favour non-violent television. But there are many other factors that affect viewing. It is entirely possible that at least some of the children who preferred violent programs were exposed to very little violent television. They may have been prevented from watching it by their parents (he really wants to watch it but we don't let him); they may not have been able to watch very often when their favourite programs were on (he loves the program but it is on after his bedtime and he only saw it once when he was allowed to stay up late); they may have siblings who have other preferences (he wants to watch the program, but his older sisters hate it so he almost never gets to watch it); and so on. Thus, while preference and exposure are presumably related, the relationship may be quite weak. This means that the pattern of results we are discussing does not indicate that exposure to violent television is related to later aggression – it indicates only that a *preference* for violent television is related to later aggression.

In this context, it is worth mentioning what the authors conclude from this result: 'These contrasting results lend considerable support to the hypothesis that preferring to watch violent television is a cause of aggressive behavior' (Lefkowitz et al., 1977: 117). This is a very odd way of putting it. How can a preference for a particular kind of television cause aggression? That I prefer to eat fatty meat does not make me get heart disease – eating the meat may, but not the preference. Many people prefer to eat red meat but have given it up for health reasons. As long as they do not eat meat, their preference for it does not increase the risk of heart attack. Obviously, preferring violent television cannot cause aggression; exposure to violent television may, but surely not the preference alone. Yet there is no evidence in this study that tells us anything about exposure. Therefore, the result is at best one step removed from the hypothesis the authors favour.

For all of these reasons, I do not think this single result should be given much weight. It is found only for boys and for one measure out of three, and deals with preference for violent television rather than with exposure. Moreover, it is essentially based on one correlation (the .31 between early preference and later peer-nominated aggression) that is so far out of line with other, similar correlations that it makes one wonder whether it is anomalous. Nevertheless, despite all these problems, I continue to think this is one of the better pieces of evidence in favour of an effect of early television on later aggression. That I consider it so weak but still think it is one of the strongest results is a reflection of just how weak I consider the other relevant results.

The results of the final wave of the study are impressive in some ways and not in others. There were eight measures of adult aggressiveness, which were considered separately for males and females. The study found that aggressiveness was remarkably stable from age eight to age thirty. Those who scored high in aggressiveness at eight tended to be high on all the adult measures. Indeed, this was the main theme of the first article written about the third wave of the study, which was titled 'Stability of aggression over time and generations' (Huesmann, Lefkowitz, Eron, & Walder, 1984). This theme was echoed in various chapters and other articles dealing with the same data. In other words, the main finding from this quite remarkable study is that aggression is extremely stable over many years.

The results relating to a possible causal connection between early preference for violent media and adult aggression are far less impressive. The crucial analyses were the relationship between early preference for television and adult behaviour after the relationship of early aggression was controlled. There were eight measures of adult aggression. For females, no relationship was found between violence preference and aggression on any of the eight measures. For males, no relationship was found on seven and a weak relationship on one. In other words, out of sixteen possible effects, only one was significant, and it was weak.

Unfortunately, the authors of this study have described their results as showing that early exposure to violent television affects adult criminality. In testimony to the U.S. Congress, Huesmann showed a graph of the results of this study that he said indicated that boys who watch a lot of violent television when they are young are much more likely to commit acts of violence when they are adults. This assertion is not justified. That graph was based on very few cases and distorted the actual findings. Actually, the twenty-two-year follow-up found no convincing evidence that early exposure causes later criminal behaviour. Rather, these results pointed in the opposite direction – there is no effect of early viewing on adult aggression.

On the other hand, to be fair, this should not be considered evidence against the causal hypothesis, because I do not think anyone seriously expected preference for violent television at age eight to be related to criminal behaviour as an adult. Or if some did expect such an effect, they would have understood that finding it was going to be very difficult given all the factors that could intervene over twenty-two years. If there had been a consistent effect, it would have been impressive, but the lack of an effect should probably not be thought of as nonsupportive.

In sum, this was an impressive study that followed children for as many as twenty-two years and developed the peer nomination measure of aggression. However, it found only one result that was consistent with the causal hypothesis – the relationship for boys between early preference for violent television and peer-nominated aggression ten years later. Despite its limitations, I believe this result should be taken seriously, even though it was not replicated for females or for the other measures. In contrast, the result for male criminal behaviour in the adult phase should be given little or no credence.

2. The cross-national project assessed the relationship between early exposure to violence and later aggression. The key results are the outcomes of multiple regressions with early aggression held constant. There was a small but significant relationship for American girls and Polish boys, a marginally significant effect for Polish girls, and a strong effect for Israeli city children. In contrast, there was no significant relationship for American boys, Finnish boys or girls, Australian boys or girls, Netherlands boys or girls, or Israeli kibbutz boys or girls.

Taken at face value, the results provide some support for the causal hypothesis but are clearly inconsistent. Of the fourteen critical tests of the hypothesis (six countries with two separate samples in Israel, and males and females for each), four were significant and one marginally significant, while nine were not significant. Also, with the exception of the Israeli city samples, the associations were quite small, explaining only a few per cent of variance more than was explained by the stability of aggressiveness over time. Although the lead authors consider the results strong support for their theory, I do not. Even without considering a variety of problems with the studies and with the analyses, the results offer at most weak support for the causal hypothesis.

However, there are problems with each of the supportive results. I will not bother with all of them but instead focus on two. Most of the groups used total violence viewing as the measure of choice. For some reason the key multiple regression analysis presented by the Polish team used only a measure of *preference* for violent television. One would have expected them to conduct the same analyses using the more standard measure – namely, total violence viewing. If they did, they didn't present the results. Without being unduly suspicious, it seems reasonable to assume that the analysis employing total violence viewing as the measure did not produce a significant effect. Thus all we have is an analysis showing that a preference for violent shows is related to later aggression. Since this is not a measure of exposure but rather of preference, it tells us little about the effect of exposure. If the exposure measure did not in fact produce a significant effect, the result provides no support for a causal effect of exposure to violence on later aggression. And since the exposure to violence measure is not presented and may therefore not have produced a significant result – the cynical might say therefore *did* not produce a significant effect – the results from Poland may not actually support the causal hypothesis.

The Israeli report has many serious problems. In the first place, unlike any other study, the Israeli study broke the sample into two groups. In several other countries the total sample contained children from two different environments (city versus suburbs, etc.). It would have been interesting to see the breakdown in terms of the two subsamples in the other countries, but these are not presented. If the Israeli study had combined the two groups, presumably there would have been no effect. The authors did not predict that the effect would occur for city and not kibbutz. If the overall effect had been significant, presumably it would have been reported; if both had been significant taken separately, presumably that would have been reported. All of this means that the statistical analyses are somewhat suspect – not that anything was done improperly, but that the effects should not be taken at face value since they have been, in a sense, selected from the full sample.

Also, the Israeli study, unlike any of the others, does not use the standard measure of aggression. The usual measure for the other five countries (with slight variations) was the number of peer nominations for aggression divided by the number of children making the nominations. This controls for the size of the group and gives a reasonable estimate of how aggressive the children rate each person. The Israeli team took this standard measure and changed it by using a ratio of the usual measure and the score for aggression avoidance (plus 1 to avoid infinite ratios). This new measure gave a great deal of weight to the single-item aggression avoidance score. This may have been entirely justified; however, it was not done elsewhere, was not validated, and in any case was different from the basic measure of the cross-national study. It seems reasonable to wonder why the authors did not present the usual measure. If they thought it had problems they could have presented their 'improved' measure in addition to the standard one, but surely the reader and the rest of the research groups would have expected to see the data presented for the standard measure. It was not, which makes one suspect that the results would have looked quite different using the standard measure. There is nothing wrong with trying different and innovative measures; but if you do not present the standard measures first, the reader should ask what the standard measure would have shown.

To summarize, among other issues, the Israeli study split the sample and found significant results for only one part, and used a unique measure for the most basic dependent variable. These problems cast serious doubt on the Israeli finding.

This is an impressive project that looked at the relationship between television viewing and many other variables and aggression in six countries. On the crucial question of whether viewing television violence has an effect on aggression, the findings were inconsistent and generally unsupportive. Of fourteen possible effects, four produced significant results and one a marginally significant result. Taking this result at face value, even without all the problems with those few significant results, it should be discouraging for the causal hypothesis. As the Dutch researchers state: 'On the basis of the data of all countries participating in this study, we may conclude that there is almost no evidence for the hypothesis that television violence viewing leads to aggressive behaviour, nor for the alternative hypothesis that aggressive behaviour leads to more television violence viewing' (Wiegman et al., 1992: 159).

3. The multiwave study had many more subjects than any of the others, and used the most carefully tested measures and the most sophisticated and complete statistical analysis. The key figures are the relationships between early television violence and later aggression once stability of aggression is entered into the equation. Of the fifteen wave-pair comparisons for the younger boys, twelve had positive relationships between early exposure and later aggression. Of these, only three were significant, and two of these were in the same panel (i.e., wave 2 to wave 4 also includes wave 3 to wave 4). When intervening television exposure was controlled, the effects were reduced so that only one relationship was significant. The effects for girls were similar though slightly weaker, and for teenage boys weaker still.

To put these results in perspective, the authors assessed the possible impact of exposure on aggression, assuming there was an effect. They did this by imagining that a boy who was in the lowest 10 per cent in terms of viewing television violence was instead in the highest 10 per cent, and then calculating how this would be expected to increase his aggression score. They did this for the longest lags between early viewing and later aggression, since the effects would be somewhat greater than for shorter lags. They calculated that the largest potential impact of increasing from the lowest to the highest viewing of television violence would be to increase his later aggression by 15 points on a scale of 400. This is a very small increase, well within the range of chance. And this is for the boy who was initially in the lowest 10 per cent of viewers. For a boy who was an average viewer of violence, the possible affect on his aggression score would be half as large.

Clearly, this large-scale study found almost no significant effects. The only possible indication of an effect was that most of the associations were positive. I shall discuss the possible meaning of this later. For now the important point is that even if this preponderance of positive associations was because there was a causal effect, that effect would be so small that it would have no appreciable impact on aggression.

4. The Manhattan study did not assess the effect of early viewing on later aggression, so it is not directly relevant. However, it did find that preference for violent television was not related to any measure of aggression or maladjustment. All of the correlations were quite small,

and none was significant even with a very large sample. Thus, this study adds no evidence in favour of the causal hypothesis, and perhaps some evidence against it.

5. The first phase of the Singer and Singer research (the nursery school study) assessed the effect of viewing television violence on aggression by computing a serious of correlations between early television and later aggression, and the reverse correlations between later television and early aggression. The authors concluded that these analyses point to a causal link between watching action programs and subsequent aggression; however, I see no justification for this conclusion. The correlations fall into no obvious pattern – certainly not one that suggests any causal effect of violence viewing on aggression or vice versa. These data offer no comfort for those who believe in the causal hypothesis. If anything, they provide evidence against it. On the other hand, given the short time period (only one year) and the small size of the samples, this lack of support should not be given a great deal of weight.

During the second wave of the study, early viewing of realistic action programs (which was the closest the study had to measure of exposure to violent television) was related to aggression and to a measure of aggression in school two years later; and it remained significant – in fact, it increased in significance – when early aggression was controlled. Unfortunately, all of the analyses were reported for the sexes combined. Since boys usually watch more action shows and are also much more aggressive, combining the sexes is likely to distort and magnify the relationship between viewing and aggression. It certainly would have been better to do separate analyses, as virtually all other studies have done. Because of this error in the key analyses, the results have to be interpreted with great caution, since we do not really know what they show. Nevertheless, taken at face value (i.e., ignoring these potential problems), the results of the multiple regressions provide some of the strongest evidence of a relationship between early television viewing and later aggression.

6. In the mediation study there was no measure of exposure to violence on television, so this study is only tangentially relevant. With males and females combined (unfortunately), there was a positive relationship between amount of television watched in year 1 and reported aggression in year 2. However, the discussion section of the paper notes that the multiple regression analysis did not find a relationship between amount of television viewing and aggression. The authors conclude that their results 'are only weakly suggestive of a link between

television viewing and aggression or restlessness.' I conclude that the study is irrelevant to the causal hypothesis, and provides neither supportive nor non-supportive results.

7. The Netherlands study had no measure of aggression at time 1, so it was not possible to control for early aggression. Nevertheless, even without controlling for the stability of aggression, there was no relationship between early exposure to or preference for media violence and any of three measures of aggression taken a year later. Unfortunately, the sexes were combined in all of these analyses. Usually this tends to inflate any relationships between media violence and aggression (because boys watch more violence and are also more aggressive). It is possible that in this case combining the sexes obscured an effect, but that seems very unlikely. With this proviso, this study provides no evidence in favour of the causal hypothesis and can be counted as evidence against it.

8. The Finnish study was a very nice study that followed its subjects for seventeen years, obtaining measures of various kinds at quite a few points along the way. The results were quite varied. The first phase of the study, years 1 to 3, was part of the cross-national study and found no effect of violence viewing on later aggression. Various analyses using aggression at year 6 and year 8 as the dependent measure suggested there might be a relationship between early television violence viewing and later aggression, but most of these produced somewhat inconsistent results and had problems as well. The key multiple-regression analysis on year 6 aggression produced contradictory results – early television violence exposure was negatively related to later aggression for boys but positively related for girls. The former might be considered evidence that exposure to violence decreases later aggression in boys, but I would not draw that conclusion. Even if one accepts the catharsis notion, I do not think anyone believes it is a long-lasting effect. So I do not believe we should consider this as evidence for a catharsis effect. The most likely explanation is that the negative relationship is due to some unknown factors or to the complex and unexplained interaction of the various factors that were entered into the analysis. The positive relationship for girls would be some evidence in favour of the causal hypothesis. However, combined with the opposite result for boys, it too is probably due to complex and unexplained interactions. There was no evidence that exposure to television violence in early years was related to later criminal behaviour once aggression was controlled.

Overall, if anything, the evidence from this extensive study is against the causal hypothesis.

Summary

Taking the results at face value, the only clear support for the causal hypothesis comes from three studies. In the first phase of the twenty-two-year study there was a strong relationship for the boys between early preference for violent television and later peer-nominated aggression. In the cross-national study there was a similar effect for boys and girls in the Israeli city sample, and considerably weaker effects for boys and girls in Poland and for girls in the United States. In the later phase of the nursery school study there was an effect for boys and girls combined.

Even accepting them at face value and without considering any non-supportive results, these findings do not provide very impressive support for the conclusion that exposure to violent media is harmful. Consider the details. The twenty-two-year study began with a sample of over 800 children, but this was reduced to 427 ten years later. Thus the effect for boys was based on just over 200 subjects. The cross-national studies had considerably smaller samples. The American sample had several hundred, which meant that the positive effect for girls was based on over 100. But the other samples were smaller, with the big effect in Israel based on only 76 children – 42 boys and 34 girls. Although supporters of the causal hypothesis sometimes say it has been supported by studies involving thousands and thousands of subjects, these supportive findings from the longitudinal studies involve a total of well under 1,000. Even if the results were consistent and strong, one would usually be quite cautious about drawing firm conclusions about the effect of social factors based on such a small sample.

Of course, the results are neither strong nor consistent. These same three studies that found the only supportive results actually produced many more non-supportive results. In the first phase of the twenty-two-year study there was no relationship for girls and none for boys on two other measures of aggression. The one supportive result was strong, but it must be weighed against five non-supportive ones. In the cross-national study there were no effects for boys or girls in Australia, the Netherlands, or Finland. In Israel there was no effect for boys or girls in the kibbutz sample. And in the United States there was no effect for boys. The five supportive results must be weighed against these nine non-supportive ones (using very similar methods and sometimes even in the same countries). The nursery school study cannot be compared with these others since it was very small in scale and employed much less sophisticated measures and analyses. In any case, the one supportive result combined the sexes, which makes it difficult to interpret. And the same study found no effect in the first phase. In other words, the three studies that obtained some supportive results also found substantially more non-supportive results.

Even without considering the other longitudinal research, these three studies provide quite unimpressive support for the causal hypothesis. If a hypothesis is correct, we expect consistency in the findings. This research does not provide it. How can one explain why the effect is found for boys on one measure but not on other measures, and is not found for girls on any measure? Yes, the peer nomination measure is probably the best measure, but one would still expect similar (though perhaps weaker) effects on the other measures. And yes, one can imagine a reason why there was no effect for girls at that time and place (the authors have produced one), but surely it would have been a stronger effect if it had held for both sexes. Similarly, and perhaps more to the point, why in the world was there an effect in Poland but not Finland, for the American girls but not the boys, and for the Israeli city sample but not the kibbutz sample? Presumably ad hoc explanations could be imagined for each of these inconsistencies, but as more and more excuses are required, the results become less and less convincing. Thus, even if these were the only longitudinal studies that had been conducted, I believe that the results would provide only minimal support for the causal hypothesis.

Yet these were, of course, not the only such studies. All the others produced non-supportive results. The Manhattan study, with a large, representative sample, found no evidence that preference for violent television was related to aggression; the Netherlands study, even with the sexes combined, found no support; the later phases of the Finnish study found no support. Most important, the massive multiwave study, with a very large sample and state-of-the-art methods and statistics, did not support the causal hypothesis. As shown in Figure 6.2, when the few supportive results are placed in the broader context of the non-supportive findings, it seems clear that overall, this line of research does not support the causal hypothesis. One could go even farther and say that the lack of strong positive findings, the inconsistency even within the studies that found positive results, and the many non-

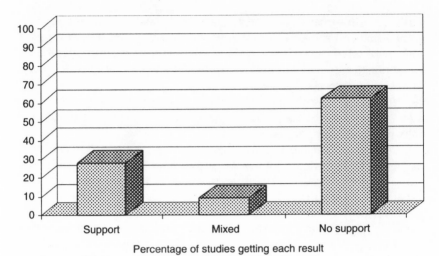

Percentage of studies getting each result

Figure 6.2. Results of longitudinal studies

supportive results provide evidence against rather than in favour of the causal hypothesis. Moreover, most of the results that seem to support the causal hypothesis have serious problems.

I conclude that the evidence from this body of research provides little support for the causal hypothesis and could be interpreted as evidence against it.

The Preponderance of Positive Relationships between Early Viewing and Later Aggression

The only result that might seem to indicate an effect of violent media on aggression is that most of the regression analyses have found positive relationships rather than negative ones between early viewing and later aggression. That is, after controlling for early aggression and taking into account the correlation between violence viewing and aggression at an early age, early violence viewing (or some measure of it) was usually positively related to later aggression. Even though many of the coefficients were close to zero and explain virtually none of the variance in aggression, the fact remains that they were not evenly divided between positive and negative relationships. How should we interpret this pattern?

One possibility is that the preponderance of positive relationships indicates that viewing violent programs has a small effect on aggression. The argument for this position is that if exposure to violence had no effect on aggression, the coefficients would be evenly split between positive and negative. That they are not leaves a causal effect as one obvious explanation. Certainly the coefficients are very small, indicating that only a tiny percentage of the variation in aggression is accounted for by exposure to violent programs. Nevertheless, the pattern is consistent with the causal hypothesis – although it indicates a much weaker effect than is usually claimed – and could be interpreted as support for it.

An alternative view is that the pattern is not due to any effect of viewing violent programs but is caused by other factors. A positive or even significant coefficient could be caused by the operation of some factor that differentially affected viewing of violent programs and aggression. If at age eight this factor had a strong effect on viewing and a weak effect on aggression, it would produce a small correlation between the two at that age. If the factor then had an increasingly strong effect on aggression, but no further effect on viewing, the statistical analyses would produce a significant coefficient between age eight viewing and age ten aggression. If the differential effect were quite weak, it might not produce a significant coefficient but would tend to produce a positive one.

To make this less hypothetical, let me describe some possible scenarios. In the multiwave study, Milavksy and colleagues suggest that the social factor could be the peer group. Suppose the group happens to favour action, adventure, and aggressiveness. On first joining the group, children are influenced mainly to engage in milder behaviours such as watching violent programs and being slightly aggressive. This would produce a small relationship between exposure to media violence and aggression (because the group encouraged both). Later, they become involved in more serious acts of aggression. This would produce the pattern of statistical effects described above – a same-age correlation between viewing violence and aggression, and a positive coefficient between early violence viewing and later aggression even after early aggression was controlled.

Another social factor might be the family situation. The multiwave study found that controlling for socioeconomic status reduced the plurality of positive effects for boys, and that controlling for school, SES (socio-economic states), and gender had the same effect for boys and girls combined. Even with these analyses, the pattern did not disappear entirely; however, perhaps other controls would have accomplished that. In any case, focusing on social and economic factors seems reasonable. In most of the research, poorer children and those with less well educated parents tend to watch more television and more violent television and also to be more aggressive. Poorer parents – especially single parents – have relatively little time and energy to spend with their children. On average, they almost certainly are less able to closely supervise and monitor their children's behaviour. (Of course, there is great variation in this. Some poor parents undoubtedly supervise their children very closely, whereas some rich parents do not.) Also, poor children have fewer toys, games, and books and have access to fewer outside activities.

If the parents spend little time with their children and the children have a limited number of leisure activities, it is likely they watch a lot of television. Moreover, they probably watch a lot of violent television, because their parents aren't available to limit their exposure to this kind of programming (unlike more affluent parents, who might impose such limits). Also, even within more affluent families, some parents spend more time than others with their children. The less supervised children may also turn to television and to violent television. So SES should be negatively related to exposure to violent television, with children from poorer families being exposed to more violent programs. More generally, amount of supervision should also be negatively related to exposure to violent television, with the less the supervision, the greater the exposure.

It is also likely that poor children and less well supervised children will be more aggressive. There are all sorts of reasons for this. Poor children live in less nice neighbourhoods, are exposed to more aggressive models, make friends who, like themselves, are not well supervised, and so on. All of the unsupervised children, both the poor and those better off financially, are likely to be less well socialized against aggressiveness than more affluent children and those who are better supervised. They also are likely to be more frustrated and more bitter, and to have various negative feelings that may translate into anger and aggression.

Thus, for a variety of reasons, on average children from poorer and one-parent homes, and less well supervised children from more affluent homes, will watch more violent television (and more television in general) and be more aggressive. This is one reason – though probably not the only one – that exposure to violent programs and aggression are correlated.

Assuming that this is at least a partial explanation of the same-age correlation between violence viewing and aggression, why would it lead to positive coefficients between early exposure and later aggression after early aggression is controlled? A simple reason is that the effects of lack of supervision on viewing violence and on aggression will follow somewhat different time courses. Children who are unsupervised and have few toys and so on will tend to watch a lot of violent television. This effect will occur as soon as the children begin to watch television. At that point it will be major factor determining the amount of exposure. There is no obvious reason for it to take time to develop. In contrast, the effect on aggression may increase over time. When the less supervised and poorer children first enter school, they may be somewhat more aggressive than other children, but the effect will be small and these family factors will be minor determinants of aggression. As time passes, they are exposed more to the neighbourhood, they become friends with other aggressive children, and they become more and more frustrated because they realize that they have less than other children in terms of possessions or care from their parents. All of this causes them to become increasingly aggressive. Thus, their exposure to violent programs does not change much over time, but their tendency to be aggressive increases. More to the point, parental supervision and other family factors become stronger determinants of their aggressiveness. This too would produce the pattern of mostly positive coefficients described above.

In my opinion these explanations are quite compelling. They are plausible, they fit what we know about the social situation, and they also fit the data. On the other hand, I am not suggesting we have any substantial evidence that any of these scenarios is correct. I offer them only to point out that many factors could produce the pattern of weak but positive coefficients that has been found. Therefore this pattern, though consistent with a causal effect of viewing violent programs on aggression, cannot be considered evidence for that effect. Moreover, even if the pattern is due to the effect of media violence on aggression, the very small size of the coefficients suggests that the effect is vanishingly weak.

Final Conclusion

The longitudinal research has produced some findings that are consistent with the causal hypothesis but many more that are inconsistent with it. There is no evidence that same-age correlations between exposure to violent media and aggression increase over time. If there had been such a pattern, it would have been consistent with and provided evidence in favour of the causal hypothesis. That there is no such pattern is inconsistent with and is evidence against the hypothesis. There are some significant coefficients indicating an association between early exposure to or preference for violent television and later aggression, but there are many more that are not significant or even substantial. If these coefficients (or the equivalent in other kinds of analyses) had been consistently large and significant, this would have been consistent with the causal hypothesis and would have been evidence in favour of it; that there are so few significant effects is inconsistent with the causal hypothesis and is evidence against it. That most of these coefficients are positive is consistent with the causal hypothesis. However, it is also consistent with many other explanations and thus cannot be considered as supporting any of these views.

In sum, the results of this research have been inconsistent and generally weak. I conclude that overall, the results of the longitudinal studies do not support the idea that viewing violent media causes aggression, and might be considered evidence against such an effect.

7

With and Without Television: Comparing Communities That Have and Do Not Have Television

Those who believe that exposure to media violence is harmful often decry the existence of television. They argue that if only there were no television at all, children would be less aggressive and the crime rate would be lower. (There would still be violence in films, but presumably the level of exposure would be much less.) I think this is rather foolish, since there was lots of aggression and crime before television and there is no evidence that children are generally more aggressive now than they were then. Nevertheless, if the causal hypothesis is correct – if television violence really does cause aggression and crime – there should be more aggression and more crime when television is available than when it is not. (Naturally, this assumes that some children will be watching violent programs, and also that the non-violent programs will not counteract the presumed harmful effects of the violent programs.) With this in mind, several studies have looked at communities that had access to television and compared them with those that did not; or they have looked at communities without television and assessed what happened after they got television.

The methods of the various studies were quite different. One study focused on changes in national crime rates after television was introduced. In other studies the research was done when television was just being introduced and some places had it while others did not. One study took advantage of the fact that in the United States new licences for television stations were frozen for three years, so that for this three-year period many communities had television while many others did not. And one study focused on a relatively remote community that had not been reached by television. In all of the studies the idea was to compare aggression or crime rates with and without television to see whether the presence or absence of television made a difference.

The main strength of this approach is that the impact of television can be studied in a natural setting over a fairly long period of time. Laboratory experiments look at effects over minutes or perhaps an hour; field experiments look at effects over days or weeks; but these with-and-without studies have looked at effects over years. Since our major concern is with the long-term effects of television violence, obviously the longer the period over which the effects are studied, the better. Moreover, this research deals with the effects, if any, of people actually watching real television programs in their homes the way they ordinarily do. Clearly, our concerns about the media involve how people are actually affected in their daily lives, not how they might be affected in the laboratory or in experiments done by psychologists. So, with respect to both the duration and the naturalness of the situation, these studies have a real advantage over both laboratory and field experiments.

The other strong point of this approach is that the communities did not choose to have or not to have television. This avoids the problem of self-selection that is present in research such as the longitudinal work that compares people who watch a lot of violent television with those who do not. In these latter studies, since the people have chosen what to watch, obviously they are different kinds of people with different tastes, personalities, preferences, and so on. Thus any differences between them in behaviour or aggression could be due not to television but to the differences between them as people or between their backgrounds, life situations, and so on. In contrast, the communities in with-and-without studies included some that had television available and some that did not, but in all cases the availability of television was due to decisions by governments rather than by the communities themselves. This does not guarantee that the have and have-not communities were identical, but it reduces the problem somewhat.

At the same time, these studies have several serious limitations and weaknesses. One limitation is that there is no control on and usually no measure of the type of television people are watching. That is, there is no way of knowing how much violent television is watched by how many people in the communities that have television. This means that the studies can provide information on the effects of television in general, but cannot narrow this down to the effects of one kind of television, specifically violent programs. Despite this, the results are directly relevant to our concerns, because if television is available, we can be certain that some of it contains violence and that some people are therefore being exposed to violent television. If the communities that have television have more aggression or crime than those that do not have television, or if crime rates increase after the introduction of television, one possibility is that television produced the effect. This finding would clearly be consistent with and provide some support for the causal hypothesis. Similarly, if the 'have' communities are not more aggressive and have no more crime than the have-not communities, it is evidence that television does not affect these behaviours. Such a finding would clearly be inconsistent with and provide some evidence against the causal hypothesis.

The most serious weakness of these studies is that there were no controls on whatever other changes were occurring at the time television was being introduced, or on other differences between those places that had television and those that did not. We can be sure that all sorts of changes were taking place before and after television became widely available, and that communities that got television early differed in many ways from those that did not. This means that any changes in crime rates after television was introduced, or differences between the haves and have-nots, may have been due to factors other than the presence of television. In some studies this was a less serious problem because many communities were involved. In Hennigan and colleagues (1982) in particular, there were probably lots of reasons why certain communities were given television licences before the freeze and others were not. But given that there were no known political reasons – or at least no known reasons that affected all the communities – the likelihood of systematic differences between them is reduced. Even with a very large group we can never be certain that any effects were due to television and not to other differences between the groups, but obviously the larger the group of communities, the better in terms of reducing the likelihood that systematic differences other than television produced the effect.

The extreme instance of this problem – one might say a fatal flaw – occurs when there is only one community in a group. In comparing one community that has television with another that does not, it is impossible to separate the effects of characteristics of the particular communities from the effects of television. The 'have' community may have more conflict, more disturbed children, less good social services and schools, less effective childrearing, or any number of other factors that could lead to increased aggression. Observing what happens when television is introduced into the 'have not' community is not much help. If aggression increases, it could be due to television, but it could also be due to increased social conflict, a rise in unemployment, an influx of aggressive children, or any one of a host of changes that may have coincided with the introduction of television. Similarly, if aggression decreased or did not change after television was introduced, those results would also be impossible to interpret. They could be due to the fact that television does not affect aggression; but they could also be due to changes in the social situation that coincided with but were not caused by the introduction of television. Perhaps unemployment decreased during the period in question, which caused a sharp drop in aggression that more than made up for an increase due to television. This fatal flaw is helped only marginally by having a large number of subjects in each community. It is, of course, better to have a large sample than a small one, because a large number of people are less likely to be affected by momentary or local factors. Nevertheless, no matter how many people are observed, they could all be affected by irrelevant and unknown factors such as those mentioned above. Thus, with only one community in a condition or even a few communities in a condition, there is no way of knowing what caused any changes that are observed.

Similarly, when the comparison is between crime rates before and after the introduction of television into one or two countries, there is no way of knowing whether any changes are due to television or to some other factor or factors. We know for certain that countries and communities are always in flux – that all sorts of social and economic changes are always occurring. Any change in behaviour in the people of one country or in one community could be caused by any one of these changes, or a combination of them. The presence or absence of television is one aspect of the social environment that can affect behaviour, but there are many other factors – some weak, some powerful – that also affect behaviour. Moreover, as discussed below, if the number of people observed in the communities is small, these possibilities become even stronger and interpretation of the results becomes even more problematic. Thus, studies that involve comparing a small number of countries or communities in one condition may be interesting, but the results should be viewed with caution. Even so, this is a very interesting group of studies.

THE STUDIES

Centerwall (1989, 1992)

This paper begins with data showing that ten to fifteen years after television was introduced in the United States and Canada, homicide rates increased sharply; and that during the same period television was not available in South Africa and homicide rates did not increase. The paper also shows that in both Canada and the United States, the timing of the increase in the homicide rate was related to the timing of the availability of television. An additional analysis indicates that the increase in crime rate occurred earlier for younger people, which Centerwall argues would be expected if the increase were due to exposure to television and if there were a lag between exposure and effect. From all this, Centerwall concluded that television caused a doubling of homicide in the United States and Canada. Indeed, as I quoted earlier, he went so far as to say that 'if hypothetically, television technology had never been developed, there would today be 10,000 fewer homicides each year in the United States, seventy thousand fewer rapes, and 700,000 fewer injurious assaults' (1992: 306). These are remarkable claims. Although this paper is almost totally ignored by psychologists who are concerned with this issue, the popular press and especially the U.S. Congress take it very seriously. So it is important for me to discuss it in some detail.

Cross-national comparison. Let me begin by disposing of the cross-national comparison between the United States and Canada on the one hand and South Africa on the other. The paper places considerable emphasis on the argument that since the United States and Canada had television and showed an increase in homicide rates, and South Africa did not have television and did not have an increase in homicide rates, television must have caused the increase in homicide in those countries that had television. This conclusion it is not valid either logically or scientifically.

South Africa differs from the other two countries in countless ways. It is interesting that South Africa did not have the same kind of increase in crime rate as the United States and Canada, but attributing the difference to the presence or absence of television requires an enormous leap of imagination. There are many possible explanations besides the absence of television in South Africa. Just to take one possibility, as noted by Centerwall, the South African government banned television because it was afraid of the social changes it might introduce. One could add that the government was afraid of social change in general and did what it could to prevent it. To the extent that social changes of various kinds can cause an increase in crime (this will be discussed at length below), the relative lack of social change in South Africa during the period in question could explain the lack of an increase in crime. One could also attribute the difference to the apartheid government in South Africa and its powerful, ruthless police.

So I consider the situation in South Africa essentially irrelevant to the argument in the paper. There are too many open questions, too few data on that country, and too many possible alternative explanations to take this comparison seriously.

Also, data from other countries directly contradict Centerwall's assertion that the availability of television causes an increase in crime. Zimring and Hawkins, who are experts on violent crime, have provided a devastating analysis (1997) based on data about television ownership and homicide rates for France, Germany, Italy, and Japan. According to Centerwall, some time after television was introduced, homicide rates in those countries should have increased. They didn't. In all of those countries, television ownership increased sharply between 1955 and 1975, but in none of those countries was there a consistent increase in homicide rates at any time after television was introduced. The dramatic increases in homicide that occurred in Canada and the United States starting around 1965 did not occur in these other countries. As Zimring and Hawkins note: 'They [the data from these four countries] *disconfirm* the causal linkage between television set ownership and lethal violence for the period 1945–1975' (1997:245; italics in original). In other words, this aspect of Centerwall's paper can be disregarded. The evidence from South Africa is meaningless, and the evidence from the other countries shows that Centerwall's central idea is wrong.

That leaves the possibility that he may be right about what happened in the United States and Canada – that for some reason, television interacted with unique factors in those countries to cause an increase in violent crime. This seems highly unlikely, but it must nevertheless be considered. Accordingly, I shall focus my discussion on the evidence from those two countries to see whether the data are consistent with the notion that television causes criminal behaviour.

Alternative explanations. In dealing with a correlational result, it is incumbent on the researcher to rule out factors that are known or thought to affect the dependent variable. Studies of the effect of diet on heart disease have looked at the amount of fat eaten in various countries and then assessed whether those populations which consume more fat are more likely to get heart disease. If they get an effect – if fat consumption is related to heart disease – the researchers do not immediately conclude that fat causes heart disease. They must first control for other factors that are known to cause heart disease. Thus, they would certainly control for smoking, exercise (if they could), and so on. In choosing which factors to control for, they would naturally consult with experts on heart disease to ensure they were controlling for all the obvious factors.

Centerwall recognized the need to deal with other explanations. He chose a few possibilities and tried to demonstrate that the increase in crime rate was not due to them. Though in my opinion his analyses are not as thorough and as convincing as they could be, let us accept that the increases were not caused by age distribution or by the economic situation (although now apparently he has decided that economic factors do affect crime rates). Unfortunately, perhaps because he is not a social scientist, he did not consider some of the most likely causes for the increase in crime. It is generally believed that environment plays a major role in personality development and has profound effects on people's behaviour both as children and as adults. Almost all developmental psychologists and criminologists probably believe that a 'bad' home life or 'poor parenting' puts children at risk for becoming aggressive and committing crimes. Similarly, a bad environment outside the home – a deteriorated, criminal, or violent neighbourhood – may put children at risk for becoming aggressive or for engaging in criminal activity. So one question that must be asked about the Centerwall study is whether there were any factors that affected the home environment and/or the neighbourhood environment during the period before the increase in homicide rates in the United States and Canada.

The answer, of course, is that there were many such factors. The post–Second World War period, during which television was introduced, was a time of revolutionary change in North American society. Many of these changes had profound effects on childrearing and on the home environment in general. Let me discuss a few of the ones that surely had strong effects and might well have led to an increase in criminal activity.

Women working outside the home. Just before the increase in the crime rate, the number of women working outside the home increased dramatically. This happened suddenly and was not accompanied by an equivalent increase in high-quality daycare or in other arrangements for providing good care for children. This was not necessarily harmful to the children: there is evidence that children who attend high-quality daycare centres do just as well socially and intellectually as children who are cared for entirely by their parents. Moreover, mothers who hold jobs outside the home may, on average, have higher self-esteem than those who do not hold such jobs, and this may have positive effects on their children. However, it is also true – or at least most experts believe that it is true – that children do not do so well when their mothers are not caring for them and when they are in low-quality daycare or in informal daycare arrangements (e.g., the neighbour takes care of them). Many of the children whose mothers were working during this period would have been receiving excellent alternative care; many would not.

Also, children who come home from school to an empty house ('latchkey children') are generally experiencing less-than-ideal childcare. These older children spend time alone either in the home or on the streets. Again, this may not be harmful in some circumstances, but there is little doubt that it is not good for many children.

This major change in North American society – this huge increase in the percentage of women working outside the home – may have resulted in many children being cared for less well than in the past, and being given less attention; in the extreme, some may have experienced serious neglect. This decline in the quality of childcare and in the quality of children's home life would be expected to lead to serious emotional and behavioural problems among at least some children; this in turn would have led to increased criminal activity by those children.

Divorce rates. Between 1950 and 1965 the divorce rate in the United States changed very little. Starting in the 1960s, attitudes and laws regarding divorce began to change. It became easier and easier to get a divorce, and also more and more acceptable to get one. The divorce rate doubled between 1965 and 1975 and then levelled off. The number of divorced women more than tripled between 1960 and 1980. The same trend was evident in Canada. Before the 1960s in both countries, relatively few children lived through a divorce or lived in a home with a divorced parent. By 1975 almost half of all marriages were ending in divorce and millions of children were involved. This must have had profound effects on many of these children.

Divorce is not always bad for the children. It is obviously difficult for them, but there is evidence that it is no worse and perhaps better than living in a home in which the parents do not get along. The divorce itself may be traumatic, but most children recover and may even be better off than they would have been if fighting parents remained together 'for the sake of the children' or because it was too difficult to get a divorce or because it was against their principles or religious beliefs. In other words, I think it would be a mistake to blame children's problems on divorce.

However, divorce often has other consequences that are almost certainly bad for children. The most obvious and most serious is that the financial situation of both parents – but especially the mother – becomes much worse. Even if before the divorce the husband and wife earned the same amount of money and divided their resources evenly, there is little question that both suffer financially from divorce. Yet this is rarely the situation. Instead, typically, the wife earns less than the husband, does not receive adequate financial support from him after the divorce, and finds herself in greatly reduced circumstances. Moreover, often the family is rather poor before the divorce, so that no matter what the financial arrangements, they are extremely poor after it. Add to this the fact that in the great majority of divorces the mother has custody and primary responsibility for the children. What this means is that children who were being raised by two parents before the divorce are being raised by one parent after it, and that parent has much less money than before. This is true now, and was even more true in the past.

The consequences for children are often devastating. Not only do they have less contact with their fathers (or none at all), but they have to live in an impoverished home with a mother who has trouble making ends meet. The now-single mother must work very hard to earn a living, while at the same time managing a household, doing all the usual chores, and taking care of her children. Poverty alone is usually thought to put children at risk for personality and behaviour problems; poverty combined with the lack of a father and a mother who has very little time for childcare can be expected to be much more damaging. Children in such a home feel deprived of many of the good things in life, are alone much of the time (or at least they don't have an adult present), spend more time on the street, and so on. All of this puts them at great risk for developing serious problems and for engaging in criminal activity.

Note that the increase in divorce rates did not precede the increase in the crime rate, but rather coincided with it. If divorce leads to more crime, one would have expected at least some of the effects to be almost immediate. Some of those involved in the divorce – and they could be either adolescents or the divorcées themselves – would be so upset by the divorce, or by the difficulties surrounding it, or by the poverty and neglect that followed it, that they committed crimes, including homicide. The effect on younger children would be cumulative, but would rarely if ever lead to homicide until the children were older. Taking the immediate and long-term effects together could easily explain the sudden increase in the crime rate, as well as the sustained rise in it over the next ten years.

Children born to young mothers, and unwanted children. As a result of the sexual revolution, and probably for many other reasons, the number of children born to women between fifteen and nineteen increased 54 per cent between 1950 and 1970. Also, the birth rates for unmarried young women increased almost 80 per cent between 1945 and 1961. For our purposes the important fact is that there were many more children born to very young women, many of whom were poor, did not have the maturity to raise a child, and often did not have the assistance of a male partner.

The effect of this was similar to but probably even more severe than the effect of the increase in divorce rates. These children lived in poverty, were not well cared for, and did not have fathers in the home, and to make it worse they had mothers who may not have wanted them and who were ill-prepared to raise them. It would be an understatement to say that these children were at risk for personality and behaviour disorders, and for engaging in criminal activity.

The use of hard drugs. Although it is difficult to obtain accurate statistics, it is widely believed by the police and others involved in law enforcement that the use of hard drugs, especially cocaine and crack cocaine, increased during the period in question. There seems little question that many homicides and other violent crimes involve drugs, either because rival drug gangs are fighting or because drug users are committing the crimes. To the extent that hard drugs, and especially crack cocaine, are the cause of crime, the increased use of these drugs could partly explain the increase in crime that began in the 1960s, and the decline in crime in the 1990s.

All of these changes and many more began after the Second World War and continued for decades. It is difficult to get precise figures on most of these changes, but it is clear they started slowly, increased in strength, and then probably levelled off in the 1970s or later. It happened that in the United States and Canada these great changes in society coincided with the introduction and spread of television. Although television may well have facilitated some of these changes, I do not think that anyone would seriously suggest that television caused them. These changes occurred during the period before and continued after the beginning of the sharp increase in homicide rates, so it is possible they caused that increase. Also, since they are widely acknowledged to affect child development and criminal behaviour, they provide a plausible, some might say highly probable, alternative to explanations that blame television. Given all this, there is no reason to believe that television played any role in the increase in crime rate.

Logic of the argument. Even when we ignore alternative explanations, the data do not support the view that television caused the increase in crime. There is no question that homicide rates began to increase some years after the introduction of television, and doubled ten to fifteen years after most people had television in their homes. Just why there was such a long lag is not explained. More to the point are the data regarding crime rates for younger people. Centerwall is impressed by the fact that the younger the group, the earlier crimes rates began to rise. His notion is that television affected young viewers, and began to affect the crime rate as these viewers got old enough to begin committing crimes.

There are several crucial points that greatly weaken this argument. First, the logic of the argument requires that exposure to television have no effect on adolescents and adults. If it did – if exposure made adolescents and adults more aggressive – the crime rate would have begun to rise immediately or soon after television was introduced. That is not what happened. By 1952 more than 25 per cent of American homes had television, yet homicide rates actually dropped slightly between 1947 and 1957. If exposure to television has as powerful an effect as Centerwall proposes, it seems highly unlikely that older people would be entirely immune to it. Perhaps an adult would be unaffected, but surely a fourteen-year-old boy should be affected. Yet if one accepts Centerwall's argument, they must be immune.

Second, even for younger viewers the data do not fit any reasonable model. By 1952, 25 per cent of homes had television. Children who were ten years old in 1952 and who had television should have begun showing the effect in 1953, since they were then in the age group that supposedly commits violent crimes. Similarly, those who were seven, eight, or nine in 1952 and who had television should have begun showing the effect in 1953, or 1957 at the latest. And when they moved into the next older group (fifteen to seventeen), they should have been showing the effects by 1955, and the effects should have grown steadily stronger as more and more reached that age. But that is not at all what the data show. The increases did not occur until 1960, eight years after many homes had television.

Even if for some mysterious reason children were unaffected by television until 50 per cent of homes had sets, the data do not fit Centerwall's theory. Let me take one example to show the lack of logic of his argument. Centerwall states that there was a six-year lag between 1954, the year in which television was in 50 per cent of the homes, and 1960, the year the effect manifested itself in an increase in the crime rate among ten- to fourteen-year-olds. (For the moment ignore the fact that there should be some effect when only 25 per cent have television.) He then says that the data are internally consistent, because children who were ten to fourteen in 1960 would have been four to eight in 1954. The ages are correct, but why should the effect take six years to appear, and why are nine-year-olds immune? Those who were 9 in 1954 entered the ten-to-fourteen group in 1955. If the nine-year-olds were affected by television, the effects should have begun showing up in 1955. Those who were eight in 1954 should have been showing the effects in 1956, and so on for the younger children. By 1958, all of those who were between six and ten in 1954 were in the ten-to-fourteen group; all of them had been exposed to television for many years; and all of them should have been committing more crimes than they would have without television. Certainly, by any reasoning, the effect on criminal activity among ten- to fourteen-year-olds should have begun to appear before 1960. That the increase did not occur until 1960 is clearly inconsistent with the notion that television caused it, and could be considered quite strong evidence against the hypothesis that television was responsible for the increase in crime rates. The same argument could be made for each of the age groups considered. In every case, the lag is too long and strongly suggests that the increase was not due to the availability of television.

Summary. I have spent much more time on this paper than I believe it is worth. It is difficult to take it seriously because it has so many flaws. Yet I felt it was necessary to discuss it in considerable detail because it has gotten a great deal of attention and is taken very seriously by many American politicians. Let me make it clear that I think this is an interesting approach to a complex issue. Used properly and carefully, it has great potential for providing interesting and perhaps even convincing arguments about the effects of media violence. However, Centerwall's data provide no evidence that television caused the increase in homicide or other crime rates. The theory is directly contradicted by data from four other industrialized countries. Even within the United States and Canada, plausible alternative explanations are available to explain the increases in crime that occurred. Moreover, a careful analysis of the relationship between the timing of the availability of television and the beginning of the increase in crime rates demonstrates that it is highly unlikely that television had any effect on crime. Indeed, rather than supporting the causal hypothesis, I believe that Centerwall's data offer substantial evidence against the causal hypothesis.

Hennigan, Del Rosario, Heath, Cook, Wharton, and Calder (1982)

This clever, innovative study took advantage of the fact that there was a freeze on new television licences in the United States between 1949 and 1952. This meant that during those three years some communities had television and some did not. The investigators surmised that if viewing television causes crime, during the three-year freeze there should be an increase in crime rates in communities with television relative to those without it. Also, after the 'without' communities finally got television, their crime rates should increase also, so that several years after all communities had television those rates should be the same across both types of communities.

Only communities in which television spread rapidly once it was introduced were chosen, since otherwise, effects would be less likely to be seen. Also, to minimize the possibility that the two types of communities were different, selection was based on the speed of spread rather than on any other factor such as size of community. This produced a list of fifty-four 'prefreeze' communities (those that had television in 1949) and forty-one 'postfreeze' communities. In addition, the researchers chose seven prefreeze states and six postfreeze states. They obtained measures of the rates for violent crime, larceny and theft, auto theft, and burglary.

The logic of the study required that the researchers compare communities and states that had television with those that did not; and then once they all had television, to compare those who got it later with those who had it earlier. These comparisons required 'interruption points' – times at which the first and second comparisons were to be made. To make sense, the first point had to represent a time at which television was widespread in the prefreeze communities and absent in the postfreeze communities; and the second point had to be when television was also widespread in the postfreeze communities. The researchers chose the time at which at least 50 per cent of prefreeze homes had television (1951) and then when at least 50 per cent of postfreeze homes had television (1955). For states, the comparable times were 1951 and 1956. The statistical analyses were complex, and it is not necessary to describe them in detail. In essence, they were designed to see if there was an increase in crime rates in the prefreeze cities in 1951 that was then repeated in the postfreeze cities in 1955.

Results. There were no effects on violent crime or on burglary at either of the chosen times. For auto theft there was an increase in the prefreeze cities but no comparable increase at the postfreeze time. These results were confirmed using a time one year later than the target date, to allow for the possibility that the effects would take time to appear. In contrast, there were consistent effects on the rate of larceny offences – they increased in the prefreeze cities and states, and then again in the postfreeze cities and states.

Discussion. For our purposes, the most important finding in this study is the total lack of effect on violent crime or on any serious crime. Not only was there no immediate effect, but presumably there was no effect later (I assume if the two groups of cities had diverged ten years later, the authors would have noted it). As noted elsewhere, the rate of violent crime increased sharply in the United States around 1965. If television had been responsible for that increase, the prefreeze cities and states would have shown the increase three years before the postfreeze communities did. Since the increase was quite dramatic, it would have shown up as a very noticeable 'bubble,' not in 1951 or 1955 but some time around 1965. So this study provides quite strong evidence that directly contradicts the idea that viewing television was the cause of the increase in the homicide rate. The results are also inconsistent with the notion that viewing television causes an increase in aggression. Again, if television had that effect, it should have shown up in the rate of violent crime, either immediately or later. So at face value, the results are inconsistent with and provide evidence against the causal hypothesis.

On the other hand, one could argue that three years is a relatively brief period to produce an effect. Although most people had television during the crucial periods, they may not have been exposed to enough violent television to affect their tendency to commit crimes. Also, many other changes to the social environment were occurring during the critical periods, and these other changes may have counteracted or obscured an effect of television. This is one of those instances in which the lack of an effect is less impressive than it would have been if there had been an effect.

Against these arguments is the fact that there was an effect on the rate of larceny. That this effect occurred demonstrates that exposure to television was enough to affect criminal behaviour and that other factors did not counteract or obscure this effect. So although we should understand the limited nature of the study, we can probably put more faith in the lack of effects on violent crime than we could have if no significant effects occurred.

Although less directly relevant to our concerns, the finding for larceny is fascinating. This study provides the first and as far as I know the only piece of evidence that television can actually affect crime rates. When television was available in 50 per cent of homes, the rate of larceny increased significantly, and this occurred in both the prefreeze and postfreeze communities. The authors explain the effect in terms of relative deprivation. Television at that time (today also, but a little less so) showed mostly attractive, white members of the middle and upper classes, even though the heaviest viewers were relatively poor. This disparity between their own lives and those shown on television could have caused the viewers to experience relative deprivation – the feeling that they had fewer material goods than others. This could lead some people to reduce the discrepancy by stealing. The authors note that it is less likely that the effect was due to direct learning or modelling of behaviour shown on television. They reject this idea, because few if any television programs at the time included any acts of larceny.

It is worth noting that the increase in larceny appeared very soon after television was widespread, and that there was no additional increase a year after the intervention point. This is somewhat difficult to understand. If television causes an increase in larceny when 50 per cent of homes have sets, it seems reasonable to expect that the increase will be greater a year later, when considerably more homes have sets. That this does not occur raises doubts about the cause of the effect. Perhaps the prefreeze and postfreeze communities differed in other ways that could explain the increases in larceny. Perhaps it was not actually watching television that caused the increase, but rather the presence of television in the homes or some other consequence of the presence of television. Perhaps the envy about possession suggested by the authors came not from watching the affluent people on television, but from knowing that some people in the community had television sets when they did not. Once more people had television, there was less reason to be envious. Alternatively, maybe people were spending so much time watching television that they were paying less attention to their possessions such as bicycles, and that made it easier for others to steal those possessions. The lack of a further increase in larceny when even more homes had television might then be explained by the fact that people were aware of the increase in larceny and were more careful to watch or protect their possessions.

I realize that all of these alternatives are rather far-fetched. I offer them because the relative deprivation explanation does not fully account for the pattern of results. Also, I hope to make the point that it is very difficult to know what causes this kind of effect and that it is almost always possible to construct a number of explanations that are consistent with the results.

Conclusion. That there was no increase in any violent (aggressive) crime in those communities with television or in the other communities when they got television is inconsistent with the idea that viewing violent television causes an increase in aggression. Various explanations for the lack of an effect are possible, but they are made less plausible by the fact that there was a significant effect on rates of larceny. In any case, there is little doubt that if the results had shown an increase in violent crime associated with the availability of television, this would have been seen by proponents of the causal hypothesis as strong evidence in its favour. Accordingly, it seems reasonable to conclude that the results of this study are inconsistent with the causal hypothesis and constitute evidence against it.

Himmelweit, Oppenheim, and Vince (1965)

A large number of children in England were interviewed early in the spread of television. One part of the study compared 1,854 children; half of them were living in homes that had television, and half in homes that did not. In addition, 370 children in Norwich were interviewed before television was available to any of them, and again a year later, at which time they were divided into those who had subsequently gotten television sets and those who had not.

Results. Unfortunately, the authors did not present the results of most interest to this review in any detail. For example, they did not present means or change scores for the Norwich sample, or for those with and without television in the rest of the sample. So I have to depend mainly on the authors' qualitative descriptions of their findings.

They report that they found no differences between viewers and non-viewers in terms of aggression, maladjustment, or delinquent behaviour. Although it is not stated explicitly, a reasonable inference is that this held for the before-and-after study in Norwich as well as for the viewers/non-viewers sample in the rest of the country. Also, there was apparently no difference in aggressiveness in the total Norwich sample before and after television was introduced. In observing children's reactions to television, the authors noted that viewing an action program or a western was sometimes followed by or accompanied by play that was related to the program. Their response to this is similar to the point I have made several times about the distinction between real and play aggression. They comment: 'These are not games of uncontrolled aggression, but are only versions of chasing and being chased – of cowboys and Indians, of cops and robbers – the oldest of childhood games, which were, of course, played long before television was thought of' (195).

Conclusions. The main result for our purposes is that as far as I can tell, none of the research found any differences in aggressiveness as a function of the presence of television in the home. This study provides no evidence for and a little evidence against the causal hypothesis.

Schramm, Lyle, and Parker (1961)

This book reports on eleven studies that were conducted between 1958 and 1960 in the United States and Canada. The samples were very large – 2,688 in one study, 1,708 in another, and so on. Overall, the work obtained data on 5,991 children, 1,958 parents of those children, and hundreds of teachers and others. The study that is probably most useful for this review involved two communities in Canada, one of which (Teletown) had television and one of which (Radiotown) did not. Each community had a population of around 5,000. The two were similar in many other ways. Teletown received mainly American television. Data were obtained from first, sixth, and tenth grade students, a total of 913.

Results. This is a very large body of work, much of it extremely interesting and helpful in understanding the role of television in children's lives. However, I am reporting only those results that relate directly to our concerns.

The children were divided into four viewing groups on the basis of how much time they spent viewing television and reading. The four groups were as follows: high users of both; high television, low reading; low television, high reading; and low users of both. In one large sample there were no differences in aggression among these four groups in grade six; in another large sample, among those in grade ten the high television/low reading group was the highest in aggression.

In Teletown and Radiotown, measures were obtained of antisocial aggression, 'prosocial' aggression, and aggression anxiety (a measure of avoiding aggression). In both grade six and grade ten, the boys and girls in Radiotown scored higher on antisocial aggression than those in Teletown. The differences were significant for both sexes in grade six, but were not significant in grade ten. There were no consistent differences between towns in terms of prosocial aggression, and there was only one substantial difference in aggression anxiety, with those in Teletown scoring higher. The authors comment: 'There is a slight indication in the data from Radiotown and Teletown that television might serve to reduce antisocial aggression ... this result, at least, provides no support for the contention that television serves to increase aggression' (132).

Conclusions. This was an early study on television and did not use as sophisticated methods as later ones did. In particular, it did not distinguish between the amount of television viewed and the amount of violence viewed. Probably the most important finding for our discussion is that a town that did not have television (Radiotown) had more aggression than one that did (Teletown). There are, of course, many reasons why this might have been true, including all sorts of unknown differences between the two towns. Thus, as with any such comparison between two communities, this result should be given little or no weight on its own. On the other hand, I have little doubt that if the result had been reversed it would have been cited as evidence of the harmful effects of television. I consider it some very weak evidence against the causal hypothesis.

Williams (1986)

This study was conducted in three small communities in Canada. One of the communities did not yet have television but would soon be receiving one channel (CBC – the Canadian Broadcasting Corporation). Knowing this, the authors decided to study the impact of television by comparing this community (which they called 'Notel' – no television) with two other communities, one of which ('Unitel') had been receiving one channel, also CBC, for many years and one of which ('Multitel') had been receiving many channels. The authors gathered data on all three communities just before television was introduced to Notel and two years after its introduction. Since only CBC was introduced into Notel, it is worth noting that at the time, that channel carried no cartoons except 'World of Disney,' no programs early on weekend mornings, and only two police detective shows a week. In other words, the television that became available to Notel was extremely low in violent content compared to what was available on the channels available in Multitel and in most American and Canadian communities.

Our concern is the impact the introduction of television into Notel had on aggression. In the first phase of the study (before television), 120 children were observed (40 in each town). In the second phase, again 120 were observed, 45 of whom had been in the first sample. The observations were made during free-play periods. Behaviour was scored for aggression, but did not distinguish between real and play aggression. In addition, all the children in grades one to five were rated by their peers and by teachers in terms of aggressiveness.

Results. Based on the observational measure, in phase 1 the children in the three towns did not differ in terms of aggression. In phase 2, after television was available in Notel, the children in all three towns had increased in aggression, but only the change in Notel was significant. The changes were striking. In Notel the scores changed from .431 aggressive acts per minute to 1.122 per minute; in Unitel from .419 to .564; and in Multitel from .444 to .640. No similar effects were found for other ratings of aggression done by the teachers or peers. Despite the lack of consistency among measures, the authors concluded that the findings demonstrated that television had caused the children in Notel to become more aggressive.

Discussion. This study has been frequently cited by those who favour the causal hypothesis. Because it is so often described as providing strong support for the causal hypothesis, detailed discussion is warranted.

To begin, it is important to remember that although the authors termed it a 'natural experiment,' it was not actually an experiment. The communities had not been randomly assigned as to whether they received television, and there was only one community and thus only one data point in each condition. There were, of course, many people in each community, but there were only three communities. The members of each community were not independent of one another, and whatever affected some would no doubt affect others. Rather than an experiment, this must be considered a case study. When there is only one community in a condition, any conclusions must be extremely tentative. No matter how good the design of the study, and no matter how consistent the results, a study of this sort can never be considered strong support for the hypothesis. Just as the similar studies by Himmelweit and by Schramm discussed earlier can be considered at best weak evidence against the hypothesis, this study at best can be considered weak evidence in favour of it. However, there are many problems with it that make even this conclusion questionable.

Real vs play aggression. The authors made a serious mistake when they decided not to distinguish between real and play aggression. As I noted earlier, it is well established that much of what children do is play fighting or play aggression, and including this along with real fighting inevitably distorts the view of children's behaviour. In this context, it should be noted that the aggression scores were extremely high in all three towns. The mean level of physical aggression in phase 1 was more than .4 acts per minute. During phase 2 it was a staggering 1.1 in Notel. In other words, on average the children in all of the towns were engaging in physical or verbal aggression more than half the time in phase 1; and in phase 2 the Notel children were engaged in physical aggression *all* the time (i.e., every minute on average they engaged in more than one act that was scored as aggression). While this level of aggressiveness is possible, it is highly unlikely that a whole group – or for that matter three whole groups – would be engaging in so much real aggression. It is, however, consistent with the notion that the children were engaged in a great deal of active play – including a lot of aggressive play – and that that is what the observers were recording.

This view is strengthened by the fact that the changes in aggression found by the observers were not confirmed by the ratings of aggression done by the teachers. Given that the mean observed scores for aggression more than doubled in Notel, one would have expected the teachers to notice that their students had become much more aggressive since television had been introduced. But if the increases seen in the playgrounds were in play aggression, the teachers would not be expected to rate the children as more aggressive, since the teachers know the difference between real and play aggression.

This suggests that any differences found by the study were in the amount of play fighting rather than in real aggression. The children in Notel were not familiar with television. Those of us young enough to remember when we first got television may remember how compelling it was at the beginning. Let us assume that in the first year or two after television was available in Notel, it was more compelling and intriguing than it was in the other towns, which had had television for many years. That being the case, the programs on television would have had a greater impact in Notel than in the other towns. Indeed, that is not far from what the authors were claiming, since presumably television was also affecting children's behaviour in Unitel and Multitel. I suggest that the impact was not to make the children in Notel more aggressive, but merely to make them more likely to act out what they saw on television. Since some of what they saw was aggressive behaviour, that is what they acted out. But they were not being truly aggressive; they were merely engaging in play aggression, just as they would have acted out a new sport or sung a new song or pretended to fly if these things had been shown on television. In other words, not distinguishing between real and play aggression makes it possible, indeed likely, that the results were due to an increase in the latter, not the former.

Alternative explanations. Even if we accept the authors' contention that they measured real aggression and that it increased greatly in Notel between phase 1 and phase 2, it need not have been caused by the introduction of television. The authors contend that it must have been caused by the introduction of television, because nothing else had changed in Notel to explain the increase. It is difficult to share their confidence, since they do not provide any information on social changes – changes that could have been very important. For example, during phase 1 the unemployment rate in Notel was considerably lower than in the other communities. If the rate had risen to become closer to that in the other communities, that would have been a very important change in social conditions and might very well have caused an increase in aggression. Alternatively, it is possible that some local event or change in the social situation occurred that increased the children's aggressiveness. Perhaps a few very aggressive children moved into town, or a few children in Notel experienced some unpleasant events in their lives that made them very aggressive. Neither occurrence would have any substantial impact on the amount of aggression, play or otherwise, in a big city or in a sample of several hundred children. But in a very small community, a few children who are more aggressive than average can greatly affect the atmosphere of the school and the social interactions among the children. That the aggressiveness (real or play) of a small group of children in Notel increased dramatically between phase 1 and phase 2 cannot be considered evidence that television made the children in Notel more aggressive. Possibly the change was not due to television at all.

Logic of the argument. Finally, let us consider the logic of the argument that the introduction of television caused a doubling of aggressiveness in Notel. Keep in mind that the other two towns had had television for some time. Presumably, any effect that television had in Notel, it would have had in the other towns, and for a longer time. Yet during phase 1, the level of aggression was the same in the three towns. Multitel, where children could watch a wide variety of violent programs, had no more aggression than Unitel, where children could watch only a limited number of violent programs, or Notel, where children could watch no television at all. If television caused aggression, there should have been the most aggression in Multitel, the next most in Unitel, and the least in Notel. That the three were so similar suggests that television had no effect on aggressiveness in those towns which had it. But we must acknowledge that we have no idea why the three communities were so similar in this measure of aggression. It could be that television had no effect, but obviously many other factors were affecting the level of aggression. The fact of the matter is that communities differ in many ways, and that any small groups of children chosen from different communities will also differ in many ways. So it would not have been surprising if the groups from each community had differed in their scores on aggressiveness, any more than it should surprise us that they did not differ. (Let me note, however, that if the three towns had differed initially in the way predicted by the causal hypothesis, this surely would have been used as evidence in its favour.)

On the other hand, if we accept the scores of the three groups as accurate indications of the level of aggressiveness of the children in the three communities – which, as I have said, I do not, but for the sake of argument, let us pretend to accept them – it is then necessary to explain why those in Notel were just as aggressive as those in the towns that had had television for years. If, as the authors believe, television causes aggression, the presence of television in Multitel and Unitel must have increased aggression in those communities. Since the children in Notel (who were not affected by television) were just as aggressive as those in Multitel and Unitel (who were affected by television), we must assume that other factors made up for the absence of television in Notel, and that these other factors had to have been at least as powerful in causing aggression as television. In other words, to account for the equality of the three towns, assuming that television causes aggression, one must assume that other factors, equal in strength to television, were present in Notel but not in the other towns.

Then how in the world can we explain the enormous increase in aggressiveness in Notel in phase 2 when the children had been exposed not to the considerable amount of violence shown in Multitel, but only the very limited amount of violence shown on CBC (and in Unitel)? Remember that the mean aggression scores in Notel more than doubled. If this was due to television, then television was a far stronger factor than any other. But that being true, the other two towns should have had more aggression in phase 1 than Notel. You can't have it both ways. If television is such an important factor, Notel should have had less aggression in phase 1. If television is not such an important factor, Notel should not have increased so greatly in aggression in phase 2.

Conclusions. As with Centerwall, I have spent more time on this study than I think it deserves. It was a serious study of changes in three small towns, but because it was a case study it cannot possibly provide strong evidence about the effect of introducing television. Also, there were many methodological problems with it, and many inconsistencies in the results, that are not usually mentioned when this study is cited.

The study's main finding is that on the observational measure, the three towns had about the same aggression scores in phase 1, but Notel obtained a much higher score in phase 2, after television was introduced. This was not shown by measures based on teachers' ratings of the children's aggression. In my opinion, the observational measure was poorly chosen and probably confused a small amount of real aggression with a great deal of play aggression. The study lacked a detailed description of the towns during the crucial period, which leaves open the possibility that events or social changes could have produced the changes in behaviour. Finally, the logic of the argument is not consistent with the pattern of the findings. For all these reasons, the key results should be viewed with considerable scepticism. I conclude that this study provides only very weak evidence in support of the hypothesis, and I consider this a generous assessment.

Overall Conclusions

All of these studies assessed the impact of television by comparing rates of crime or aggression when television was available with rates when it was not. Centerwall showed that crime increased after television became available, but the time lag and other reasons make it highly implausible that there was a causal connection. Hennigan found no effect on violent crime. Three of the studies compared specific communities with and without television. Himmelweit and Schramm found no evidence for more aggression with than without television – if anything, the opposite. Based on direct observation of a small number of children, Williams did find an increase in observed aggression after television was introduced, but this finding was not replicated by teachers' rating of the children's aggressiveness, and there are many reasons to be sceptical of the former result. So this body of research provides little or no evidence that supports the causal hypothesis.

On the contrary, there is some rather strong evidence that contradicts the hypothesis. A detailed analysis of Centerwall's data indicates that the time lags between the availability of television and the beginning of the increase in crime rates are inconsistent with a causal effect. If television violence contributed to crime, the increase in the crime rate should have occurred far earlier than it did. If television has an effect on adolescents and adults, the increase should have begun as soon as people had television, or at most a year or two later. Instead, there was no increase in adult crime rates for many years, which indicates that television does not affect the aggressiveness of these age groups. If television affects children under ten, the effects on crime rates should appear as soon as they enter the ten-to-fourteen age group. Yet this age group showed no increase for six to eight years after most people had television. Taken together, this pattern is inconsistent with an effect of television on crime and is thus evidence against the causal hypothesis. Moreover, the data from four other industrialized countries directly contradict the hypothesis by showing no increase in homicide rates after the introduction of television.

Similarly, the lack of effect on violent crime in the Hennigan study is difficult to understand if television violence causes aggression. Although three years is not a long time, one would presumably expect an increase in crime during that period. That one did not occur in the communities with television compared to those without it, is also inconsistent with the causal hypothesis and constitutes evidence against it.

I conclude that taken as a whole, the results of these studies are inconsistent with the causal hypothesis and generally contradict it.

8

Other Approaches to
Assessing Causality

I have discussed many different kinds of research that have attempted to gather evidence on whether exposure to media violence causes aggression. Every method has provided some interesting and useful information. Yet despite the wide variety of methods, it seems it is always possible for ingenious people to find other approaches to the problem. This section describes these other approaches that do not fit neatly into the more usual categories of research.

Belson (1978)

It is difficult to know how to classify this study. In one sense it is simply another survey that obtained information on exposure to media, measures of aggression, and a great deal of other data. As such, it would fit into the group of survey studies described in chapter 3. However, the purpose of this study was to assess the causal relationship (if any) between exposure to violent media and aggression, and Belson claimed that he had done that. Since I try to accept authors' views of their work, at least as a first step, I have placed this study in this eclectic section that deals with novel attempts to answer the question of causality.

Method. The sample consisted of a representative group of 1,565 boys between twelve and seventeen living in London. The boys were interviewed at home and in the research office. Their mothers were also interviewed.

Great care was taken in developing the key measures and collecting the data. Unfortunately, the measures had not been used before, and as far as I know have not been used since. Therefore, we do not have any detailed information about their validity or reliability. This is especially important because the boys were asked to think back many years in describing their behaviour, and ordinarily retrospective accounts of this kind are not very accurate.

Exposure to violent television was assessed by showing the boys a list of sixty-eight television programs that had appeared between 1959 and 1971, which was most of the lifetime of the boys in the sample. The boys indicated which ones they had seen and how often. The programs were all rated independently for violent content, and from these ratings and the boys' answers, the author calculated scores for total viewing of television and total viewing of violent television. There were also measures of exposure to violent content in movies and comic books, as well as a measure of exposure to newspapers.

Aggression was measured by having the boys sort cards containing statements about their involvement in violent acts and by asking some questions directly. From their answers, several scores for violent actions were computed.

Results. The usual measure of an association between two factors is a correlation, but unfortunately, as far as I can tell, no simple correlations were computed. So we don't know the association between any of the exposure scores and any of the violent behaviour scores. Instead of calculating correlations, Belson simply divided the subjects into those with high and those with low exposure to violent television (or whatever other exposure measure was being investigated) and then compared the two groups in terms of scores on violent behaviour (this was called the forward hypothesis – going from exposure to aggression). In addition, the boys were divided into high and low violence and were compared in terms of scores on exposure (called the reverse hypothesis). As I understand it – and I admit that I found some of the logic difficult to follow – the forward hypothesis was considered to have been supported only when it was significant and when the reverse hypothesis either was not significant or showed a weaker effect.

Exposure and violent behaviour. On almost all measures of exposure to any kind of media, the high-exposure group had higher scores for overall violence. For example, those who were higher on exposure to violent television had violence scores of 57, against 51 for those who were lower on exposure to violent television. The same difference occurred for exposure to comic books (57 vs 49), violent films (57 vs 49), and, oddly, newspapers (57 vs 49). However, for most of these comparisons – and especially for exposure to violent television and films – the reverse effects were also significant. From this the author concluded that although the results were consistent with exposure to violent media causing violent behaviour, it was possible that the results were due to a personality effect or to violent behaviour causing the boys to watch more violent television and movies. In other words, the author decided that there was no clear support for the causal hypothesis.

In contrast, the same comparisons for serious violent behaviour found that high exposure to violent television was related to high scores on serious violence, and that the reverse comparison was not significant. On this measure, there was no 'effect' of violent films or newspapers. However, the results also showed that overall exposure to television – and, more strikingly, exposure to non-violent television – produced almost the same pattern as was produced by exposure to violent television. For both total exposure and exposure to non-violent television, the high-exposure group had significantly higher scores on serious violence, and the reverse hypothesis was not significant. Moreover, the size of the effect for these measures of exposure was almost identical to the effect for violent television, both in actual magnitude and in statistical significance. Obviously, if exposure to non-violent television produces the same 'effect' as exposure to violent television, there is no reason to believe that violent content plays any role in violent behaviour.

Belson recognized this as a serious problem that made any conclusions about causality difficult. To deal with this he conducted an analysis he termed 'massive matching,' in which various subgroups of subjects were matched on various other measures and then compared on the score of serious violence. I will not attempt to describe this procedure in detail, but for now will note merely that the author believed this analysis demonstrated that it was exposure to violent television and not to television in general that was related to serious violent behaviour.

Exposure to violence in the media and attitudes toward violent behaviour. The study began with a series of hypotheses regarding the effect of exposure to media violence on attitudes toward violent behaviour. It was predicted that high exposure to television violence would make the boys think about, or make them preoccupied with, the acts of violence they saw on television; that it would make the boys more likely to want to commit the acts of violence they saw on television; that it would increase their willingness to commit those acts; and that all of these predictions would also be true of exposure to violent comic books, violent movies, and newspapers. None of these hypotheses received any support.

Discussion. The most important point to make is that despite the author's claims to the contrary, this study provides no evidence of a causal connection between any of the variables studied. By its nature the study could not possibly have provided any substantial evidence for or against a causal effect. Since all of the measures were taken at one time and related to the same time period, there were no grounds for assessing causal effects. Given the nature of the data, it might have been possible to do the same kind of analyses as were done in the longitudinal studies. Perhaps the author could have computed scores for exposure to violence and for violent behaviour at various ages. In other words, the boys could have been asked about their exposure to violence and their aggression when they were, say, eight and twelve and at present. Having gathered these different scores, it would then have been possible to conduct regression analyses to establish whether early exposure is related to later violence when early aggression is controlled. Of course, since these scores would all be based on retrospective data, they would probably be quite inaccurate and unreliable. I am not seriously suggesting that this procedure would have produced strong results. But at least it would have provided some minimal information relevant to causality. When there is only one score at one time for each measure, no causal information is available.

Belson contended that having found a relationship, he could rule out other factors by the unusual analyses he employed. Without getting into a discussion of his method and accepting it as stated, it still could not rule out other explanations. For purposes of argument, let us assume that it could rule out the factors Belson considered. The difficulty is that although he considered quite a few factors, there are many more that he did not consider. A few obvious examples are the extent to which there was violence in the home, whether the boys had psychopathic or aggressive personalities, and the incidence of gang violence in the boys' neighbourhoods. Any of these could have caused the boys to watch more violent television and also to be more violent themselves. Thus, without considering other problems with the study, there is no question that it provides no real evidence of causality and should rightly be considered merely one more survey study that, unfortunately, did not provide correlations of the kind that would have been helpful.

Besides this basic limitation, the study relied entirely on retrospective self-reports for its data. The boys were asked how often they had watched television programs as much as ten years earlier. The accuracy of their answers must be considered rather low. Of perhaps greater importance, answers to questions about exposure to violent media and about their own violent behaviour were likely to affect each other and so produce spurious correlations. Moreover, although the boys were promised anonymity, they were responding to a real person, and at least some of them must have been concerned about the impression they were giving (they were, after all, adolescents, who are usually extremely concerned about self-presentation). Some of them may have avoided describing themselves as violent and as liking violent media; others may have *wanted* to seem tough in both behaviour and viewing preferences. Any tendency to avoid seeming tough or to want to appear tough would inflate any correlation that existed and would produce one even in the absence of a real correlation, especially if some had one tendency and some had the other. This is always a problem with self-reports, and was probably especially so in this study.

Finally, remember that the subjects were teenagers. Although Belson attempted to measure their exposure to violent media throughout their lives, it is likely that the measures were affected mainly by more recent exposure. Almost everyone believes that whatever effect exposure to violent media has, it is mainly on children rather than on teenagers and adults. Thus, one would expect the effects to be weaker for the subjects in this study than in studies involving younger children.

Conclusions. This study provides more evidence that exposure to violent television is related to aggressive behaviour, and adds evidence that exposure to violent films, comic books, and even newspapers also is related to violent behaviour. The study produced no evidence of any causal connection between any type of exposure and any kind of violent behaviour. I conclude that it offers no support for the causal hypothesis, but also no evidence against it.

Kruttschnitt, Heath, and Ward (1986)

This study employed a technique usually called the case control method, which is quite common in medical research but relatively rare in psychological research. People who meet certain criteria are selected and compared to those who do not meet these criteria. The idea is to look back into the history of those with and without the condition to see if there are life experiences or any other factors that distinguish the groups. If there are, it raises the possibility that those experiences are what caused the condition. For example, people with lung cancer might be compared to those without lung cancer, with the two groups matched on as many other variables as possible. One would expect to find that those with lung cancer were heavier smokers than those without. There also might be differences in terms of diet, lifestyle, family background, exposure to pollutants, and so on. This method was used by Kruttschnitt but focused on people who had been convicted of violent criminal acts.

One hundred men incarcerated for violent criminal acts were compared to sixty-five who were not incarcerated, had not committed violent criminal acts, and came from the same neighbourhoods and backgrounds as the criminal group. Information was obtained on the men's exposure to violent media, parental violence, sibling aggression, family attachment, and school performance and activities.

Results. A series of regression analyses indicated that school experiences and parental violence were significantly related to violent criminal behaviour. Exposure to media violence was not related to violent criminal behaviour.

Discussion. Although the results clearly provide no evidence in favour of the causal hypothesis, I would not give these results much weight, because the study has a number of serious weaknesses. Of most concern are that the samples are not matched perfectly and that all of the information comes from retrospective reports from the subjects. Thus, even if exposure to violent media had been significantly related to violent behaviour, it would have been at most suggestive of a real effect. This kind of study is probably more useful when the information obtained is more concrete and therefore less subject to inaccuracy and distortion. People are probably capable of answering accurately, and willing to do so, when asked if they smoke, if they live near a garbage dump, if they eat a high-fat diet, and other such questions. They are less likely to answer accurately when asked to recall how much violent television they watched as children, whether they fought with their siblings, and whether their parents were violent. They are also better at reporting accurately on recent experiences (e.g., at the age of fifty whether they have smoked during the past ten years) than on less recent experiences (e.g., how attached they were to their parents when they were children, and how much violent television they watched when they were six). So while certainly a useful method of research for many purposes, it seems to have less utility when it comes to studying the effects of exposure to violent media.

Conclusion. This study provides no evidence that exposure to violent television in childhood makes people more likely to commit violent crimes. It thus offers no support for the causal hypothesis. For the reasons given above, I would not give this result much weight. However, I should mention – as I have with other such results – that if the study had found a significant association between exposure and crime, those favouring the causal hypothesis would surely have considered it evidence in favour of their position.

Messner (1986)

This study was based on the idea that if exposure to violent television increases the likelihood of committing a crime, greater exposure should be associated with more crime. Messner then reasoned that areas in which there was greater exposure to violent television programs should have higher crime rates. To assess whether this was correct, he obtained measures of exposure to violent television programs in various geographical areas and related them to rates of crime in those areas.

Method. Using content analyses done by the National Coalition on Television violence (NCTV), the most violent regular, prime-time series were identified. Exposure to these programs was based on Nielsen data for average number of viewers of each program, converted to standard metropolitan statistical areas (SMSAs). In this way each of the 281 SMSAs in the United States was given a score for exposure to violence. That is, the score was a measure of the average viewing of violent programs in the area.

Measures of crime were based on FBI data. They consisted of the rates of violent crime (criminal homicide, forcible rape, robbery, and aggravated assault) and property crime (burglary, larceny, and auto theft) for each SMSA for the period in question.

Since other factors could affect crime rates, measures were obtained for each SMSA of various social and demographic factors: percentage of people below the poverty line, percentage of adults with less than a high school education, percentage of the population that was Black, the Gini coefficient – which measures the level of economic inequality – and the average monthly payment to recipients of AFDC (aid to families with dependent children). Also, measures were obtained of population density, percentage of population eighteen to thirty-four, number of males per 100 females, and total population.

Results. The most important results for our purposes were correlations (actually regression coefficients) between the measure of exposure to violent television and rates of the four types of violent crime, as well as the rate of violent crime in total. Surprisingly, all of the coefficients were negative, indicating that the rates of all of these violent crimes were lower in areas with higher exposure to violent television. The coefficients were small – none higher than –.17 – but all were significant except the one involving aggravated assault. When 'variance inflation factors' were controlled, the results remained essentially the same but the coefficients were larger – –.17 to –.25 – and were all significant. Similar though considerably weaker results were found when total television was related to the rates of violent crime. Again, the regression coefficients were all negative, although the highest was only –.14. Another analysis looked at the relationship between exposure to television violence and non-violent crimes. Once more, the regression coefficients were all negative, and these were even stronger than those involving violent crime: –.25 to –.35.

In contrast, other factors were associated with increased rates of violent crime. The Gini coefficient, which measures economic disparity, was strongly correlated with homicide (.41), rape (.28), robbery (.36), assault (.36), and total violent crimes (.42). The male/female ratio was also associated with increased crime rates, although the correlations were lower – all between .13 and .19. Interestingly, economic level by itself, measured as either per cent poor or in terms of AFDC payments, was unrelated to the rate of violent crime.

Discussion. The results are the opposite of what would be predicted by the causal hypothesis. The author concludes that the results raise 'serious questions about the claim that high rates of urban crime can be attributed in any simple and direct way to heavy exposure to television violence.' It is difficult to disagree with this conclusion. These results are clearly inconsistent with the causal hypothesis and directly contradict it.

However, as with almost any study of this kind, there are various problems and limitations that must be taken into account. As the author acknowledges, the data for exposure are based on a relatively short time period, and there is no longitudinal analysis of how exposure may affect crime rates over time. On the other hand, the factors that correlated positively with crime rates were those that usually do. If the crime data had been poor, the study would not have found such strong correlations between the Gini coefficient and crime rates, or any of the other strong positive correlations. The fact that these social factors produced strong positive correlations with crime rates should give us more confidence in the negative correlations between violence viewing and crime. Therefore, none of these concerns seems terribly important. They do not change the basic finding that at least for this period and with these data, exposure to violent television was negatively related to crime rates.

Of greater importance is that the author did not conduct multiple regressions in which factors other than exposure were controlled. Controlling for variance inflation factors is helpful, but it would have been more revealing to investigate whether the relationship between exposure to violent television and crime rates remained negative once the social and demographic factors were controlled. Although it seems quite unlikely that this would have changed the results substantially, this type of analysis is usually done when there are so many interrelated variables.

In my opinion the most serious limitation of the study is that it concerns mainly or perhaps entirely adults. The measure of exposure to television violence is based on viewing of prime-time popular programs. Though they may be watched by children, the Nielsen measure assumes that most viewers are adults. It is likely that in homes in which adults watch a lot of violent programs the children also watch a lot of violent television (including these programs); however, the focus of the measure is certainly on adult viewing. So one way of interpreting the result is that heavy viewing of violent television by adults is not related to the likelihood that they will commit crimes, and instead seems to be negatively related to this likelihood.

This is by no means a trivial result. It is the opposite of what the causal hypothesis would predict and is difficult to understand if exposure really does increase aggression. By the time people reach adulthood, presumably their tendency to be aggressive or to commit crimes is fairly well established. Nevertheless, it would be expected that additional violent television at this stage would increase the likelihood that they would behave aggressively. Some of the experimental research is based on that premise, because it consists of exposing adults or adolescents to one or more violent programs and measuring their aggressiveness. If exposure to a few violent programs really does increase aggressiveness – as some of the authors suggest – then surely a diet that is richer in violent television should also be expected to increase aggressiveness, and, aggregated over many people, to increase crime rates. That it does not in this study is evidence against the causal hypothesis. It also contradicts some of the experimental findings – or at least some of the interpretations of those studies in terms of a causal effect on aggression.

One could also interpret the results more broadly. Even though the measures of exposure and of crime rates were taken at one time, there is no reason to expect they would have varied greatly from year to year. Rather, both measures were probably typical of what the SMSAs would have reflected in other years. An area that scored high in violent viewing in this study almost certainly scored high the year before that and the year before that and so on. Similarly, areas that had high rates of crime in this study probably had high rates of crime in the years before and after the period in question. This means that the lack of positive correlation can be interpreted to mean not only that exposure during the target year did not increase crime during that year, but also that prior exposure to violent television in previous years probably did not produce an increase in crime either immediately or later. If exposure during the previous five years had caused a gradual increase in the likelihood that adults and especially children would commit crimes, areas with high violence exposure scores should have had high rates of crime. That they did not suggests that there was no negative effect of exposure.

Let me put this another way. If the results had shown a positive correlation between exposure and crime rate, we can be sure that this would have been interpreted by many as indicating that violent programs cause aggression and also that the effect occurs over many years (since the effect is generally thought to be cumulative). However, there was a negative correlation, not a positive one. I hesitate to interpret this as meaning that viewing violent programs decreases aggression or crime, but certainly it is evidence against the notion that it increases aggression or crime.

Conclusion. The results provide no evidence in favour of the causal hypothesis and constitute some fairly strong evidence against it.

Lynn, Hampson and Agahi (1989)

This study was designed to test what the authors call a genotype-environment correlation and interaction theory of the relationship between viewing television violence and aggression. One basic idea behind this approach is that genetically determined propensities affect behaviour and personality, but that there are at least two processes by which this occurs. First, the propensity may have a direct effect; second, this effect may be magnified by the environment. The authors use intelligence as an example. Highly intelligent parents tend to transmit to their biological children a genetic tendency to be intelligent – a direct effect. In addition, highly intelligent parents tend to provide an environment that enhances the intelligence of their children – an indirect effect. Moreover, according to the theory, genetically different children react differently to the same environment. Genetically intelligent children will do well in school, will be rewarded for that, will work harder and read more and so on, and will become even more intelligent. In contrast, children whose intelligence is lower for genetic reasons will do poorly in school, will become discouraged, will not work hard, will not read and so on, and their intelligence will be reduced or at least not enhanced as much as that of the others. The application of this approach to the television violence issue is complex and probably need not be explained in detail here. The essence of it is that both between-sibling correlations and between-family correlations can be used to test aspects of the model.

Method. The study obtained information about television violence viewing, aggression, and various other factors from pairs of siblings. It began with 2,039 children between eleven and sixteen. All of them lived in Northern Ireland and attended rural or small-town schools. From this sample 99 pairs of brothers, 113 pairs of sisters, and 174 brother-sister pairs were selected.

Aggression was measured by the aggression questionnaire of the Interpersonal Behaviour Survey. This scale has been shown to have a heritability of approximately 60 per cent. Television violence viewing was measured by having the children indicate how often they watched forty-three popular programs, weighting the programs in terms of their violence, and calculating the total amount of violence watched by multiplying the violence weighting by the frequency of viewing. The children were also asked twelve questions about their liking of various violent aspects of programs. Their answers were then summed to give an 'enjoyment of violence' score.

Results. As would be expected, males were more aggressive, watched more television violence, enjoyed television violence more, and scored higher on psychoticism than females. The correlations between violence viewing and aggression were .08 for males and .15 for females. These figures are at the lower end of the usual continuum but well within the range of previous results. In contrast, aggression was strongly correlated with psychoticism (.53 for males, .48 for females) and with the enjoyment of television violence (.35 and .34), and was negatively correlated with intelligence (−.11 and −.20). A multiple regression with aggression as the dependent variable found that psychoticism was most strongly related, followed by enjoyment of television violence, and then (considerably weaker) neuroticism. In this analysis there was no relationship between aggression and the amount of television violence viewed.

The authors considered the results for siblings crucial for their hypothesis. There were high correlations between siblings for IQ, extroversion, television violence viewing, and total television viewing. However, between-siblings correlations were very low for aggression and for enjoying television violence. The high correlation for viewing violence and the low correlation for enjoying it suggest to the authors that siblings watch television as a family, but that their reactions to it are different. The authors conclude that this pattern is inconsistent with the causal hypothesis, but consistent with the idea that both propensity to be aggressive and tendency to enjoy violent television are genetically determined.

Perhaps the most important finding for our purposes is that the sibling who was higher in aggression was no more likely to watch violent television than the less aggressive sibling (correlations of .04, .08, and −.02 for brothers, sisters, and mixed-sex pairs respectively). As the authors note, this indicates that 'when all shared family variables are controlled, i.e., all the genetic and environmental factors which tend to make siblings alike, the amount of viewing of television violence has no effect on aggression.'

The authors offer six ways in which the data are inconsistent with the causal hypothesis (which they call something else). They conclude that the hypothesis is untenable.

Discussion. The results provide no support for the causal hypothesis and are, in fact, generally inconsistent with it. Virtually every relevant finding is either neutral or contradicts the predictions that would be made from the hypothesis. In contrast, they are generally consistent with an explanation in terms of personality or predisposition or some other similar factor. Whether the results provide clear support for the alternative hypothesis could be argued.

On the other hand, there were quite a few limitations to this study. In the first place, the measure of aggression was apparently based entirely on self-reports by the subjects themselves. This is a legitimate way of measuring aggression, but it is probably less valid and more prone to distortion than the peer nomination measure used in many other studies. Of greater importance is that the subjects ranged in age from eleven to sixteen. Again, it is entirely legitimate to look at the relationship between television violence viewing and aggression in this age group, but it is probably not the group in which the effects would be expected to be most pronounced. Those who favour the causal hypothesis would probably argue that by the time a child turns eleven, his or her tendency to act aggressively has been established, and the role of television violence in shaping that tendency is largely or entirely complete – that the effect of viewing television violence on aggressive behaviour occurs mostly at relatively young ages. Thus, although the results are not consistent with the causal hypothesis, they do not provide a strong test of it.

Nevertheless, many experimental studies and some non-experimental ones have involved teenagers or even older subjects. Those conducting this research obviously believed that television violence can affect aggression at these ages, and some of the experimental work has shown effects. That the present study failed to find any support for a causal link between exposure to television violence and aggression calls into doubt the significance of these laboratory studies. It supports the interpretation that the laboratory effects are due not to a direct effect of exposure to violence, but rather to other mechanisms such as experimental demand or arousal.

Conclusion. This study, which admittedly is not state-of-the-art in terms of its measures, and does not involve the age group of main concern, provides no evidence that exposure to violent television causes aggression. The results are inconsistent with the causal hypothesis, and some of them directly contradict it.

Rowe and Herstand (1985)

This study was similar to the previous one in that it used data from siblings to assess the contribution of environmental and genetic factors in producing aggressive behaviour. The idea was to look at correlations within families (between siblings) as well as correlations between families. The term 'between-family (BF) influences' was used to refer to those factors (environmental or genetic) that operate to make siblings similar to each other; and the term 'within-family (WF) influences' to refer to those that make siblings dissimilar.

Method. The subjects were 124 pairs of siblings between fourteen and eighteen attending a high school in Elyria, Ohio. Television violence viewing was measured by asking the participants how often they watched nine popular programs that contained a considerable amount of violence. Scores could range from 0 (never watched any of them) to 27 (never missed any of them). There was also a measure of identification with aggression, which tapped the extent to which the subjects imitated television aggression and enjoyed it. Aggression was measured by self-reported aggressiveness. In addition, there were two measures of the consequences of aggression, one concerning the consequences for the heroes of television programs and one for the participants in their actual lives. The authors also obtained measures of conflict and control in the home, a measure of the extent to which the siblings shared activities, and measures of the parents' social class and education.

Results. Television violence viewing did not correlate significantly with aggression for either males or females. The members of the same-sex pairs were quite similar in terms of viewing violence and aggression;

the opposite-sex pairs were similar only in terms of viewing. The major finding was that both within and between families, the strongest correlations with aggression were with aggression consequences for the self and identification with aggression.

Discussion. The authors interpret their results mainly as indicating that individual differences play a major role in determining aggressive behaviour. They base this on several findings. First, television violence viewing was unrelated to aggression, whereas identification and consequences to self were strongly related. They explain this pattern by saying that programs are watched for many reasons, not just their violent content, so the relationship between program choices and aggression would be reduced. Of course, this assumes that it is the choice of program that matters rather than a direct effect of its content, but they do not make quite that point. They say also that identification captures the individual's reactions to violence and that these may be what matter. Their most interesting discussion concerns the strong correlation between aggression and consequences to self, and the lack of a correlation between aggression and consequences to hero. On this, they comment that adolescents should have 'little trouble distinguishing the real consequences of their own aggression ... from the unrealistic consequences for program heroes, which were almost uniformly positive. This suggests that the influence of television viewing may be relatively limited precisely because its content is fictional.'

Conclusions. This study provides no evidence in favour of the causal hypothesis and a considerable amount of evidence against it. However, this is quite a limited study. The sample is small, the measures are problematic, and all the data are based on self-reports. Of even greater importance, the subjects were all adolescents and we would expect the effect of television violence to be strongest among younger children. So, the findings should probably not be given much weight.

On the other hand, this is one more study that gets results that do not support the causal hypothesis. Moreover, although we would expect the effects of television violence to be stronger among younger children, many of the experimental studies have involved adolescents and even older subjects. As with the previous study, the lack of effect of television violence viewing in this study casts doubt on how those experiments have been interpreted. The results of both of these studies suggest that rather than a direct effect of television violence (due to modelling or learning) as proposed by those who favour the causal hypothesis, the effects in those experiments may be due to other mechanisms, such as experimenter demand or arousal. Finally, the present results provide one more piece of evidence that the relationship between television violence and aggression may be due to some other factor, such as an aggressive personality, that is related to both of them.

Summary and Conclusions

These five studies employed somewhat different methodologies than the others I have reviewed. Belson conducted a typical survey but employed unusual statistical analyses to demonstrate causality. Kruttschnitt and colleagues compared known criminals with noncriminals to see if they differed in their exposure to violent media when they were children. Messner looked at the relationship in American metropolitan areas between viewing of violent television programs and the crime rates in those areas. The other two studies obtained data on siblings and attempted to determine which factors caused the participants to be aggressive. In my opinion the Messner study is quite important, although it is almost never cited by anyone reviewing the research in this area. The other studies contribute less to our understanding of the issues, although they are innovative.

These studies provided no evidence to support the view that exposure to media violence causes aggression. In fact, almost without exception the results were inconsistent with or directly contradicted the causal hypothesis. I believe that taken together they provide evidence against it. The results of the Messner study in particular should be considered quite strong evidence against it.

9

Desensitization: Does Exposure to Media Violence Reduce Responsiveness to Subsequent Media Violence and/or Real Violence?

Most of the research on the effects of exposure to violent media has focused on the possibility that it causes aggression or crime. A somewhat different but related idea, which I shall call the desensitization hypothesis, is that exposure to media violence causes people to become callous or indifferent to violence. The notion is that seeing acts of violence on television or in the movies makes them seem commonplace. Someone who has not seen violence in the media will presumably be shocked and upset at witnessing an act of violence. In contrast, so the argument goes, someone who has seen hundreds or thousands of murders and fights on television is likely to be unimpressed by an act of violence and thus less shocked and upset.

Although it has received little attention in the way of research, the desensitization hypothesis deals with an effect that is potentially extremely important. When people see a real act of violence, we hope they will respond with concern and do what they can to stop it. We want them to feel that violence is bad, that people should not commit violence, and that they themselves should never be violent. Most North Americans have witnessed few if any acts of real violence and have not had a chance to become desensitized to it. In contrast, they have witnessed a great many acts of violence in the media. If exposure to this media violence causes them to be less concerned about real violence, this would be almost as serious as if it caused them to commit violence themselves.

In considering the desensitization hypothesis, it is essential to distinguish it from what might be called an habituation effect, which is reduced responsiveness to additional portrayals of violence in the media. It is possible that people who have seen violent scenes in a movie or on television are less sensitive to other such scenes in the media. Exposure to media violence may cause people to become less impressed by, excited by, and surprised by, and generally less responsive to, subsequent media violence. Someone who has never seen a murder or a beating or a fistfight on television or film might respond more strongly to the portrayal of one than someone who has seen many of them. The more you see it, the less impact additional exposure to it has. Similarly, a thrilling chase scene is less exciting after you have just seen another thrilling chase scene. And wonderful scenery, while still enjoyable, produces less wonder after you have viewed a lot of wonderful scenery. The same is probably true of any kind of content in the media. This effect, which concerns only reactions to other media portrayals, is not the same as desensitization to real-world violence.

The desensitization hypothesis refers to reduced responsiveness to actual violence caused by exposure to media violence. Desensitization to real violence would have enormous implications. People who are unconcerned or less concerned about actual violence are less likely to intervene when they witness aggression, less likely to take action to prevent aggression, and perhaps more likely to engage in aggression themselves (although that is less clear and is, in any case, dealt with more directly by the other research). In many recent discussions of the effects of media violence, the possibility of desensitization to violence has been mentioned almost as often as the possibility of increased aggression by viewers. In these discussions, desensitization is often taken as a proven phenomenon. So it is important to consider what the research shows.

Although the desensitization hypothesis has been around for many years, surprisingly little relevant research has been published. In this review I have considered the few studies that were conducted primarily to assess the hypothesis, as well as any other studies I could find that contain some data that pertain to it.

Drabman and Thomas (1974a, 1974b, 1975, 1976)

Drabman and Thomas conducted the first experiments that attempted to demonstrate the desensitization effect. Although their findings were published in several different articles, I will describe and comment on them together since they are very similar. As far as I can tell, Drabman and Thomas conducted three experiments on this issue, with two groups in one of them.

Method. The design was to expose some children to a violent film and others to a non-violent film (or in one study to no film). Experiment 1 used as the violent program an eight-minute western featuring Hopalong Cassidy and containing violence of various kinds, and the control group was not shown a film. Experiments 2 and 3 used a fifteen-minute excerpt from 'Mannix,' a detective program with many acts of violence, as the violent program, and a fifteen-minute excerpt of a baseball game as the non-violent program. (Note that I am assuming that experiment 3 used the 'Mannix' excerpt – the article states only that it was a fifteen-minute segment from a detective series.) The children then watched a television set, which they were told was monitoring two younger children in another room. A tape played on the set showing the other children first playing together nicely, but then getting into more and more serious conflict until they began to fight. The children in the study were told to watch the monitor and get help if they saw the kids getting into trouble. The measure was whether the children went to get help and the latency of getting help.

The subjects in experiment 1 were twenty-two boys and twenty-two girls from the third and fourth grades; in experiment 2 they were forty first-grade and forty third-grade children evenly divided into males and females; and in experiment 3 they were twenty boys and twenty girls from the fifth grade.

Results. In experiment 1 almost all the children went to get help. However, significantly more of those in the violent film group than in the no-film group waited until the children were actually fighting. Also, those in the film group responded significantly less quickly overall than those in the no-film group. The median latencies for the boys were 104 vs 63 seconds for the film and no-film groups; for the girls the comparable figures were 119 and 75 seconds.

In experiment 2, the third-graders who saw the violent film were significantly less likely to get help and significantly slower to respond (145 seconds vs 88 seconds) than those who saw the baseball program. Among first-graders, there were no significant effects of type of film. In fact, those who saw the violent film responded slightly faster than those who saw the baseball excerpt (146 seconds vs 162 seconds).

In experiment 3, those who saw the violent program responded significantly less quickly than those who saw the baseball program (for boys 136 vs 75; for girls 137 vs 107).

Thus, three of the four groups of subjects responded more slowly after watching a violent program; one showed the opposite effect, though not significantly. The significant effects were not large, averaging a little more than half a minute. Nevertheless, taken at face value, these three experiments provide fairly consistent evidence in favour of the desensitization hypothesis.

Discussion. The authors interpret the result as indicating that watching the violent movie made the children less sensitive to actual aggression. This is a possible interpretation, but there are others. In the first place, it seems implausible that watching a brief clip of 'Hopalong Cassidy' or 'Mannix' made the children insensitive to violence in the real world. Given the average level of exposure to television and to westerns and detective programs on television, it is highly likely that all or most of these children had watched many westerns and lots of violent programs in their lives. It is difficult to understand why watching one more relatively mild and brief program should have had any substantial effect on their sensitivity to real violence.

The same point can be made regarding laboratory experiments on television violence and aggression. Why should one more violent film affect the aggression of people who have presumably seen hundreds if not thousands of similar programs? But in that context, at least one can imagine exposure to a violent program triggering an aggressive impulse or aggressive act. It is more difficult to imagine exposure to a violent film (after a great many such exposures in the past) having a noticeable effect on reactions to acts of violence. If exposure to years of violent television has made children insensitive to real-life violence, it makes no sense for this to be affected by just one more exposure. Moreover, if there has been this desensitization effect over the years, it does not seem to have affected the children in these studies, almost all of whom on observing fighting went to get help within a minute or two.

Experimenter demand offers a plausible alternative explanation of the effect. Perhaps the experimenter has, in a sense, told some of the children that violence is not a big deal or at least that it is acceptable. Some of them are shown a violent program and are given no explanation for it. A reasonable inference for the children to draw is that the experimenter likes this program and approves of or accepts its contents – otherwise why show it to them? Perhaps they even conclude that the experimenter was defining what he meant by violence, and was setting the standard quite high. When they then observe some arguing, they perceive it in terms set by the experimenter – namely, that it is not very serious. When it does get serious, they get help. In contrast, those in the baseball or no-film condition do not have any reason to believe that the experimenter accepts a certain amount of violence, and do not have aggression defined for them. Without this context, the arguing seems more serious, and they are more likely to respond to it. This explanation is consistent with the fact that the subjects almost all respond quite quickly once the situation gets serious, even though they have presumably seen a great deal of violence on television. In other words, they have not been desensitized to violence by either their habitual viewing of television or by the brief exposure in the experiment.

These two interpretations – desensitization and experimenter-defined context – may seem similar, but they are worlds apart. The former assumes that a brief exposure to a familiar type of program can actually change the child's standard of serious aggression or sensitivity to aggression; the latter assumes only that in an unfamiliar situation, the child's responses are determined in part by the adult who is in charge. If the latter interpretation is correct, there is no reason to believe that exposing these children to the western would affect their sensitivity to violence once the experiment is over.

Another explanation that others have suggested is that the effect was due to the degree to which the children were distracted. There was no serious attempt to equate the violent programs with the non-violent one, and in one of the experiments the control group saw no program at all. It is likely that the violent programs were more enjoyable and almost certainly more exciting and arousing that the other programs. This could have caused the subjects who were shown the violent programs to be more distracted and to pay less attention to the television set than the others. Even a slight distraction could have produced the difference in latency, which was on average considerably less than a minute.

Conclusion. The results of these studies are generally consistent with what would be expected from the desensitization hypothesis. However, the results are rather weak, the number of subjects is very small, and other explanations of the effect are plausible.

Horton and Santogrossi (1978)

Horton was one of the authors of the earlier study by Thomas and colleagues. Horton and Santogrossi attempted to replicate the Drabman and Thomas finding of a desensitization effect. The study was designed also to investigate the effects of adult commentary on reducing the effect of the violent film.

The subjects were thirty-two second to third grade boys. They watched a violent or non-violent film. During the violent film, an adult made anti-aggressive, non-aggressive, or neutral comments. Then, as in the previous studies, all the subjects watched a television set that was supposedly monitoring two young children who were shown getting into a fight.

Results. The boys were faster to seek help when the adult had made either anti-aggressive or non-aggressive comments than when the adult had made neutral comments. However, those who watched the non-violent film did not differ from those who watched the violent film in speed of getting help. That is, there was no desensitization effect.

Discussion. The authors explain the lack of effect as being due to the adult commentary confusing or distracting the boys and thus reducing the impact of the violent film. They also note that their violent film may have been less violent than the ones used in the earlier research. Both explanations are possible, and there is no way to evaluate them.

Conclusion. Although there may well be a reasonable explanation for the lack of effect, the fact remains that this study, which was conducted by one of the authors involved in the earlier research, did not replicate the results of that research. It found no desensitization effect. Whatever the reason for this failure, it casts doubt on the strength and reliability of the earlier findings.

Molitor and Hirsch (1994)

This study also was meant to be a replication of Drabman and Thomas. The design was identical, and the 'real life' tape was very similar. Children watched scenes from either *The Karate Kid* or *16 Days of Glory*, a documentary about the 1984 Olympic games. They then all saw a tape of children getting into a fight. The subjects were forty-two fourth and fifth grade children, with an equal number of boys and girls.

Results. All but one child went to get help. Those who had watched the violent film were somewhat slower to seek help, but the effect was not significant ($p = .08$).

Discussion. The result was in the same direction as the original results but was considerably weaker. The median difference in response times between the two conditions was less than twenty seconds. This was not significant by the usual standards, using a non-parametric test. Although the authors interpret the results as a replication, one could as easily interpret it as a failure to replicate. In any case, the slight difference between the conditions could easily have been caused by equally slight differences in distraction caused by the differences between the films; or by the message conveyed by the showing of the films regarding the acceptability of aggressive behaviour.

Conclusion. The result can be considered a failure to replicate or a marginally significant replication. In either case, instead of strengthening the original finding, it weakens it.

Woodfield (1988)

As far as I can discover, this study was presented at a conference and has not been published in a journal. I include it here only because it was discussed by Molitor and Hirsch and is directly relevant. This description is based entirely on their description.

According to Molitor and Hirsch, this was one more attempt to replicate the Drabman and Thomas studies. It used an excerpt from *The Karate Kid* and a different film of 'real life' violence. The study did not obtain statistically significant differences in responding between those who had watched the violent and non-violent films.

Woodfield explained the lack of effect as being due to children being exposed to so much violence on television that the 'additional increment represented by the truncated *Karate Kid* material just did not affect them' (in Molitor and Hirsch, 1994:194). Molitor and Hirsch suggest that the failure might have been because the film of the 'real life' violence was not believable and was too short.

Conclusion. I cannot evaluate the study or the possible explanations for the lack of effect. Its only significance for our purposes is that it failed to replicate the earlier studies and showed no desensitization effect.

Linz, Donnerstein, and Penrod (1988)

This study differed from the previous ones in many ways. It involved undergraduates, not children; it used full-length films watched outside the laboratory, not brief excerpts seen in the laboratory; the violent films contained strong sexual elements, not just violence; and the measure was reactions to a legal case, not the time it took to respond to scenes of children fighting. However, the authors made the same predictions – namely that watching the violent films would produce desensitization to real violence. The focus was on sexual violence both in the films and in the dependent measure. The idea was that male undergraduates who watched films that contained violence in the context of erotic scenes would be less sensitive to the crime of rape.

There were three types of films. Some subjects watched R-rated violent films that depicted mainly violence against women. Although the violence was not itself sexual, it typically occurred in the context of mildly erotic scenes. Films like these have sometimes been referred to as 'slasher' films. Other subjects watched R-rated non-violent films involving the sexual exploits and activities of teenagers. A third group watched X-rated, non-violent, sexually explicit films. Although the paper does not discuss this, the first two types of films were extremely popular during the period in question and included some well-known films such as *Friday the 13th* (type 1) and *Porky's* (type 2). Films of the third type were not shown commercially. It should be noted also that of the subjects originally asked to participate in the study, only a handful refused when they were given detailed information about the films they would be viewing. The subjects viewed either two or five films, one every other day.

After viewing all of the films in their condition, they were informed that the last film they were supposed to view had not arrived. They were then asked to participate in another study. They sat in a courtroom at the Law School and watched a videotaped trial involving the alleged rape of a woman during a fraternity party. Then they responded to a variety of questions about the trial.

Results. Much of the paper is devoted to how the films affected the subjects emotionally, and how they responded after watching more than one film. This is not our main concern, but it is worth noting that regardless of the type of film, subjects responded less strongly to the second film and to subsequent films than to the first one. This was especially true of the slasher (violent) films. Generally, the declines occurred after even one film, and did not require all five films. In fact, for those shown the violent films the decline in self-rated depression was actually greater after fewer films than after more films. Whatever the explanation, there is some indication that the effect on mood was less once they had seen even one film of the type.

In terms of their reactions to the trial, the film conditions had only small effects on any of the measures. There was some tendency for those who had viewed the violent films to score lower on victim sympathy and rape empathy scales. However, there were no effects on any of the other variables, including verdicts, rape myth acceptance, victim responsibility, and sentence. In other words, no matter how many films they watched, there was no general effect on their reactions to the trial; and there was no indication at all that what slight effects did occur were greater after more films.

Discussion. There is only a hint of evidence that exposure to the violent films produced desensitization to the victim of rape, and none at all that exposure to more films produced more such desensitization. If there really were a change in attitudes toward women or toward sexual violence or toward rape, one would expect (as the authors did) effects on reactions to the trial. That no such effects occurred is evidence against a negative effect of exposure to any of the films. Moreover, the fact that those exposed to five violent films did not differ from those exposed to two is quite strong evidence against the notion that whatever slight effects occurred were due to desensitization.

Conclusion. The study provides little or no evidence that exposure causes desensitization to actual violence.

Goldstein and Colleagues (1976)

This study was conducted to test the causal hypothesis, but I believe its main relevance is to the desensitization hypothesis. The study looked at men's reactions to violent crime before and after exposure to various kinds of films. The study was conducted in four countries: Canada, England, Italy, and the United States. Adult men were approached either while they were waiting to enter a movie theatre or just after leaving the theatre. The films were either aggressive, or sexual, or neither. The men were asked what they thought the minimum sentence should be for people convicted of assault and battery, rape, robbery, and murder.

Results. There was some tendency for the severity of the sentences to increase after aggressive movies, to decrease after neutral movies, and not to change after sexual movies. However, the only effect that was significant was for the crime of murder – the effects for the other crimes did not even approach significance. For murder, sentences increased after both aggressive and sexual movies. The increase was greater after aggressive movies than after sexual movies, but this difference was not significant.

Discussion. The authors interpret their results in terms of aggressiveness, considering longer sentences as more aggressive. This interpretation of the measure seems implausible. I do not think that length of sentence is a measure of aggressiveness, nor do I think that giving a longer sentence is being more aggressive. So I did not include this study in my review of the research on the causal hypothesis.

In my view, the significance of this finding has to do with desensitization rather than with aggression. The results show that after aggressive movies, men are no less concerned about crime than before them. For three crimes, the men choose just as severe sentences after seeing films as they did before; and for murder, they choose longer sentences. Not one result in any country for any crime indicates that the men were less concerned – were desensitized – to crime or to violence after seeing an aggressive film. The one significant change in their attitudes was in the other direction. Admittedly, choosing a minimum sentence for a crime is not a direct measure of how upset they would be if they actually witnessed a crime, and it is not precisely the same as measuring how upset they would be if they heard or read about a crime. But it can reasonably be interpreted as a measure of how much they care about these crimes and how serious they think they are. If they were desensitized, they might be less bothered by the idea of the crimes and would presumably be more likely to give less severe sentences. Indeed, that was one of the predictions made by Linz and colleagues in their study. They argued that exposure to violent films would desensitize men to the crime of rape and that they would therefore give less severe sentences to someone who had committed rape. They did not find that in their study, and neither did Goldstein and colleagues. Rather, the one effect in the Goldstein study was in the opposite direction from the one predicted by the desensitization hypothesis – an increase in the severity of sentences for murder, not a decrease.

Conclusion. Men who saw a violent film chose no less severe sentences for three crimes and somewhat more severe sentences for the crime of murder than men who saw a neutral film. This result does not support the desensitization hypothesis and instead constitutes evidence against it.

Belson (1978)

As described in the previous chapter, this was a large survey study of a representative sample of teenage boys in London. A great deal of information was collected, most of it dealing with the relationship between exposure to violence in the media and aggression. But in addition Belson was very interested in the idea that exposure to violence leads to desensitization. With this in mind, he designed the study to collect information that would be relevant to this hypothesis and provide a test of it. Belson predicted that exposure to violence in the media would lead to desensitization toward violent behaviour, and he thought this would be true of all media. Exposure to violence on television, in the movies, and in comic books, and exposure to newspapers, were all expected to produce this effect.

The idea was that high exposure would 'harden' the boys and make them more callous when they were confronted with both 'near' and 'distant' violence. 'Near' violence was conceptualized as violence such as occurs in the home, on the street, and in areas that boys frequent. It was the kind of violence they might experience – as witness, victim, or perpetrator – in their daily lives. 'Distant' violence was conceptualized as violence experienced only indirectly through the media, and that would not ordinarily be part of their daily lives.

Method. Callousness toward near violence was tested by showing the boys pictures of the following: a boy about to trip a man who was walking with a cane, a man beating up a woman, a boy being attacked by a gang in an alley, a youth cutting the face of another youth with a broken bottle, a boy being held down while another boy kicks him, and a man flogging a dog. Callousness toward distant violence was tested by showing the boys pictures of the following: plane crash wreckage with a caption saying that seventy-two people had died, police activity under a headline about attempts to kill a witness, a ship on fire with a caption saying that eighty-four were trapped, a picture of Vietnamese children running from a bombed village, Bangladeshi troops bayoneting people, and a girl in Northern Ireland tied to a pole with her head shorn and tarred under a caption about IRA revenge. Of the six pictures for each type of violence, each boy was shown three.

The procedure was designed to obtain the boys' spontaneous responses to the pictures. For example, a boy was shown the picture of the boy tripping the man and asked to study it and then to read aloud the following: 'You are walking down the street when you happen to see a boy you don't know about to trip an old man who is walking with a cane.' The boy was then asked to tell the interviewer what he saw in the picture. Finally, the boy was shown twelve statements (one at a time) that described possible reactions to the event, and was asked whether each statement described how he would feel, or did not describe how he would feel, or whether he didn't know how he would feel. Two examples of the statements are: 'I would try and find a policemen or a teacher or an adult,' and 'This sort of thing happens all the time; I might not take any notice of it.' Other statements were used for the 'distant' events. Each statement was scored by an independent group in terms of the degree of callousness it indicated. The boy's total callousness score was based on the scores of those questions he agreed with.

Results. There was no support for the desensitization hypothesis for either near or distant violence or for exposure to any of the media. In terms of their reactions to violence, the boys who were exposed to a lot of violent television or violent movies or violent comic books or newspapers did not differ from those who were less exposed. Despite the many possible comparisons between the high and low exposure boys, there was not a hint of a difference in terms of their reactions to the events. As summarized by the author: 'The present body of evidence does not support the view that high exposure to television violence increases boys' callousness to either "near" or "distant" violence' (477).

Discussion. Several considerations are relevant in judging how much weight to give this result. It is important to remember that the boys did not actually witness an event or respond to one. They were shown hypothetical events and then asked how they thought they would respond to them. This was done with great care and attention to detail, but it was still hypothetical rather than real. We have no way of knowing whether the boys' responses were accurate reflections of how they would have responded to witnessing an actual violent event or to reading about an actual violent event. So we should interpret the results with some caution.

On the other hand, the other results from this study indicate that the measures have some validity. Generally, boys who described themselves as high in exposure to media violence also described themselves as high in violent acts. This makes sense and suggests that the boys were responding consistently. Moreover, at least some of the boys were willing to describe themselves as quite violent and as watching a lot of violent television. One would imagine that a boy who said he engaged in violent acts himself would have little difficulty saying he was not bothered when he witnessed such acts by others. Also, there were reasonable relationships between the measure of callousness and other factors in the boys' lives. For example, older boys were more callous than younger ones; boys who were often truant from school were more callous than those who were not truant; boys who did not enjoy school were more callous than those who did; and those who had stolen sweets were more callous than those who had not. Thus, the absence of a relationship between exposure and callousness was probably not due to the boys trying to present themselves as more caring than they were, or to a total lack of validity of the measures.

For present purposes, the main limitation of this study is that the measures of callousness were based on self-reports rather than actual behaviour. Having said that, this was a large-scale survey with a representative sample of teenage boys, the measures were carefully constructed and were made with considerable attention to detail, and the rest of the results fell into a logical pattern.

Conclusion. The results offer not the slightest support for the desensitization hypothesis but rather contradict it. I conclude that this study provides the strongest evidence available against the hypothesis, and I would give the results considerable weight.

Other Relevant Results

In Feshbach and Singer (1971), various measures of attitudes toward aggression were obtained throughout the course of the study. The results were complex and differed for different measures and schools. But, overall, boys who were allowed to watch only non-violent programs tended to develop more favourable attitudes and values toward aggression than boys exposed to violent programs. There may have been other reasons for this, such as the boys in the non-violent condition being frustrated because they could not watch their favourite shows. Nevertheless, this finding is the opposite of what would be expected from the desensitization hypothesis. It certainly provides no support for it and could be considered to contradict it.

In some of the studies described by Schramm (1961), a measure was taken called 'aggression anxiety.' It was supposed to measure the tendency to avoid aggression or to be repelled or upset at aggressive behaviour. The only relevant result using this measure concerns a difference between Teletown (the town with television) and Radiotown (the one without television). On this measure, Teletown scored higher. That is, those who had television in their homes were more likely to avoid and to be upset by aggressive behaviour. This measure may not be identical to a measure of desensitization, but it is similar to it. The result is the opposite of what would be predicted by the desensitization hypothesis.

Hartnagel and colleagues (1975) surveyed a large number of junior and senior high school students. Although the study focused on the relationship between exposure to violent television and aggression, the students were also asked questions regarding their attitudes toward violence – specifically, their approval of it. The correlations between exposure to violent media and these measures of approval were essentially zero. Approval of violence is not quite the same as desensitization to violence, but the two are fairly similar. People who were desensitized to violence would presumably be more accepting of it. So the lack of appreciable correlations between exposure to violence and these measures of approval of violence is inconsistent with the desensitization hypothesis and to some extent contradicts it.

Summary

There are six very similar laboratory studies that are relevant to the desensitization hypothesis. Using almost identical methods and materials, they tested whether children who had watched a brief excerpt from a movie containing violence would respond less quickly to a real violent scene than would children who had not seen a violent movie. In the original set of three studies, three groups showed the predicted effect, and one group showed a non-significant effect in the opposite direction. All of the research done by other experimenters failed to find the predicted effect. Molitor and Hirsch found a non-significant effect in the predicted direction; the other two attempts found no significant difference in response times between those who had seen a violent program and those who had seen a non-violent one. When we consider that the total number of subjects in all of these experiments was very small, and take into account that the original work was not replicated, these experimental findings provide at most weak evidence for desensitization.

Other studies provide evidence against the idea that exposure to media violence causes desensitization to real violence. Linz and colleagues found only very weak evidence that exposure to films containing sex and violence made people less responsive or less empathic toward a victim of rape and no evidence that such exposure actually affected their reactions to a rape trial. Similarly, Goldstein and colleagues found that after seeing an aggressive movie, men showed no indication that they were less concerned about violent crime. In fact, interviewed immediately after leaving the movie and therefore right after being exposed to media violence, they were if anything more concerned about murder and more punitive toward those who commit it. This was a very large sample of men in four different countries, and there was not a hint of any desensitization.

The Belson study (1978) is of considerable importance. With a very large, representative sample, Belson reported no correlation between exposure to violent media and callousness toward either near or distant violence. If the boys who had been exposed to a lot of media violence had been desensitized, presumably this would have shown up. That there was no such effect is strong evidence against desensitization in the real world.

Hartnagel and colleagues, also with a large sample, found no correlations between exposure to violent television and approval of violence. When Schramm (1961) compared towns with and without television, those with television scored higher on aggression anxiety, a measure of being upset by or repelled by violence. And Feshbach and Singer (1971) found that boys who watched almost no violent television for several weeks became more favourable toward aggression compared to boys who watched only violent television.

Clearly, the only support for the desensitization effect was in the three experiments conducted by Drabman and Thomas. The results were not entirely consistent, and the effects failed to replicate in three studies done by other experimenters. Moreover, even if the laboratory effects were consistent, they would not necessarily demonstrate desensitization. In the first place, an explanation in terms of desensitization is quite implausible. It makes little sense that children who had been exposed to a great deal of violent television would become insensitive or even less sensitive to violence because they were exposed to one more brief violent program. In fact, the data show that the children were not insensitive. Almost all of them – including those exposed to the violent program – went for help as soon as they witnessed fighting.

In contrast, both distraction and experimenter demand are plausible explanations. The violent film could have caused the subjects to think the experimenter was implicitly approving of a certain degree of violence; this would have made them go for help only after the conflict escalated to the point of fighting, thus producing the slight delay that was found. Alternatively or in addition, the violent film could have caused the children to be distracted, because it was almost certainly more exciting and involving than no film or an excerpt from a baseball game. A slight distraction could have produced the small delay in going for help. Neither of these explanations would require that the subjects be generally insensitive to violence, so both are consistent with the rather fast responses of almost all of the subjects.

In any case, the important question is whether long-term exposure to violence in the media produces desensitization to real violence. The few studies that involved large numbers of subjects found no evidence of such an effect. The literature provides no evidence that people who are exposed to a lot of media violence are less sensitive to, care less about, or are less concerned about real violence than those who are exposed to less media violence.

In sum, there is little or no support for the desensitization hypothesis. Taken at its strongest, the research might provide some slight indication of short-term desensitization after watching violent programs, and provide evidence against any long-term effect of habitual viewing of violent programs. However, the evidence on both issues is quite limited. I believe that a more clearly justified conclusion is that there is no reason to believe in either a short- or long-term desensitization effect.

Habituation. It may be that repeated exposure to media violence causes habituation to further media violence. Cline and colleagues (1973) found some evidence that those with high exposure to television in their daily lives were less responsive physiologically to violent scenes on television than those with lower exposure to television. Thomas and colleagues (1977) reported somewhat contradictory results. Subjects with high exposure to violent television were less responsive to both violent and non-violent programs. But when they watched first a violent program and then 'real' aggression, those with high exposure to violent television were more (not less) responsive than those who generally saw less violent television.

In two experiments, Thomas and colleagues (1977) investigated the effect of viewing a short program containing violence on subsequent responsiveness to violence. In the first experiment, children who had first seen a violent program were less responsive (by GSR) to 'real' aggression than those who watched a non-violent program. In a second experiment, males who had watched the violent program were less responsive to a film of an actual riot, but females showed the opposite pattern. Linz and colleagues (1988) found some evidence that after exposure to one violent (or sexual) film, men were less responsive to exposure to subsequent films of the same kind. This result suggests a habituation effect. Yet there was no cumulative effect – that exposure to one film produced the same decrement as exposure to three. This is difficult to understand. If exposure is really causing habituation, more exposure should cause more of it. Or to put this more carefully, there should be a cumulative effect of exposure at least up to some point of maximum habituation.

All of these studies together involved very few subjects, so we cannot have much confidence in their results. Also, both the correlational and experimental results are inconsistent, with some showing habituation and some showing the opposite. Nevertheless, overall, this small body of research provides some evidence that exposure to violent media causes people to be less responsive to subsequent media violence.

Although the evidence is meager, this seems plausible. People who are exposed to almost any stimulus tend to get used to it (to habituate to it). Whatever response it produced when it was novel tends to decline with familiarity. To produce the same level of response, then, requires a stronger stimulus. A violent fight sequence that might have been quite arousing the first time it was viewed will be less arousing the second or tenth time; and violent scenes that are strongly arousing to someone unfamiliar with television may be unexceptional and not very arousing to someone who has watched television for years. The same would be true of scenes involving chases, sex, beautiful scenery, or almost anything else. So, I would not be surprised if future research demonstrated that heavy viewers of violence in the media were less aroused by violence in the media – less aroused than they once were, and less aroused than people who are less heavy viewers.

However, even if there is some habituation to media violence, there is no evidence that this carries over to responses to violence in the real world. As noted earlier, there is no evidence that heavy viewers of television are desensitized to real-life violence. In short, at the moment the evidence does not support the desensitization hypothesis – there is little or no evidence that exposure to media violence causes desensitization (lowered responsiveness) to real violence. Rather, what little evidence there is generally argues against the desensitization hypothesis.

10

Summary and Conclusions

This review has considered in detail a great deal of research on the effects of exposure to media violence. Each study was described, analyzed, criticized, and evaluated. The previous sections summarized the results of each type of research. Several conclusions seem to be warranted.

First, the survey research, combined with the longitudinal studies, provides fairly good evidence that exposure to media violence – or perhaps only preference for more violent programs – is related to aggressiveness. Those who are exposed to more violence in the media and/or who prefer more violence in the media tend to be more aggressive than those who are exposed to or prefer less violence. The evidence for this is not entirely consistent, and the size of the relationship varies greatly from study to study. Nevertheless, most of the studies do find a correlation, and its magnitude seems to be between .1 and .2, although conceivably it is as high as .3. This means that between 1 per cent and, at the very high end, 9 per cent of the variation in aggression is predicted by exposure to media violence. This is not a big effect – especially at the low end – but it *is* a relationship, and if it were as high as 9 per cent it would be a substantial one.

Of course, as explained in detail in this review, the existence of this relationship only raises the possibility that media violence causes aggression. There is a temptation to think that because there is a correlation, there must be a causal link. That is not correct. The correlation alone tells us nothing about causality: the relationship could be produced without any causal effect of media violence. All of the other research discussed in this review was designed to establish whether there is a causal link – whether exposure to violent media makes people more aggressive.

Second, the rest of the research does not demonstrate that exposure to media violence affects aggression. Some studies using each type of research have found some support for the causal connection, but far more have not found support. The largest group of studies are the laboratory experiments. Of these, 39 per cent found results that were consistent with the causal hypothesis, and 41 per cent obtained results that were not consistent with it and did not support it. Moreover, when studies that used questionable measures of aggression were eliminated, only 81 per cent of the remaining experiments supported the hypothesis, whereas 55 per cent did not and the rest produced mixed results. This is not a pattern of results that scientists expect when a hypothesis is correct, nor is it one that would cause them to accept the hypothesis.

There were some significant effects in the laboratory experiments; however, this should not be interpreted to mean that exposure to media violence does cause aggression but not always. The significant effects that did occur were probably due to factors other than the violent content of the programs used in the experiments. In particular, I suggest that the violent programs were almost always much more interesting and more arousing than the non-violent programs. Few of the experiments even tried to equate the two types of films, even though it should have been clear that this was a crucial problem that had to be solved. You cannot show one group a film of a prizefight and another group a film of canal boating and argue that the only difference between the two films is the amount of violence. Almost all the laboratory experiments suffered from this problem; this casts doubt on the interpretation of the results in terms of the amount of violence in the films.

The most obvious difference between the violent and non-violent films was that the former were usually more arousing and exciting. This presents a very serious problem, because it is well established that differences in arousal affect behaviour. People who are more aroused tend to perform any activity more strongly than those who are less aroused. Given a bag to punch, they will punch it harder; given something to squeeze, they will squeeze it harder; and given almost any activity, they will do more of it. In the experiments at hand, subjects were often given a doll to punch or a button to press or a dial to turn. If we knew nothing about the subjects except their level of arousal, we would certainly expect those who were more aroused to punch the doll, press the button, or turn the dial more than those who were less aroused. Since the violent film produced more arousal, that alone could explain the effects of the films.

Perhaps an even more important problem with the laboratory experiments is that almost all of them had strong demand factors that, in essence, gave the subjects permission to behave aggressively or even instructed them to behave aggressively. When people are brought into a laboratory, they are very sensitive to what the experimenter does. If he shows them a film, they will wonder why that film was chosen. If no good explanation is provided, they will assume that the experimenter has a reason. And if the film is a violent film, many if not most people will infer that the experimenter likes the film, or approves of violence, or wants them to behave aggressively. This inference will be strengthened when they are later given a chance to behave aggressively – not something they would ordinarily expect to do in a laboratory. Having drawn that inference, they will be more likely to behave aggressively (since that is apparently what the experimenter wants). In other words, simply because of demand pressures, subjects shown violent films are more likely to behave aggressively than those shown non-violent films.

Psychologists are well aware of the problem of demand factors and usually make great efforts to eliminate or at least minimize them in laboratory research. Yet for some reason, in this group of experiments very little effort was made to do so. As a result, demand factors alone could explain the differences in aggressiveness that sometimes occurred.

In sum, the laboratory experiments produced inconsistent results, with more of them being non-supportive than supportive. And the results that were obtained were, in my opinion, more likely due to factors other than the violence in the programs. In any case, I firmly believe that the laboratory experiments tell us little about how exposure to violence in the media affects people in the real world – which is presumably our main concern.

The field experiments were in some sense the strongest test of the causal hypothesis. They involved relatively long-term effects, and full-length movies or actual television programs rather than short excerpts. Also, they were conducted in more natural settings: the programs were viewed and the behaviours were observed in locations that were familiar to the subjects. Perhaps most important, they were experiments, so any significant effects would have causal implications. For all these reasons, the field experiments were the best hope of getting evidence to support the causal hypothesis.

The results were, in fact, even less supportive of the hypothesis than were the results of the laboratory experiments. Only three of eleven field experiments obtained even slightly supportive results – three of twenty-four if one counts all the separate experiments. Those who favour the causal hypothesis often cite the research by the Leyens/ Parke group as providing strong support. I agree that two of these studies (but not the third) produced results that are consistent with the hypothesis. However, as I discussed earlier, these studies suffered from having too few independent groups and from employing statistical procedures that were without question inappropriate (as admitted by Leyens). Yet even if these studies had produced strong, consistent results supporting the causal hypothesis, they would have been swamped by those that found either no effect of media violence on aggression, or a reverse effect, or a mixture of effects with most being inconsistent with the causal hypothesis. Moreover, the studies that obtained supportive results involved very small samples of subjects, whereas many of those that obtained non-supportive results had quite large samples. Even more so than with the laboratory experiments, this is an extremely discouraging pattern of results for the causal hypothesis.

The rest of the research related to the causal hypothesis is non-experimental. This means that regardless of the results, it could never provide terribly strong evidence that exposure to media violence causes aggression. Nevertheless, since the ideal experiment cannot be conducted, scientists can try to build a case for a causal effect using other methods. In this context, I consider longitudinal studies extremely important. They provide information relevant to two predictions from the causal hypothesis. First, they show whether the correlations between exposure to violent media and aggression change with age. If the causal hypothesis is correct, the correlations should probably increase as children get older. Even if this is not absolutely required by the hypothesis, there is little question that increasing correlations with age would be consistent with the hypothesis and provide some support for it. However, the longitudinal studies found no evidence for such a pattern. I consider this to be inconsistent with the hypothesis. In any case, it certainly does not support it.

An even more important aspect of these studies is that they provide evidence as to whether early exposure to media violence is associated with increased aggression at a later age after early aggression is held constant. The reasoning underlying this prediction and the statistical analyses have been discussed earlier. The basic point is that if children are equally aggressive at age eight but watch different amounts of media violence, those who watch more should become more aggressive than the others two or seven years later. As noted before, this spreading apart in terms of aggressiveness is the major prediction from the causal hypothesis. This prediction is tested with multiple regression analyses (or similar statistical analyses) that hold aggression constant at age eight and look at the remaining relationship between violence exposure at age eight and aggression at the later age. If this relationship is positive and significant, it is consistent with and to some extent supports the causal hypothesis. If it is not significant, it is inconsistent with the causal hypothesis.

As with all of this research, the results have been mixed. The supportive results were for males on one measure in the twenty-two-year study; from the cross-national study, for boys and girls in the Israeli city sample, and considerably weaker effects for boys and girls in Poland and for girls in the United States; and for boys and girls combined in the later phase of the nursery school study. Some of these results are open to serious criticisms, so they are less clear than they might appear. Moreover, both the twenty-two-year study and the cross-national study produced more non-supportive results than supportive ones. So considering only the results that are most consistent with the causal hypothesis, they are not impressive.

But even if one were to accept these supportive results entirely, there are many more studies that obtained results that are inconsistent with the causal hypothesis. The twenty-two-year study found no effect for girls or for boys on two other measures; the cross-national study found no effect for boys or girls in Australia, for boys or girls in the Netherlands, for boys or girls in Finland, for boys or girls in the Israeli kibbutz sample, or for boys in the United States. The nursery school study found no effect in the first phase. And none of the other studies found any support for the hypothesis. Although this body of research provides some supportive evidence, it obviously did not produce the kind of consistent support that would give one confidence in the hypothesis. Rather, the pattern of evidence generally fails to support the hypothesis.

Some studies compared communities that had television with those that did not and looked for differences in aggression. This research is perhaps the most discouraging for the causal hypothesis. One study reported an increase in aggression after television was introduced, but it is a flawed study, the results were inconsistent, and there are many possible explanations for the result. None of the other studies provided any evidence in favour of the causal hypothesis; in fact, they provided some quite strong evidence against it.

Finally, there was a small group of studies using a variety of methods. These studies offer no support at all for the causal hypothesis, and several of them provide quite convincing evidence against it.

It should be obvious from the individual reviews that the results of the research have been generally non-supportive of the causal hypothesis. Some studies of each type found results that could be considered as supporting the hypothesis, but more found results that did not support it. What should we make of this pattern of results?

Science depends on consistency. Before a theory or hypothesis can be considered correct, the research testing it must produce results that support it with great consistency. Ideally, every single study will support the hypothesis. More realistically – especially when dealing with complex hypotheses and situations – we would probably consider a hypothesis to be supported as long as the great majority of the studies support it. If 90 per cent of the studies obtain the results predicted by the hypothesis, we can be reasonably confident that the hypothesis is correct. We may wish to know why the others failed, but even if we cannot establish why, we will still accept the hypothesis. If the results are less consistent than that – if, say, only 70 per cent support the hypothesis and 30 per cent do not – we will be considerably less confident. We may feel that the hypothesis is probably correct, but we will have serious concerns about the failures. And if only 50 per cent support the hypothesis, we will be very unlikely to believe the hypothesis is correct. We may still think there is some slight truth to the hypothesis, but it will be clear that the effects are unreliable, probably very weak, and perhaps not there at all. In fact, if the results are this inconsistent, our focus may well shift to explaining why there were any positive results. We may then look for problems in the research that produced the effects even though the hypothesis is incorrect. If we still believe in the hypothesis despite the inconsistency and the lack of support, that belief is based on faith and hope rather than on the scientific results.

Turning to the research on media violence and aggression, it should be clear that not one type of research provided the kind of supportive evidence that is ordinarily required to support a hypothesis. Not one found 90 per cent supportive or 80 per cent or 70 per cent or even 50 per cent. In fact, regardless of the method used, fewer than half the studies found results that supported the hypothesis – sometimes considerably fewer than half. The results of this research have sometimes been described as overwhelmingly supportive of the causal hypothesis. That is not correct. Rather, the research is discouraging for the hypothesis, with most of the research not supporting it. I conclude that the scientific research does not support the hypothesis that exposure to violent media causes aggression.

Third, the small body of research on desensitization has tested two quite different effects. There is some evidence that exposure to media violence causes habituation and therefore reduced responsiveness to further media violence. The results are rather weak and inconclusive, but the effect may be real. Regarding the more important effect on actual violence, three small-scale studies found some support for this, but the effect failed to replicate and other studies did not support it. I conclude that there is little or no evidence for a desensitization effect and there is some evidence that directly contradicts it.

Where does this leave us? On the one hand, we have considerable justification for rejecting the hypotheses. If they were correct, we should expect to see a pattern of results that consistently support them. We do not get that pattern, so the hypotheses are almost certainly incorrect. On the other hand, those who continue to believe in them can argue that the research is flawed, or that one should not expect perfect consistency, or even that the existence of some supportive results shows that the hypotheses are correct. This is not very good science, but it cannot easily be rejected.

However, those who believe in the hypotheses cannot argue that the research provides overwhelming or even strong support for them. I hope it is clear that the research does not support either hypothesis. After so much research, with many of the studies being of very high quality, if the hypotheses were correct, I believe that we would have found the evidence to support them.

Accordingly, this comprehensive review of the scientific evidence leads to two clear conclusions. First, despite the way it has sometimes been described, the research does not provide overwhelming support for either the causal hypothesis or the desensitization hypothesis. On the contrary, the evidence for both hypotheses is weak and inconsistent, with more non-supportive results than supportive results. Second, following from the first conclusion, exposure to media violence does not cause aggression, or if it does the effects are so weak that they cannot be detected and must therefore be vanishingly small. I would not make such a strong statement about the desensitization hypothesis, because there has been too little relevant research. Instead I would conclude that it is probably not true, but the case is not yet closed.

If Not, Why Not

The purpose of this review was to discover what the scientific evidence showed regarding the hypothesis that exposure to media violence causes aggression. I hope it is clear that the evidence does not support this hypothesis. Indeed, the majority of the studies produced evidence that is inconsistent with or even contradicts the hypothesis. In addition, the evidence does not support the hypothesis that exposure to media violence makes people less sensitive to real world violence. Again, the majority of the studies are inconsistent with this hypothesis. Thus, those who believe in these hypotheses should not and cannot base their belief on the scientific evidence.

Those who favour the causal hypothesis have time and again compared this debate to the one about smoking and cancer. They say, correctly, that just as with smoking and cancer, no perfect experiment can be done and therefore you must rely on other kinds of evidence. And they say that just as with smoking and cancer, there is overwhelming evidence supporting the causal hypothesis but that despite the mass of evidence, some people have refused to accept that media violence causes aggression.

This is false. It is an insult to those who have studied the effect of tobacco on cancer. It is misleading to the point of being irresponsible and dishonest. I am not an expert on smoking research, but it is perfectly clear that it bears almost no relationship to the research on media violence. Mentioning them together reminds me of the joke in which Fred says to Frank, 'When I watch you play golf, it reminds me of Tiger Woods.' Frank, who loves golf and fancies himself better at it than he is, says 'Really, how come?' And Fred says, 'When I see you play golf, I always say to myself, he sure doesn't play anything like Tiger Woods.'

The laboratory research in the two fields is vastly different, with vastly different results. In the laboratory, animals exposed to smoke have developed cancers, and this has happened in virtually every experiment. The effects are dramatic, recognizable, and deadly; they are also consistent and replicable. In the laboratory, those exposed to media violence at most have been rated as somewhat more aggressive than those not exposed. Not one experiment has shown that exposure causes people to commit serious acts of violence. Most of the experiments do not involve real aggression, and none involve true violence. Moreover, the results are not consistent and not replicable. A majority of studies have failed to find any effects on aggression.

Outside the laboratory, research has found that people who smoke are much more likely to develop cancer than those who do not smoke. The effects are huge. The National Cancer Institute says that the risk of dying of lung cancer is twenty-two times higher for male smokers and twelve times higher for female smokers than for people who have never smoked. As mentioned earlier, Khuder (2001) found that smokers are thirty-eight times as likely as non-smokers to get certain kinds of lung cancer. In addition, the more people smoke, the higher their risk; the longer they smoke, the higher the risk; and if they stop smoking, the risk goes down. This dose–response relationship is crucial for the argument and is powerful evidence that smoking is the cause of the lung cancer. Research on media violence has shown nothing of the kind. The most favourable findings have been that those who watch a lot of media violence early in life have a slight tendency to be more aggressive later than those who watch less. The results have not been consistent, and more studies fail to find this than do find it. Not one study has shown that those who are exposed to more media violence are more likely to become criminals, to hurt anyone, to commit any violent crime or any serious aggressive act. And there is no dose–response relationship – there is not the slightest indication that watching media violence for more years leads to more aggression, or that ceasing to watch leads to a decrease in aggression.

In other words, the smoking–cancer effect has been supported by a wide variety of studies that have found strong, consistent evidence of the kind that scientists find very convincing. In contrast, the media violence–aggression effect has not been supported by a majority of studies, has never shown a strong effect, and does not have the kind of evidence or the kind of consistency that scientists demand. Thus, the comparison of the two bodies of research makes precisely the opposite point from the one proposed by the supporters of the causal hypothesis. Both effects, smoking and lung cancer, and media violence and aggression, are long-term and cannot be tested with a straightforward experiment; both effects can therefore be tested only by a combination of methods. There the similarity ends. The findings on smoking and cancer have been powerful, consistent, and replicable and have indi-

cated a clear dose–response relationship; the findings on media violence and aggression have been weak, inconsistent, and non-replicable
and have never indicated a clear dose–response relationship. The comparison demonstrates that it is possible to make a strong and convincing – indeed, overwhelming – case for an effect using good scientific
methods even without the perfect experiment. It has been done with
the effect of smoking on lung cancer; it could have been done with the
effect of media violence on aggression but it has not been done. The
case for the former effect has been made and is closed; the case for the
latter effect has not been made and is open only in the sense that some
may choose not to accept the disappointing findings.

I know that many people believe very strongly that media violence
causes aggression and that they do so notwithstanding what the scientific research has shown. Their beliefs may be bolstered to some extent
by their incorrect impression that the evidence supports them; but the
evidence is not of major concern to them. They are unlikely to change
their views just because the evidence is not consistent with them. In a
sense, this issue may be what a friend of mine calls 'data-proof.' As long
as the data seem to support a position, those who hold it refer to the
data and seem to rely on it; but once the data no longer support it, those
who hold it simply stop referring to the data and maintain their beliefs.

Perhaps those who hold these views, though they are impervious to
the fact that the evidence does not support them, might be influenced
by softer, more intuitive arguments. Accordingly, although it is beyond
the scope of this review, and is not really part of the scientific argument,
let me try to offer some reasons why it makes sense that media violence
has no effect on aggression.

When I talk about the research with politicians (and others), they
compare media violence to advertising. Since advertising affects attitudes and behaviour, it seems obvious that violent programs should do
the same. One congressman noted that companies spend billions on
advertising. If television has no effect, why should they do this – are
they stupid? He asked whether he should stop paying for television
advertising when he campaigns.

There is no question that the media are very powerful in many ways.
It would be foolish to suggest otherwise. Advertising does work, and
political advertising can have an enormous impact on the outcome of
an election (although bad ads can hurt the candidate running them just
as good ads can help). There is, however, a vast difference between
advertising and programs or films. The difference is that ads have a

message – a clear, unmistakable message – which is to buy the product or vote for the candidate. The people who see an ad know its purpose; if they do not, if it is not absolutely clear, it is not a good ad and will probably have no effect. When people see an ad for a Ford, they receive the message that the Ford is a good car and that they should buy it. When they see an ad for a political candidate, they receive the message that he or she is a good candidate or that the opponent is a bad candidate. These ads may or may not contain information; if they do, the information may or may not be useful or truthful or convincing. But whatever the ad, whatever the product, the message cannot be missed – buy me, not the other product; vote for me, not the other candidate.

Films and television programs that contain violence are not designed to convey the message that violence is good or that people should engage in violent acts. They do not contain information that is likely to convince anyone of anything; they do not contain explicit messages in favour of aggression or violence. They are just entertainment. The programs are not meant to be persuasive, just popular. So it should not be surprising that they have no effect on people's aggressive behaviour or on their attitudes toward violence.

What about *implicit* messages? Though most people would agree that the media almost never deliver a message that explicitly encourages violence, some people argue that violence in the media carries the implicit message that violence is acceptable. When Batman punches the bad guy, perhaps the message is that one must resort to violence to solve problems. When the Roadrunner turns the tables on the Coyote and blows him up, perhaps children are being taught to use violence against their enemies rather than other means of settling disputes. When Bruce Willis or the police or the Power Rangers use violence against terrorists or criminals or evil monsters, perhaps the implicit message is that only violence will work and therefore you (the viewer) should also be violent. Or maybe the message is not so much that violence works as that violence is acceptable or even desirable. If all these nice, honest, good people are committing acts of violence, maybe this says to the viewer that this kind of behaviour is all right. These messages – that violence is the only way to settle disputes, that violence is acceptable – might influence attitudes and behaviours. If viewers who get these messages accept them, we can expect their own attitudes toward violence to become more positive, and that they will be likely to become violent themselves.

There are several responses to this idea. First, I do not think these programs carry the message that violence is the only way to settle disputes, or that violence is generally acceptable. To the extent they convey any messages about violence, those messages are quite different from these. One possible message is that when a bad person or a bad monster or a bad animal starts a fight or commits a crime or threatens you or those you love, those who are entrusted with protecting society may have to use violence in return. In the great majority of all films and television programs containing violence, all or most of the violence committed by the good guys is committed by police or crimefighters or others who are allowed to use violence. And they use violence only after it has been used by the bad guys; the good guys almost never (perhaps never) start the fight. While we would prefer a society without any violence, few of us would deny the police (and mythical protectors of society) the right to use violence when necessary. It would be nice if the police and other good guys could be shown trying a little harder to talk the bad guys out of the fight, convincing them to give up, and so on. Still, it is not realistic to expect many criminals, terrorists, monsters, and so on to be convinced by talk of this kind to give up their weapons and stop doing whatever bad stuff they are doing. The fact is that there is violence in our society and often it is dealt with by violence of some sort. I do not believe that those who watch these programs are getting the message that violence is the only way to deal with problems. If they get any message at all along these lines, it is that we should all be thankful that the good guys – those who are there to protect us – can also use violence when necessary. They are certainly not getting the message that they, the viewers, should engage in violence. So there is no reason to expect their behaviour to be affected.

A somewhat different concern of those who worry about the effects of media violence is that aggression is shown as effective. If so, viewers may come to believe this and may accordingly behave more aggressively themselves. The authors of the National Television Violence Study (NTVS) are especially adamant on this point. They assert that when violence is not punished – or even worse, when it is rewarded – it is especially likely to make viewers more aggressive. As we have seen, there is no scientific evidence to support this assertion. Despite that, it is repeated over and over as if it were a known fact. Scientific evidence of causation aside, the NTVS provides a highly useful picture of what occurs on television. It found that television programs often contain violent acts that are not punished immediately. However, the same study shows that bad characters in serious shows are almost always punished eventually. Although the authors of the study are concerned about the lack of immediate punishment, I think the viewers all know that punishment is coming. Much of the tension in the stories we watch on television comes from wondering when and how the bad guys will get punished, but there is no question that in almost every program, in almost every story, the bad people who start the violence will get what they have coming to them. One could argue that television presents an unrealistic picture in this respect: criminals on TV get caught and punished far more often than they do in the real world. So if viewers learn anything, if they get any message, it is that violence committed for a bad or illegal reason in a serious context will be punished.

The other possible message from most of the programs is that it is a bad idea, not a good one, to be the one who first uses violence. In almost every television program that has violence, and in most films, the person who starts the fight (the bad guy) eventually loses. The authors of the study are concerned that good characters are rarely punished after using violence. Naturally! They are allowed to use violence when it is necessary, so they should not get punished. When Batman punches a crook, should Batman get hurt? When Bruce Willis fights criminals, should Willis lose? When police officers get in a shoot-out with criminals, should the police get punished? Obviously not. In fact, to the extent that crime fighter shows have any message, it is not that police officers should get punished for using violence, but that it is dangerous to be a police officer or anyone who fights crime. This does not teach anyone that it is okay to use violence or that violence will be rewarded – if anything, it teaches the opposite.

Some have argued that the media glamorize violence. Certainly, some heroes are violent and glamorous. This is true of many of the comic book heroes (Batman, Superman, Power Rangers, Wonder Woman) and the non-cartoon versions of these characters. It is also true of some other characters, such as James Bond. But many violent heroes are anything but glamorous. Bruce Willis in *Die Hard*, most police officers in cop shows, and so on get dirty, are often hurt, and are typically shown doing their jobs, which are important but not at all glamorous. In fact, one theme that runs through many of the more realistic shows is that law enforcement people have tough, dangerous jobs and are not appreciated enough by the public or by politicians. Is there any evidence that the supposed glamour of these violent characters has caused more people to apply for jobs in law enforcement? I doubt it. So I do not accept that, in general, violence has been glamorized in the media. I agree that it is not made as awful and ugly as it really is, but not that it has been made especially attractive. Therefore, I am not surprised that children have not been influenced by the glamour of violence to engage in it.

I cannot prove that media violence carries no message or that it does not glamorize violence. But I ask those who believe it does to think seriously about whether the programs and films they know really urge people, explicitly or implicitly, to engage in violence; or suggest that violence is glamorous. A few films and programs may do this, but I think any reasonable view of the full range of programs would show that they do not encourage viewers to be violent themselves. They certainly do not directly try to sell violence the way ads for products try to sell those products. I cannot think of one television program that contains the explicit message that viewers should go out and commit violence.

One reason why some people are so convinced that media violence causes aggression is that they think they have seen it happen themselves. They know that children in schoolyards are imitating the Power Rangers and other television heroes who engage in martial arts. They see children watch a violent program and then get involved in fighting. Since they have witnessed it first-hand, they are totally convinced. At a congressional hearing, a congressman said he did not need any scientific evidence to prove that media violence causes aggression. The reason was that he had come home recently and been met at the door by his young son aiming a karate kick at him. Q.E.D. What more evidence does anyone need?

I understand the power of personal experience. However, it is important to step back and try to figure out what the experience means. The congressman's story is a perfect example. I did not get a chance to respond to him, but I would have said the following: Congressman, I assume that you and your son have a good relationship. I assume he did not harm you and that he did not mean to harm you. (If he meant to harm you, please get some professional help right away.) Congressman, your son was playing. He was not fighting; he did not hurt you; he was playing. He had probably seen someone on television doing karate kicks – or maybe he saw it in the schoolyard – and he was imitating them. Years ago, he might have pretended to punch you or to shoot you with a bow and arrow or with a gun. Would you have been as upset if he had put his fingers into the shape of a gun – as so many boys do – and said 'bang, bang'? Then I suppose you would have known he was playing, but it would have been the same thing. The precise behaviour is surely influenced by the media, but it is not aggression – it is play. You might not like that kind of play; you might prefer him to throw you a ball or do something really imaginative. If you want to complain that television does not foster imagination and creativity, you may have a point. But aggression? No.

Also, for those who have watched kids get into trouble after a violent program, maybe the effect is due entirely to the fact that they are excited. Violent programs tend to get kids aroused. When they are aroused, they engage in more active behaviour, and some of that may be aggressive. But it is the arousal that affects them, not the content of the show. Any show that aroused them would have had the same effect. There is even a study showing that kids are more aggressive after watching 'Sesame Street.' I can believe it. There is no aggression in the program. It is hard to imagine a more prosocial, educational, imaginative show. But it is a very active, lively, fast-paced show – that's one of the reasons children like it so much. If they are more aggressive after it, obviously it is not because of any aggressive content, but rather because of the arousal. Yes, children may be more aggressive after watching violent programs, but they may be equally aggressive after any action program or any program that is lively and exciting. You may prefer children to be quieter. I'm not so sure. I think it is probably good for them to get excited and aroused even if it sometimes leads to more trouble for the parents. Bored children can get into real trouble; interested, excited kids are probably better off in the long run. So don't blame media violence for increased action and sometimes increased aggression, unless you want to blame everything – movies, television programs, books, any arousing, exciting activity.

Another argument I hear is that since the advent of television, crime and aggression have increased. Supposedly the connection is obvious. I dealt with this at some length in my discussion of Centerwall's paper. The main point is that all sorts of things have changed since television was available, and these other changes are much more likely than television to have produced the increase in crime. I do not want to rehash these arguments, but I urge those who see a connection to keep in mind that there are explanations other than television violence. Let me add that both aggression and crime have been with us for a long time, since well before television and movies. There is no indication that in general, either aggressiveness or crime has increased since the invention of movies or television. Moreover, the homicide rates in the

United States and Canada have gone through many cycles. What people tend to focus on is that the rate of violent crime – for homicide in particular – increased sharply from about 1965 to 1980. That's true. But the rate then levelled off, and has been dropping sharply since around 1992. The rate is now back to about what it was in the early 1970s, not much above its low point in the 1960s. It is the increase that makes some people think it must be due to television, because the increase came soon after the introduction and spread of television. However, an almost identical pattern – a sharp increase followed by a sharper decrease – occurred in the early part of this century, long before there was any television. The increase then was certainly not due to television, but rather to social factors of various kinds. If that earlier increase occurred in the absence of television, why think that the later increase was due to television? It makes no sense.

Then there is the recent decrease in violent crime. All of the studies indicate that television and films have just as much violence as they used to, or more, and that the violence is more graphic than ever. Also, violent video games started to become available and popular in the early 1990s and are now a major element in many children's lives. And I suppose the lyrics in popular music, especially rap music, are much more violent than they have ever been. Yet despite the continuing media violence, and the new violence in video games and music, the rates for homicide and other violent crimes have dropped seven years in a row. If media violence caused the increase, how can one explain the decrease? A more likely explanation is that media violence did not cause either the increase or the decrease; both of these were caused by major social forces.

Finally, it is important to remember that the research I have reviewed dealt almost exclusively with the effects of fictional or fictionalized programs and films. There has been almost no systematic research on the effects of exposure to real violence or to media coverage of real violence. Some ingenious work by Phillips (1979, 1983) suggests that watching prizefights may increase homicides and that hearing about suicides may cause an increase in suicides. This work has been criticized on methodological grounds, and in my earlier review I found many of the details of the results implausible. Phillips has answered the criticisms, and he may be right that highly publicized violent events of these kinds cause an increase in similar events. Although there is no systematic evidence to support it, many people believe that media coverage of horrific crimes causes some people to imitate those crimes.

The killings at Columbine High School received an enormous amount of media attention and were followed by a number of similar attacks in other schools. It is possible that the later crimes were caused to some extent by coverage of the earlier one.

We do not know very much about the effects of coverage of actual violent events. However, I want to make it absolutely clear that this review does not deal with this issue. The lack of scientific support for the causal hypothesis relates entirely to fictional material. Indeed, I think it is likely that real violence and the coverage of real violence do affect aggression and crime. Children may imitate violence they observe directly. Both children and adults may be influenced by their knowledge that their society or their neighbourhood has a lot of violence. Moreover, it seems likely that repeated exposure to real violence, either directly or in the media, causes desensitization to subsequent real violence. I believe that when there is a murder on the front page of the newspaper every day or as the lead story on the television news every day, people are less shocked than when murders are rare events. Thus, both the causal hypothesis and the desensitization hypothesis may be correct with respect to real violence or media coverage of real violence, and perhaps that is what people should be worrying about.

Let me end by acknowledging again that to many people it seems self-evident that media violence causes aggression. I think I have shown in this comprehensive, detailed review that the scientific evidence does not support that view. Perhaps some of the arguments in this chapter will make it seems less obvious, and people will be willing to change their views. In any case, I hope that neither organizations nor individuals will ever again say that the evidence for a causal effect of media violence is overwhelming or that the case is closed. Perhaps people will even begin to accept the clear fact that the evidence does not support the notion that exposure to media violence causes aggression or desensitization to aggression.

References

Albert, R.S. (1957). The role of mass media and the effect of aggressive film content upon children's aggressive responses and identification choices. *Genetic Psychology Monographs, 55,* 221–283.

Anderson, C.A. (1997). Effects of violent movies and trait hostility on hostile feelings and aggressive thoughts. *Aggressive Behavior, 23,* 163–178.

Andison, F.S. (1977). TV violence and viewer aggression: A cumulation of study results. *Public Opinion Quarterly, 41,* 314–331.

Atkin, C. (1983). Effects of realistic TV violence vs. fictional violence on aggression. *Journalism Quarterly, 60,* 615–621.

Atkins, A., Hilton, I., Neigher, W., & Bahr, A. (1972). Anger, fight, fantasy, and catharsis. *Proceedings of the American Psychological Association, 7,* 241–242.

Bandura, A. (1965). Influence of models' reinforcement contingencies on the acquisition of imitative responses. *Journal of Personality and Social Psychology, 1,* 589–595.

Bandura, A., Ross, D., & Ross, S.A. (1961). Transmission of aggression through imitation of aggressive models. *Journal of Abnormal and Social Psychology, 63,* 575–582.

Bandura, A., Ross, D., & Ross, S.A. (1963a). Imitation of film-mediated aggressive models. *Journal of Abnormal and Social Psychology, 66,* 3–11.

Bandura, A., Ross, D., & Ross, S.A. (1963b). Vicarious reinforcement and imitative learning. *Journal of Abnormal and Social Psychology, 67,* 601–607.

Belson, W.A. (1978). *Television violence and the adolescent boy.* Westmead: Saxon House.

Berkowitz, L., & Alioto, J.T. (1973). The meaning of an observed event as a determinant of its aggressive consequences. *Journal of Personality and Social Psychology, 28,* 206–217.

Berkowitz, L., Corwin, R., & Heironimus, M. (1963). Film violence and subsequent aggressive tendencies. *Public Opinion Quarterly, 27,* 217–229.

Berkowitz, L., & Geen, R.G. (1966). Film violence and the cue properties of available targets. *Journal of Personality and Social Psychology, 3*, 525–530.

Berkowitz, L., & Geen, R.G. (1967). Stimulus qualities of the target of aggression: A further study. *Journal of Personality and Social Psychology, 5*, 364–368.

Berkowitz, L., Parke, R.D., Leyens, J., & West, S.G. (1974). Reactions of juvenile delinquents to 'justified' and 'unjustified' movie violence. *Journal of Research in Crime and Delinquency, 11*, 16–24.

Berkowitz, L., & Rawlings, E. (1963). Effects of film violence on inhibitions against subsequent aggression. *Journal of Abnormal and Social Psychology, 66*, 405–412.

Black, S.L., & Bevan, S. (1992). At the movies with Buss and Durkee: A natural experiment on film violence. *Aggressive Behavior, 18*, 37–45.

Boyatzis, C.J., Matillo, G.M., & Nesbitt, K.M. (1995). Effects of 'The Mighty Morphin Power Rangers' on children's aggression with peers. *Child Study Journal, 25*, 45–55.

Bushman, B.J. (1995). Moderating role of trait aggressiveness in the effects of violent media on aggression. *Journal of Personality and Social Psychology, 69*, 950–960.

Bushman, B.J. (1998). Priming effects of media violence on the accessibility of aggressive constructs in memory. *Personality and Social Psychology Bulletin, 24*, 537–545.

Bushman, B.J., & Geen, R.G. (1990). Role of cognitive-emotional mediators and individual differences in the effects of media violence on aggression. *Journal of Personality and Social Psychology, 58*, 156–163.

Buvinic, M.L., & Berkowitz, L. (1976). Delayed effects of practiced versus unpracticed responses after observation of movie violence. *Journal of Experimental Social Psychology, 12*, 383–393.

Centerwall, B.S. (1989). Exposure to television as a cause of violence. In G. Comstock (Ed.), *Public communication and behavior: Vol. 2* (pp. 58) San Diego, CA: Academic Press.

Centerwall, B.S. (1992). Television violence: The scale of the problem and where to go from here. *Journal of the American Medical Association, 267*, 3059–3063.

Cline, V.B., Croft, R.G., & Courrier, S. (1973). Desensitization of children to television violence. *Journal of Personality and Social Psychology, 27*, 360–365.

Collins, W.A. (1973). Effect of temporal separation between motivation, aggression and consequences. *Developmental Psychology, 8*, 215–221.

Collins, W.A., & Getz, S.K. (1976). Children's social responses following modeled reactions to provocation: Prosocial effects of a television drama. *Journal of Personality, 44*, 488–500.

Comstock, G. (1982). Violence in television content: An overview. In Pearl, D., Bouthilet, L., & Lazar, J. (Eds.), *Television and Behavior: Ten years of Scientific Progress and Implications for the Eighties* (pp. 108–125). Washington, D.C.: U.S. Government Printing Office.

Comstock, G., & Fisher, M. (1975). *Television and human behavior: A guide to the pertinent scientific literature*. Santa Monica, CA: Rand Corporation.

Cook, T.D., Kendzierski, D.A., & Thomas, S.A. (1983). The implicit assumptions of television research: an analysis of the 1982 NIMH report on television and behavior. *Public Opinion Quarterly, 47*, 161–201.

Day, R.C., & Ghandour, M. (1984). The effect of television-mediated aggression and real-life aggression on the behavior of Lebanese children. *Journal of Experimental Child Psychology, 38*, 7–18.

de Konig, T.I., Conradie, D.P., & Neil, E.M. (1980). The effect of different kinds of television programming on the youth. Pretoria, RSA: Human Sciences Research Council Report No. Comm-20.

Dominick, J.R. (1984). Videogames, television violence, and aggression in teenagers. *Journal of Communication, 136*–147.

Donnerstein, E., Donnerstein, M., & Barrett, G. (1976). Where is the facilitation of media violence: The effects of nonexposure and placement of anger arousal. *Journal of Research in Personality, 10*, 386–398.

Doob, A.N., & Climie, R.J. (1972). Delay of measurement and the effects of film violence. *Journal of Experimental Social Psychology, 8*, 136–142.

Drabman, R.S., & Thomas, M.H. (1974). Does media violence increase children's toleration of real-life aggression? *Developmental Psychology, 10*, 418–421.

Drabman, R.S., & Thomas, M.H. (1974). Exposure to filmed violence and children's toleration of real life aggression. *Personality and Social Psychology Bulletin, 1*, 198–199.

Drabman, R.S., & Thomas, M.H. (1975). Does TV violence breed indifference? *Journal of Communication, 25*, 86–89.

Drabman, R.S., & Thomas, M.H. (1976). Does watching violence on television cause apathy? *Pediatrics, 57(3)*, 329–331.

Drabman, R.S., & Thomas, M.H. (1977). Children's imitation of aggressive and prosocial behavior when viewing alone and in pairs. *Journal of Communication, 27*, 189–198.

Dubanoski, R.A., & Parton, D.A. (1971). Imitative aggression in children as a function of observing a human model. *Developmental Psychology, 4*, 489–99.

Ellis, G.T., & Sekyra, F. III (1972). The effect of aggressive cartoons on the behavior of first grade children. *The Journal of Psychology, 81*, 37–43.

Eron, L.D. (1963). The relationship of TV viewing habits and aggressive behavior in children. *Journal of Abnormal and Social Psychology, 67*, 193–196.

Eron, L.D, Huesmann, L.R., Lefkowitz, M.M., & Walder, L.O. (1972). Does television violence cause aggression? *American Psychologist*, 253–263.

Eron, L.D., Walder, L.O., & Lefkowitz, M.M. (1971) *Learning of aggression in children*. Boston: Little, Brown: 1971.

Fechter, J.V. Jr. (1971). Modeling and environmental generalization by mentally retarded subjects of televised aggressive or friendly behavior. *American Journal of Mental Deficiency*, *76*, 266–267.

Feshbach, S. (1961). The stimulating versus cathartic effects of a vicarious aggressive activity. *Journal of Abnormal and Social Psychology*, *63*, 381–385.

Feshbach, S., and Singer, R.D. (1971). *Television and aggression*. San Francisco: Jossey-Bass.

Freedman, J.L. (1984). Effect of television violence on aggressiveness. *Psychological Bulletin*, *96*, 227–246.

Friedman, H.L., & Johnson, R.L. (1972). Mass media use and aggression: A pilot study. In G.A. Comstock & E.A. Rubinstein (Eds.), *Television and Social Behavior: Vol. 3* (pp. 337–360) Rockville, MD: NIMH.

Friedrich, L.K., & Stein, A.H. (1973). Aggressive and prosocial television programs and the natural behavior of preschool children. *Monographs of the Society for Research in Child Development*, *38*, 4.

Gadow, K.D., & Sprafkin, J. (1987). Effects of viewing high versus low aggression cartoons on emotionally disturbed children. *Journal of Pediatric Psychology*, *12*, 413–427.

Gadow, K.D., Sprafkin, J., & Ficarrotto, T.J. (1987). Effects of viewing aggression-laden cartoons on preschool-aged emotionally disturbed children. *Child Psychiatry and Human Development*, *17*, 257–274.

Geen, R.G., & Berkowitz, L. (1966). Name-mediated aggressive cue properties. *Journal of Personality*, *34*, 456–465.

Geen, R.G., & Berkowitz, L. (1967). Some conditions facilitating the occurrence of aggression after the observation of violence. *Journal of Personality*, *35*, 666–676.

Geen, R.G., & O'Neal, E. (1969). Activation of cue-elicited aggression by general arousal. *Journal of Personality and Social Psychology*, *11*, 289–292.

Goldstein, J.H., Rosnow, R.L., Raday, T., Silverman, I., & Gaskell, G.D. (1976). Punitiveness in response to films varying in content: A cross-national field study of aggression. *European Journal of Social Psychology*, *5*, 149–165.

Gorney, R., Loye, D., & Steele, G. (1977). Impact of dramatized television entertainment on adult males. *American Journal of Psychiatry*, *134*, 170–174.

Greenberg, B.S. (1974). British children and televised violence. *Public Opinion Quarterly*, *38*, 531–548.

Hall, W.M., & Cairns, R.B. (1984). Aggressive behavior in children: An outcome of modeling or social reciprocity? *Developmental Psychology*, *20*, 739–745.

Hanratty, M.A., Liebert, R.M., Morris, L.W., & Fernandez, L. E. (1969). Imitation of film-mediated aggression against live and inanimate victims. *Proceedings of the American Psychological Association, 457–458.*

Hapkiewicz, W.G., & Roden, A.H. (1971). The effect of aggressive cartoons on children's interpersonal play. *Child Development, 42,* 1583–1585.

Hapkiewicz, W.G., & Stone, R.D. (1974). The effect of realistic versus imaginary aggressive models on children's interpersonal play. *Child Study Journal, 4,* 47–58.

Hartmann, D.P. (1969). Influence of symbolically modeled instrumental aggression and pain cues on aggressive behavior. *Journal of Personality and Social Psychology, 11,* 280–288.

Hartnagel, T.F., Teevan, Jr, J.J., & McIntyre, J.J. (1975). Television violence and violent behavior. *Social Forces, 54,* 341–351.

Hennigan, K.M., Del Rosario, M.L., Heath, L., Cook, T.D., Wharton, J.D., & Calder, B.J. (1982). Impact of the introduction of television on crime in the United States: Empirical findings and theoretical implications. *Journal of Personality and Social Psychology, 42,* 461–477.

Hicks, D.J. (1965). Imitation and retention of film-mediated aggressive peer and adult models. *Journal of Personality and Social Psychology, 2,* 97–100.

Himmelweit, H.T., Oppenheim, A.N., & Vince, P. (1965). *Television and the child: An empirical study of the effect of television on the young.* London: Oxford University Press.

Horton, R.W., & Santogrossi, D.A. (1978). The effect of adult commentary on reducing the influence of televised violence. *Personality and Social Psychology Bulletin, 4,* 337–340.

Huesmann, L.R. (1982). Television violence and aggressive behavior. In Pearl, D., Bouthilet, L., & Lazar, J. (Eds.), *Television and behavior: ten years of scientific progress and implications for the eighties* (pp. 126–137). Washington, D.C.: U.S. Government Printing Office.

Huesmann, L.R. (1986). Psychological processes promoting the relation between exposure to media violence and aggressive behavior by the viewer. *Journal of Social Issues, 42,* 125–139.

Huesmann, L.R., & Eron, L.D. (1986). *Television and the aggressive child: A cross-national comparison.* Hillsdale, NJ: Erlbaum

Huesmann, L.R., Lefkowitz, M.M., Eron, L.D, & Walder, L.O. (1984). Stability of aggression over time and generations. *Developmental Psychology, 20,* 1120–1134.

Huston-Stein, A., Fox, S., Greer, D., Watkins, B.A., & Whitaker, J. (1981). The effects of TV action and violence on children's social behavior. *The Journal of Genetic Psychology, 138,* 183–191.

Josephson, W.L. (1987). Television violence and children's aggression: Testing the priming, social script, and disinhibition predictions. *Journal of Personality and Social Psychology, 53*, 882–890.

Kaplan, R.M., & Singer, R.D. (1976). Television violence and viewer aggression: A reexamination of the evidence. *Journal of Social Issues, 32*, 35–70.

Khuder, S.A. (2001) Effect of cigarette smoking on major histological types of lung cancer: a meta-analysis. *Lung Cancer, 31*, 139–148.

Kniveton, B.H. (1973). The effect of rehearsal delay on long-term imitation of filmed aggression. *British Journal of Psychology, 64*, 259–265.

Kniveton, B.H., & Stephenson, G.M. (1970). The effect of pre-experience on imitation of an aggressive film model. *British Journal of Clinical Psychology, 9*, 31–36.

Kniveton, B.H., & Stephenson, G.M. (1973). An examination of individual susceptibility to the influence of aggressive film models. *British Journal of Psychology, 122*, 53–56.

Kniveton, B.H., & Stephenson, G.M. (1975). The effects of an aggressive film model on social interaction in groups of middle-class and working-class boys. *Journal of Child Psychology and Psychiatry and Allied Disciplines, 16*, 301–313.

Kruttschnitt, C., Heath, L., & Ward, D.A. (1986). Family violence, television viewing habits, and other adolescent experiences related to violent criminal behavior. *Criminology, 24*, 235–267.

Kuhn, D.Z., Madsen, C.H., Jr., & Becker, W.C. (1967). Effects of exposure to an aggressive model and 'frustration' on children's aggressive behavior. *Child Development, 38*, 739–745.

Lando, H.A., & Donnerstein, E.I. (1978). The effects of a model's success or failure on subsequent aggressive behavior. *Journal of Research in Personality, 12*, 225–234.

Langham, J., & Stewart, W. (1981). Television viewing habits, and other characteristics of normally aggressive and non-aggressive children. *Australian Psychologist, 16*, 123–133.

Lefcourt, H.M., Barnes, K., Parke, R., & Schwartz, F. (1966). Anticipated social censure and aggression-conflict as mediators of response to aggression induction. *Journal of Social Psychology, 70*, 251–263.

Lefkowitz, M.M, Eron, L.D., Walder, L.O., and Huesmann, L. R. (1977). *Growing up to be violent: A longitudinal study of the development of aggression.* New York: Pergamon.

Leyens, J.P., Camino, L., Parke, R.D., & Berkowitz, L. (1975). The effects of movie violence on aggression in a field setting as a function of group dominance and cohesion. *Journal of Personality and Social Psychology, 32*, 346–360.

Leyens, J., & Dunand, M. (1991). Priming aggressive thoughts: The effect of the anticipation of a violent movie upon the aggressive behaviour of the spectators. *European Journal of Social Psychology, 21*, 507–516.

Leyens, J., Herman, G., & Dunand, M. (1982). The influence of an audience upon the reactions to filmed violence. *European Journal of Social Psychology, 12*, 131–142.

Leyens, J.P., & Parke, R.D. (1975). Aggressive slides can induce a weapons effect. *European Journal of Social Psychology, 5*, 229–236.

Leyens, J., & Picus, S. (1973). Identification with the winner of a fight and name mediation: Their differential effects upon subsequent aggressive behaviour. *British Journal of Social and Clinical Psychology, 12*, 374–377.

Liebert, R.M., & Baron, R.A. (1972). Some immediate effects of televised violence on children's behavior. *Developmental Psychology, 6*, 469–475.

Liebert, R.M., Sprafkin, J.N., & Davidson, E.S. (1982). *The early window: Effects of television on children and youth.* New York: Pergamon Press.

Linz, D.G., Donnerstein, E., & Penrod, S. (1988). Effects of long-term exposure to violent and sexually degrading depictions of women. *Journal of Personality and Social Psychology, 55*, 758–768.

Lipsey, M.W. (1992). Juvenile delinquency treatment: A meta-analytic inquiry into the variability of effects. In T.D. Cook, H. Cooper, D.S. Cordray, H. Hartmann, L.V. Hedges, R.J. Light, T.A. Louis, and F. Mosteller (Ed.), *Meta-analysis for explanation: A casebook* (pp. 212–42). New York: Russell Sage Foundation.

Liss, M.B., Reinhardt, L.C., & Fredriksen, S. (1983). TV heros: The impact of rhetoric and deeds. *Journal of Applied Developmental Psychology, 4*, 175–187.

Lovaas, O.I. (1961). Effect of exposure to symbolic aggression on aggressive behavior. *Child Development, 32*, 37–44.

Loye, D., Gorney, R., & Steele, G. (1977). An experimental field study. *Journal of Communication, 27*, 206–216.

Lynn, R., Hampson, S., & Agahi, E. (1989). TV violence and aggression: A genotype-environment, correlation and interaction theory. *Social Behavior and Personality, 17*, 143–164.

Manning, S.A., & Taylor, D.A. (1975). Effects of viewed violence and aggression: stimulation and catharsis. *Journal of Personality and Social Psychology, 31*, 180–188.

McCarthy, E.D., Langner, T.S., Gersten, J.C., Eisenberg, J.G., and Orzeck, L. (1975). Violence and behavior disorders. *Journal of Communication, 25*, 71–85.

McHan, E.J. (1985). Imitation of aggression by Lebanese children. *Journal of Social Psychology, 125*, 613–617.

McIntyre, J.J., Teevan, Jr., J.J. and Hartnagel, T. (1972). Mass media use and aggression: A pilot study. In G.A. Comstock & E.A. Rubinstein (Eds.), *Television and Social Behavior: Vol. 3* (pp. 383–435). Rockville, MD: NIMH.

McLeod, J.M., Atkin, C.K., & Chaffee, S.H. (1972). Adolescents, parents and television use: Adolescent self-report measures from Maryland and Wisconsin samples. In G.A. Comstock & E.A. Rubinstein (Eds.), *Television and Social Behavior: Vol. 3* (pp. 173–238). Rockville, MD: NIMH.

Messner, S.F. (1986). Television violence and violent crime: An aggregate analysis. *Social Problems, 33,* 218–234.

Meyer, T.P. (1972a). Effects of viewing justified and unjustified real film violence on aggressive behavior. *Journal of Personality and Social Psychology, 23,* 21–29.

Meyer, T.P. (1972b). The effects of verbally violent film content on aggressive behavior. *AV Communication Review, 20,* 160–169.

Milavsky, J.R., Kessler, R.C., Stipp, H.H., and Rubens, W.S. (1982). Television and aggression: Results of a panel study. In Pearl, D., Bouthilet, L., & Lazar, J. (Eds.), *Television and behavior: Ten years of scientific progress and implications for the eighties* (pp. 138–157). Washington, D.C.: U.S. Government Printing Office.

Milavsky, J.R., Stipp, H.H., Kessler, R.C., and Rubens, W.S. (1982). *Television and aggression: A panel study.* New York: Academic Press.

Milgram, S., & Shotland, R.L. (1973). *Television and antisocial behavior: Field experiments.* New York: Academic Press.

Molitor, F., & Hirsch, K.W. (1994). Children's toleration of real-life aggression after exposure to media violence: A replication of the Drabman and Thomas studies. *Child Study Journal, 3,* 191–203.

Mueller, C.W., & Donnerstein, E. (1983). Film-induced arousal and aggressive behavior. *Journal of Social Psychology, 110,* 61–67.

Mueller, C.W., Donnerstein, E., & Hallam, J. (1983). Violent films and prosocial behavior. *Personality and Social Psychology Bulletin, 9,* 83–89.

Mussen, P., & Rutherford, E. (1961). Effects of aggressive cartoons on children's aggressive play. *Journal of Abnormal and Social Psychology, 62,* 461–464.

National Television Violence Study, Executive Summary. (1995). Studio City, CA: Mediascope Inc.

Noble, C. (1973). Effects of different forms of filmed aggression on children's constructive and destructive play. *Journal of Personality and Social Psychology, 26,* 54–59.

O'Carroll, M., O'Neal, E., McDonald, P., & Hori, R. (1977). Influence upon imitative aggression of an imitating peer. *Journal of Social Psychology, 101,* 313–314.

Paik, H., & Comstock, G. (1994). The effects of television violence on antisocial behavior: A meta-analysis. *Communication Research, 21*, 516–546.

Parke, R.D., Berkowitz, L., Leyens, J.P., West, S.W., & Sebastian, R.J. (1977). Some effects of violent and nonviolent movies on the behavior of juvenile delinquents. In L. Berkowitz (Ed.), *Advances in Experimental Social Psychology: Vol. 10* (pp. 135–172). New York: Academic Press.

Pearl, D., Bouthilet, L., & Lazar, J. (Eds.). (1982). *Television and Behavior: Ten years of Scientific Progress and Implications for the Eighties.* Washington, D.C.: U.S. Government Printing Office.

Perry, D.G., & Perry, L.C. (1976). Identification with film characters, covert aggressive verbalization, and reactions to film violence. *Journal of Research in Personality, 10*, 399–410.

Phillips, D. (1979). Suicide, motor vehicle fatalities, and the mass media: Evidence toward a theory of suggestion. *American Journal of Sociology, 87*, 1340–1359.

Phillips, D. (1982). The impact of mass media violence on U.S. homicides. *American Sociological Review, 48*, 560–568.

Potts, R., Huston, A.C., & Wright, J.C. (1986). The effects of television form and violent content on boys' attention and social behavior. *Journal of Experimental Child Psychology, 41*, 1–17.

Robinson, J.P., & Bachman, J.G. (1972). Television viewing habits and aggression. In G.A. Comstock & E.A. Rubinstein (eds.), *Television and Social Behavior: Vol. 3* (pp. 372–382). Rockville, MD: NIMH.

Rowe, D.C., & Herstand, S.E. (1985). Familial influences on television viewing and aggression: A sibling study. *Aggressive Behavior, 12*, 111–120.

Sanson, A., & Di Muccio, C. (1993). The influence of aggressive and neutral cartoons and toys on the behaviour of preschool children. *Australian Psychologist, 28*, 93–99.

Savitsky, J.C., Rogers, R.W., Izard, C.E., & Liebert, R.M. (1971). Role of frustration and anger in the imitation of filmed aggression against a human victim. *Psychological Reports, 29*, 807–810.

Sawin, D.B. (1981). The fantasy-reality distinction in televised violence: Modifying influences on children's aggression. *Journal of Research in Personality, 15*, 323–330.

Schramm, W., Lyle, J., & Parker, E.B. (1961). *Television in the lives of our children.* Stanford, CA: Stanford University Press.

Sebastian, R.J., Parke, R.D., Berkowitz, L., & West, S.G. (1978). Film violence and verbal aggression: A naturalistic study. *Journal of Communication, 28*, 164–171.

Siegel, A.E. (1956). Film-mediated fantasy, aggression and strength of aggressive drive. *Child Development, 27*, 365–378.

Signorelli, N., Gross, L., & Morgan, M. (1982). Violence in television programs: Ten years later. In Pearl, D., Bouthilet, L., & Lazar, J. (Eds.), *Television and behavior: Ten years of scientific progress and implications for the eighties* (pp. 158–174). Washington, D.C.: U.S. Government Printing Office.

Singer, J.L. and Singer, D.G. (1981). *Television, imagination and aggression.* Hillsdale, NJ: Lawrence Erlbaum

Singer, J.L., Singer, D.G., & Rapaczynski, W.S. (1984). Family patterns and television viewing as predictors of children's beliefs and aggression. *Journal of Communications, 34,* 73–89.

Singer, J.L., Singer, D.G., Desmond, R., Hirsch, B., & Nicol, A. (1988). Family mediation and children's cognition, aggression, and comprehension of television: A longitudinal study. *Journal of Applied Developmental Psychology, 9,* 329–347.

Sprafkin, J., Gadow, K.D., & Grayson, P. (1987). Effects of viewing aggressive cartoons on the behavior of learning disabled children. *Journal of Child Psychology and Psychiatry, 28,* 387–398.

Sprafkin, J., Gadow, K.D., & Grayson, P. (1988). Effects of cartoons on emotionally disturbed children's social behavior in school settings. *Journal of Child Psychology and Psychiatry, 29,* 91–99.

Steuer, F.B., Applefield, J.M., & Smith, R. (1971). Televised aggression and the interpersonal aggression of preschool children. *Journal of Experimental Child Psychology, 11,* 442–447.

Talkington, L.W., & Altman, R. (1973). Effects of film-mediated aggressive and affectual models on behavior. *American Journal of Mental Deficiency, 77,* 420–425.

Thomas, M.H. (1982). Physiological arousal, exposure to a relatively lengthy aggressive film, and aggressive behavior. *Journal of Research in Personality, 16,* 72–81.

Thomas, M.H., & Drabman, R.S. (1975). Toleration of real life aggression as a function of exposure to televised violence and age of subject. *Merrill-Palmer Quarterly of Behavior and Development, 24,* 227–232.

Thomas, M.H., Horton, R.W., Lippincott, E.C., & Drabman, R.S. (1977). Desensitization to portrayals of real-life aggression as a function of exposure to television violence. *Journal of Personality and Social Psychology, 35,* 450–458.

Thomas, M.H., & Tell, P.M. (1974). Effects of viewing real versus fantasy violence upon interpersonal aggression. *Journal of Research in Personality, 8,* 153–160.

Thornton, W., & Voigt, L. (1984). Television and delinquency: A neglected dimension of social control. *Youth and Society, 15,* 445–468.

Van der Voort, T.H.A. (1986). *Television violence: A child's-eye view*. Amsterdam: Elsevier

Viemero, V. (1986). Relationships between filmed violence and aggression. Department of Psychology at Abo Akademi, Monograph Supplement 4.

Viermo, V. (1996). Factors in childhood that predict later criminal behavior. *Aggressive Behavior, 22,* 87–97.

Walters, R.H., & Thomas, E.L. (1963). Enhancement of punitiveness by visual and audiovisual displays. *Canadian Journal of Psychology, 17,* 244–255.

Walters, R.H., Thomas, E.L., & Acker, C.W. (1962). Enhancement of punitive behavior by audio-visual displays. *Science, 136,* 872–873.

Walters, R.H., & Willows, D.C. (1968). Imitative behavior of disturbed and nondisturbed children following exposure to aggressive and nonaggressive models. *Child Development, 39,* 79–89.

Wells, W.D. (1973). Television and aggression: Replication of an experimental field study. Unpublished manuscript, Graduate School of Business, University of Chicago.

Wiegman, O., & Kuttschreuter, M. (1992). A longitudinal study of the effects of television viewing on aggressive and prosocial behaviours. *British Journal of Social Psychology, 31,* 147–164.

Wiegman, O., Kuttschreuter, M., & Baarda, B. (1986). *Television viewing related to aggressive and prosocial behaviour*. The Hague: SVO

Wilkins, J.L., Scharff, W.H., & Schlottmann, R. S. (1974). Personality type, reports of violence, and aggressive behavior. *Journal of Personality and Social Psychology, 30,* 243–247.

Williams, T.M. (Ed.). (1986). *The impact of television: A natural experiment in three communities*. New York: Academic Press.

Wood, W., Wong, F.Y., & Chachere, J.G. (1991). Effects of media violence on viewers' aggression in unconstrained social interaction. *Psychological Bulletin, 109,* 371–383.

Woodfield, D.L. (1988). Mass media viewing habits and toleration of real life violence. Paper presented at the meeting of the Southeastern Psychological Association, New Orleans.

Worchel, S., Hardy, T.W., & Hurley, R. (1976). The effects of commercial interruption of violent and nonviolent films on viewers' subsequent aggression. *Journal of Experimental Social Psychology, 12,* 220–232.

Zillmann, D. (1971). Excitation transfer in communication-mediated aggressive behavior. *Journal of Experimental Social Psychology, 7,* 419–434.

Zillmann, D., & Johnson, R.C. (1973). Motivated aggressiveness perpetuated by exposure to aggressive films and reduced by exposure to nonaggressive films. *Journal of Research in Personality, 7,* 261–276.

Zillmann, D., Johnson, R.C., & Hanrahan, J. (1973). Pacifying effect of happy ending of communications involving aggression. *Psychological Reports, 32,* 967–970.

Zillmann, D., & Weaver, J.B. III. (1999). Effects of prolonged exposure to gratuitous media violence on provoked and unprovoked hostile behavior. *Journal of Applied Social Psychology, 29,* 145–165.

Zimring, F.E., & Hawkins, G. (1997). Crime is not the problem: Lethal violence in America. New York: Oxford University Press.

Index